Companion Workbook

math expressions

Dr. Karen C. Fuson

Watch the moose come alive in its snowy environment as you discover and solve math challenges.

Download the Math Expressions AR app available on Android or iOS devices.

Grade 3

This material is based upon work supported by the
National Science Foundation
under Grant Numbers
ESI-9816320, REC-9806020, and RED-935373.

Any opinions, findings, and conclusions, or recommendations expressed in this material
are those of the author and do not necessarily reflect the views of the National Science Foundation.

Contents

© Houghton Mifflin Harcourt Publishing Company

Contents

Contents

© Houghton Mifflin Harcourt Publishing Company

Contents

© Houghton Mifflin Harcourt Publishing Company

Dear Family:

In this unit and the next, your child will be practicing basic multiplications and divisions. *Math Expressions* uses studying, practicing, and testing of the basic multiplications and divisions in class. Your child also should practice at home.

Homework Helper Your child will have math homework almost every day. He or she needs a Homework Helper. The helper may be anyone — you, an older brother or sister (or other family member), a neighbor, or a friend. Please decide who the main Homework Helper will be and ask your child to tell the teacher tomorrow. Make a specific time for homework and give your child a quiet place to work.

Study Plans Each day your child will fill out a study plan, indicating which basic multiplications and divisions he or she will study that evening. When your child has finished studying (practicing), his or her Homework Helper should sign the study plan.

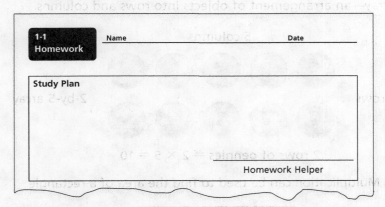

Practice Charts Each time a new number is introduced, students' homework will include a practice chart. To practice, students can cover the products with a finger or pencil. They will say the multiplications, sliding the finger or pencil down the column to see each product after saying it. Students can also start with the last problem in a column and slide up. It is important that your child studies count-bys and multiplications at least 5 minutes every night. Your child should study each division on the Mixed Up column by covering the first factor.

Keep all materials in a special place.

	In Order	Mixed Up
	1 × 5 = 5	9 × 5 = 45
	2 × 5 = 10	5 × 5 = 25
	3 × 5 = 15	2 × 5 = 10
	4 × 5 = 20	7 × 5 = 35
5s	5 × 5 = 25	4 × 5 = 20
	6 × 5 = 30	6 × 5 = 30
	7 × 5 = 35	10 × 5 = 50
	8 × 5 = 40	8 × 5 = 40
	9 × 5 = 45	1 × 5 = 5
	10 × 5 = 50	3 × 5 = 15

To help students understand the concept of multiplication, the *Math Expressions* program presents three ways to think about multiplication.

- **Repeated groups**: Multiplication can be used to find the total in repeated groups of the same size. In early lessons, students circle the group size in repeated-groups equations to help keep track of which factor is the group size and which is the number of groups.

4 groups of bananas

$$4 \times \boxed{3} = 3 + 3 + 3 + 3 = 12$$

- **Arrays**: Multiplication can be used to find the total number of items in an *array*—an arrangement of objects into rows and columns.

5 columns

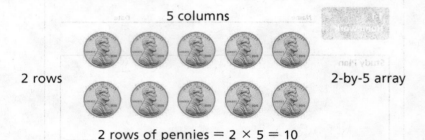

2 rows   2-by-5 array

2 rows of pennies = $2 \times 5 = 10$

- **Area**: Multiplication can be used to find the area of a rectangle

3 units

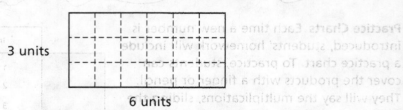

6 units

Area: 3 units $\times$ 6 units = 18 square units

Please contact me if you have any questions or comments.

Thank you.

Sincerely,
Your child's teacher

Estimada familia:

En esta unidad y en la que sigue, su niño practicará multiplicaciones y divisiones básicas. *Math Expressions* usa en la clase el estudio, la práctica y la evaluación de las multiplicaciones y divisiones básicas. También su niño debe practicar en casa.

Ayudante de tareas Su niño tendrá tarea de matemáticas casi a diario y necesitará un ayudante para hacer sus tareas. Ese ayudante puede ser cualquier persona: usted, un hermano o hermana mayor, otro familiar, un vecino o un amigo. Por favor decida quién será esta persona y pida a su niño que se lo diga a su maestro mañana. Designe un tiempo específico para la tarea y un lugar para trabajar sin distracciones.

Planes de estudio Todos los días su niño va a completar un plan de estudio, que indica cuáles multiplicaciones y divisiones debe estudiar esa noche. Cuando su niño haya terminado de estudiar (practicar), la persona que lo ayude debe firmar el plan de estudio.

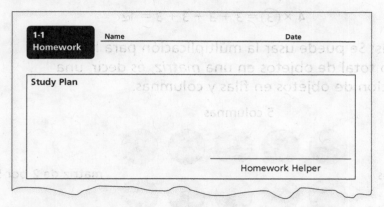

Tablas de práctica Cada vez que se presente un número nuevo, la tarea de los estudiantes incluirá una tabla de práctica. Para practicar, los estudiantes pueden cubrir los productos con un dedo o lápiz.Los niños dicen la multiplicación y deslizan el dedo o lápiz hacia abajo para revelar el producto después de decirlo. También pueden empezar con el último problema de la columna y deslizar el lápiz o el papel hacia arriba. Es importante que su niño practique el conteo y la multiplicación por lo menos 5 minutos cada noche. Su niño debe estudiar cada división en la columna de Desordenados cubriendo el primer factor.

Guarde todos los materiales.

5s	In Order	Mixed Up
	$1 \times 5 = 5$	$9 \times 5 = 45$
	$2 \times 5 = 10$	$5 \times 5 = 25$
	$3 \times 5 = 15$	$2 \times 5 = 10$
	$4 \times 5 = 20$	$7 \times 5 = 35$
	$5 \times 5 = 25$	$4 \times 5 = 20$
	$6 \times 5 = 30$	$6 \times 5 = 30$
	$7 \times 5 = 35$	$10 \times 5 = 50$
	$8 \times 5 = 40$	$8 \times 5 = 40$
	$9 \times 5 = 45$	$1 \times 5 = 5$
	$10 \times 5 = 50$	$3 \times 5 = 15$

Para ayudar a los estudiantes a comprender el concepto de la multiplicación, el programa *Math Expressions* presenta tres maneras de pensar en la multiplicación. Éstas se describen a continuación.

- **Grupos repetidos**: La multiplicación se puede usar para hallar el total con grupos del mismo tamaño que se repiten. Cuando empiezan a trabajar con ecuaciones de grupos repetidos, los estudiantes rodean con un círculo el tamaño del grupo en las ecuaciones, para recordar cuál factor representa el tamaño del grupo y cuál representa el número de grupos.

4 grupos de bananas

$$4 \times (3) = 3 + 3 + 3 + 3 = 12$$

- **Matrices**: Se puede usar la multiplicación para hallar el número total de objetos en una *matriz*, es decir, una disposición de objetos en filas y columnas.

5 columnas

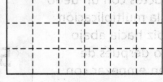

2 filas   matriz de 2 por 5

2 filas de monedas de un centavo = $2 \times 5 = 10$

- **Área**: Se puede usar la multiplicación para hallar el área de un rectángulo.

3 unidades

6 unidades

Área: 3 unidades $\times$ 6 unidades = 18 unidades cuadradas

Si tiene alguna duda o algún comentario, por favor comuníquese conmigo. Gracias.

Atentamente,
El maestro de su niño

area

Associative
Property of
Multiplication

array

column

Associative
Property of
Addition

Commutative
Property of
Addition

The property that states that changing the way in which factors are grouped does not change the product.

Example:

$(2 \times 3) \times 4 = 2 \times (3 \times 4)$

$6 \times 4 = 2 \times 12$

$24 = 24$

The total number of square units that cover a figure.

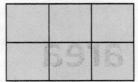

Example:

The area of the rectangle is 6 square units.

A part of a table or array that contains items arranged vertically.

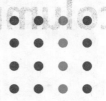

An arrangement of objects, pictures, or numbers in columns and rows.

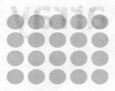

The property that states that changing the order of addends does not change the sum.

Example:

$3 + 7 = 7 + 3$

$10 = 10$

The property that states that changing the way in which addends are grouped does not change the sum.

Example:

$(2 + 3) + 1 = 2 + (3 + 1)$

$5 + 1 = 2 + 4$

$6 = 6$

Commutative Property of Multiplication

division

Distributive Property

divisor

dividend

equal groups

The mathematical operation that separates an amount into smaller equal groups to find the number of groups or the number in each group.

Example:
$12 \div 3 = 4$ is a division number sentence.

The property that states that changing the order of factors does not change the product.

Example:
$5 \times 4 = 4 \times 5$
$20 = 20$

The number that you divide by in division.

Example:
$12 \div 3 = 4$ $3\overline{)12}^{\,4}$

divisor   divisor

You can multiply a sum by a number, or multiply each addend by the number and add the products; the result is the same.

Example:
$3 \times (2 + 4) = (3 \times 2) + (3 \times 4)$
$3 \times 6 \quad = \quad 6 \quad + \quad 12$
$18 \quad\quad = \quad\quad 18$

Two or more groups with the same number of items in each group.

The number that is divided in division.

Example:
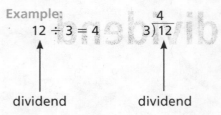
$12 \div 3 = 4$ $3\overline{)12}^{\,4}$

dividend   dividend

equation

function table

even number

Identity Property of Addition

factor

Identity Property of Multiplication

A table of ordered pairs that shows a function.

For every input number, there is only one possible output number.

Rule: add 2	
Input	Output
1	3
2	4
3	5
4	6

A mathematical sentence with an equals sign.

Examples:
11 + 22 = 33
75 − 25 = 50

If 0 is added to a number, the sum equals that number.

Example:
3 + 0 = 3

A whole number that is a multiple of 2. The ones digit in an even number is 0, 2, 4, 6, or 8.

The product of 1 and any number equals that number.

Example:
10 × 1 = 10

Any of the numbers that are multiplied to give a product.

Example:
4 × 5 = 20

factor factor product

(>) is greater than

odd number

(<) is less than

pictograph

multiplication

product

A whole number that is not a multiple of 2. The ones digit in an odd number is 1, 3, 5, 7, or 9.

A symbol used to compare two numbers.

Example:

6 > 5

6 *is greater than* 5.

A graph that uses pictures or symbols to represent data.

Favorite Ice Cream Flavors

Peanut Butter Crunch	
Cherry Vanilla	
Chocolate	

Each 🍦 stands for 4 votes.

A symbol used to compare two numbers.

Example:

5 < 6

5 *is less than* 6.

The answer when you multiply numbers.

Example:

$4 \times 7 = 28$

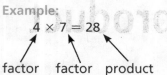

factor   factor   product

A mathematical operation that combines equal groups.

Example:

$4 \times 3 = 12$

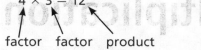

factor   factor   product

$3 + 3 + 3 + 3 = 12$

4 times

quotient

variable

row

Zero Property of Multiplication

square unit

A letter or symbol used to represent an unknown number in an algebraic expression or equation.

Example:

$2 + n$

n is a variable.

The answer when you divide numbers.

Example:

$35 \div 7 = 5$ $7\overline{)35}$ ← quotient

↑
quotient

If 0 is multiplied by a number, the product is 0.

Example:

$3 \times 0 = 0$

A part of a table or array that contains items arranged horizontally.

A unit of area equal to the area of a square with one-unit sides.

1 unit

1 unit
1 square unit

PATH to FLUENCY **Practice with Equal Groups**

Complete each function table.

11

Number of Tricycles	Number of Wheels
1	
2	
3	
4	
5	

12

Number of Rabbits	Number of Ears
1	
2	
3	
4	
5	

13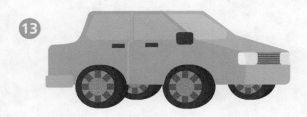

Number of Cars	Number of Wheels
1	
2	
3	
4	
5	

14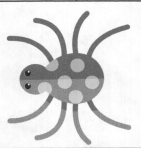

Number of Spiders	Number of Legs
1	
2	
3	
4	
5	

✓ **Check Understanding**

Draw an equal shares drawing to find the number of markers in 8 packages of markers with 5 markers in each package.

Dear Family:

Over the next few weeks your child will bring home a Practice Chart for each new number to practice multiplications and divisions. Other practice materials will also come home:

- **Home Study Sheets:** A Home Study Sheet includes 3 or 4 practice charts on one page. Your child can use the Home Study Sheets to practice all the count-bys, multiplications, and divisions for a number or to practice just the ones he or she doesn't know for that number. The Homework Helper uses the sheet to test (or retest) your child by giving problems. The Homework Helper should check with your child to see which basic multiplications or divisions he or she is ready to be tested on. The helper should mark any missed problems lightly with a pencil.

If your child gets all the answers in a column correct, the helper should sign that column on the Home Signature Sheet. When signatures are on all the columns of the Home Signature Sheet, your child should bring the sheet to school.

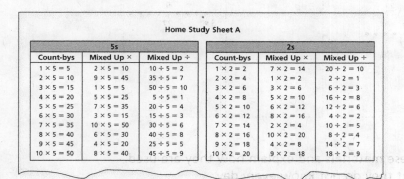

Home Study Sheet A

5s			2s		
Count-bys	Mixed Up ×	Mixed Up ÷	Count-bys	Mixed Up ×	Mixed Up ÷
1 × 5 = 5	2 × 5 = 10	10 ÷ 5 = 2	1 × 2 = 2	7 × 2 = 14	20 ÷ 2 = 10
2 × 5 = 10	9 × 5 = 45	35 ÷ 5 = 7	2 × 2 = 4	1 × 2 = 2	2 ÷ 2 = 1
3 × 5 = 15	1 × 5 = 5	50 ÷ 5 = 10	3 × 2 = 6	3 × 2 = 6	6 ÷ 2 = 3
4 × 5 = 20	5 × 5 = 25	5 ÷ 5 = 1	4 × 2 = 8	5 × 2 = 10	16 ÷ 2 = 8
5 × 5 = 25	7 × 5 = 35	20 ÷ 5 = 4	5 × 2 = 10	6 × 2 = 12	12 ÷ 2 = 6
6 × 5 = 30	3 × 5 = 15	15 ÷ 5 = 3	6 × 2 = 12	8 × 2 = 16	4 ÷ 2 = 2
7 × 5 = 35	10 × 5 = 50	30 ÷ 5 = 6	7 × 2 = 14	2 × 2 = 4	10 ÷ 2 = 5
8 × 5 = 40	6 × 5 = 30	40 ÷ 5 = 8	8 × 2 = 16	10 × 2 = 20	8 ÷ 2 = 4
9 × 5 = 45	4 × 5 = 20	25 ÷ 5 = 5	9 × 2 = 18	4 × 2 = 8	14 ÷ 2 = 7
10 × 5 = 50	8 × 5 = 40	45 ÷ 5 = 9	10 × 2 = 20	9 × 2 = 18	18 ÷ 2 = 9

> Children practice by covering the answers with their finger or a pencil and sliding down their finger or pencil to check each answer as soon as they say it.

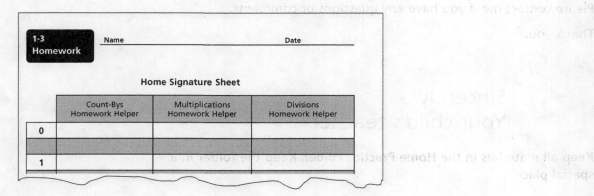

1-3 Homework

Name _____ Date _____

Home Signature Sheet

	Count-Bys Homework Helper	Multiplications Homework Helper	Divisions Homework Helper
0			
1			

Put all practice materials in the folder your child brought home today.

- **Home Check Sheets:** A Home Check Sheet includes columns of 20 multiplications and divisions in mixed order. These sheets can be used to test your child's fluency with basic multiplications and divisions.

- **Strategy Cards:** Your child should use the Strategy Cards to practice multiplication and division by trying to answer the problem on the front. That card is put into one of three piles: *Know Quickly, Know Slowly,* and *Do Not Know.* The *Know Slowly* and *Do Not Know* cards are practiced until they are known quickly.

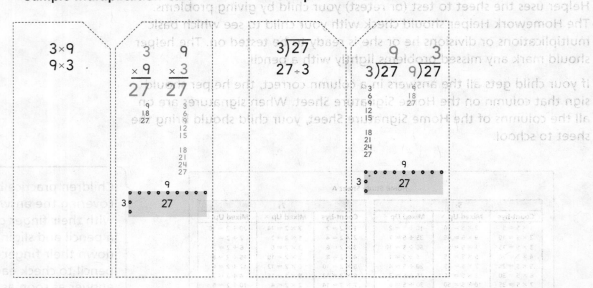

Sample Multiplication Card   **Sample Division Card**

Ask your child to show you these materials and explain how they are used. Your child should practice what they do not know every day.

Please contact me if you have any questions or comments.

Thank you.

Sincerely,
Your child's teacher

Keep all materials in the Home Practice Folder. Keep the folder in a special place.

Estimada familia:

Durante las próximas semanas su niño llevará a casa una tabla de práctica para cada número nuevo para practicar multiplicaciones y divisiones. Otros materiales de práctica también se llevará a casa:

- **Hojas para estudiar en casa:** Una hoja para estudiar en casa incluye 3 ó 4 tablas de práctica en una página. Su niño puede usar las hojas para practicar todos los conteos, multiplicaciones y divisiones de un número, o para practicar sólo las operaciones para ese número que no domine. El ayudante de tareas usa la hoja para hacerle una prueba (o repetir una prueba) con problemas. Esa persona debe hablar con su niño para decidir sobre qué multiplicaciones o divisiones básicas el niño puede hacer la prueba. La persona que ayude debe marcar ligeramente con un lápiz cualquier problema que conteste mal. Si su niño contesta bien todas las operaciones de una columna, la persona que ayude debe firmar esa columna de la hoja de firmas. Cuando todas las columnas de la hoja de firmas estén firmadas, su niño debe llevar la hoja a la escuela.

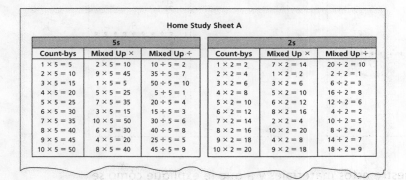

Los niños practican cubriendo las respuestas con su dedo o un lápiz y deslizan su dedo o lápiz hacia abajo para revelar cada respuesta después de decirlo.

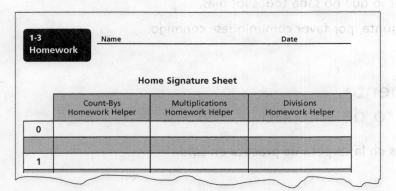

Guarde todos los materiales de práctica en la carpeta que su hijo trajo a casa hoy.

© Houghton Mifflin Harcourt Publishing Company

- **Hojas de verificación:** Una hoja de verificación consta de columnas de 20 multiplicaciones y divisiones sin orden fijo. Estas hojas se pueden usar para comprobar el dominio de su niño con las multiplicaciones y divisiones básicas.

- **Tarjetas de estrategias:** Su niño debe usar las Tarjetas de estrategias para practicar la multiplicación y división al responder el problema del frente. Esa tarjeta se pone en una de las tres pilas: *Contesta Rápidamente, Se Demora En Contestar y No Sabe*. Las tarjetas de *Se Demora En Contestar* y *No Sabe* se practican hasta que las contesten rápidamente.

Ejemplo de tarjeta de multiplicación   Ejemplo de tarjeta de división

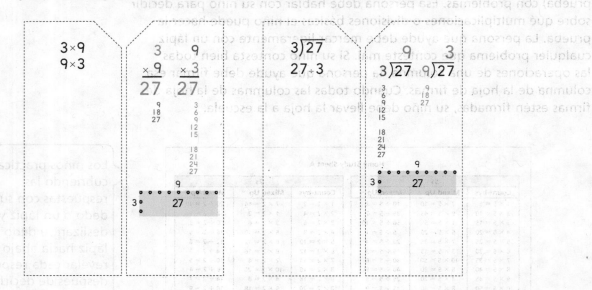

Pida a su niño a que le muestre estos materiales y a que le explique cómo se usan. Su niño debe practicar lo que no sabe todos los días.

Si tiene alguna duda o pregunta, por favor comuníquese conmigo.

Atentamente,
El maestro de su niño

Guarde todos los materiales en la carpeta de práctica en casa.

Name _____

Signature Sheet

	Count-Bys Partner	Multiplications Partner	Divisions Partner	Multiplications Check Sheets	Divisions Check Sheets
5s				1:	1:
2s				1:	1:
10s				2:	2:
9s				2:	2:
				3:	3:
3s				4:	4:
4s				4:	4:
1s				5:	5:
0s				5:	5:
				6:	6:
6s				7:	7:
8s				7:	7:
7s				8:	8:
				9:	9:
				10:	10:

Name _____

Dash Record Sheet

Dash Number	Accurate	Fast	Really Fast	Dash Number	Accurate	Fast	Really Fast
1				13			
2				14			
3				15			
4				16			
5				17			
6				18			
7				19			
8				19A			
9				19B			
9A				19C			
9B				19D			
9C				20			
10				20A			
10A				20B			
10B				20C			
10C				20D			
11				21			
11A				21A			
11B				21B			
11C				21C			
12				22			
12A				22A			
12B				22B			
12C				22C			

Name _____

PATH to FLUENCY

Study Sheet A

5s

Count-bys	Mixed Up ×	Mixed Up ÷
1 × 5 = 5	2 × 5 = 10	10 ÷ 5 = 2
2 × 5 = 10	9 × 5 = 45	35 ÷ 5 = 7
3 × 5 = 15	1 × 5 = 5	50 ÷ 5 = 10
4 × 5 = 20	5 × 5 = 25	5 ÷ 5 = 1
5 × 5 = 25	7 × 5 = 35	20 ÷ 5 = 4
6 × 5 = 30	3 × 5 = 15	15 ÷ 5 = 3
7 × 5 = 35	10 × 5 = 50	30 ÷ 5 = 6
8 × 5 = 40	6 × 5 = 30	40 ÷ 5 = 8
9 × 5 = 45	4 × 5 = 20	25 ÷ 5 = 5
10 × 5 = 50	8 × 5 = 40	45 ÷ 5 = 9

2s

Count-bys	Mixed Up ×	Mixed Up ÷
1 × 2 = 2	7 × 2 = 14	20 ÷ 2 = 10
2 × 2 = 4	1 × 2 = 2	2 ÷ 2 = 1
3 × 2 = 6	3 × 2 = 6	6 ÷ 2 = 3
4 × 2 = 8	5 × 2 = 10	16 ÷ 2 = 8
5 × 2 = 10	6 × 2 = 12	12 ÷ 2 = 6
6 × 2 = 12	8 × 2 = 16	4 ÷ 2 = 2
7 × 2 = 14	2 × 2 = 4	10 ÷ 2 = 5
8 × 2 = 16	10 × 2 = 20	8 ÷ 2 = 4
9 × 2 = 18	4 × 2 = 8	14 ÷ 2 = 7
10 × 2 = 20	9 × 2 = 18	18 ÷ 2 = 9

10s

Count-bys	Mixed Up ×	Mixed Up ÷
1 × 10 = 10	1 × 10 = 10	80 ÷ 10 = 8
2 × 10 = 20	5 × 10 = 50	10 ÷ 10 = 1
3 × 10 = 30	2 × 10 = 20	50 ÷ 10 = 5
4 × 10 = 40	8 × 10 = 80	90 ÷ 10 = 9
5 × 10 = 50	7 × 10 = 70	40 ÷ 10 = 4
6 × 10 = 60	3 × 10 = 30	100 ÷ 10 = 10
7 × 10 = 70	4 × 10 = 40	30 ÷ 10 = 3
8 × 10 = 80	6 × 10 = 60	20 ÷ 10 = 2
9 × 10 = 90	10 × 10 = 100	70 ÷ 10 = 7
10 × 10 = 100	9 × 10 = 90	60 ÷ 10 = 6

9s

Count-bys	Mixed Up ×	Mixed Up ÷
1 × 9 = 9	2 × 9 = 18	81 ÷ 9 = 9
2 × 9 = 18	4 × 9 = 36	18 ÷ 9 = 2
3 × 9 = 27	7 × 9 = 63	36 ÷ 9 = 4
4 × 9 = 36	8 × 9 = 72	9 ÷ 9 = 1
5 × 9 = 45	3 × 9 = 27	54 ÷ 9 = 6
6 × 9 = 54	10 × 9 = 90	27 ÷ 9 = 3
7 × 9 = 63	1 × 9 = 9	63 ÷ 9 = 7
8 × 9 = 72	6 × 9 = 54	72 ÷ 9 = 8
9 × 9 = 81	5 × 9 = 45	90 ÷ 9 = 10
10 × 9 = 90	9 × 9 = 81	45 ÷ 9 = 5

18

Name _____

What's the Error?

Dear Math Students,

Today I found the unknown number in this division equation by using a related multiplication. Is my calculation correct?

$40 \div 5 = \boxed{}$ $\boxed{9} \times 5 = 40$

If not, please correct my work and tell me what I did wrong. How do you know my answer is wrong?

Your friend,
Puzzled Penguin

5 Write a response to Puzzled Penguin.

_____

_____

_____

_____

_____

(PATH to FLUENCY) **Relate Division and Multiplication Equations with 5**

Find the unknown numbers.

6 $20 \div \boxed{5} = \boxed{}$ $\boxed{} \times \boxed{5} = 20$

   $20 \div \boxed{4} = \boxed{}$ $\boxed{} \times \boxed{4} = 20$

7 $10 \div \boxed{5} = \boxed{}$ $\boxed{} \times \boxed{5} = 10$

   $10 \div \boxed{2} = \boxed{}$ $\boxed{} \times \boxed{2} = 10$

8 $15 \div \boxed{5} = \boxed{}$ $\boxed{} \times \boxed{5} = 15$

   $15 \div \boxed{3} = \boxed{}$ $\boxed{} \times \boxed{3} = 15$

What's the Error?

Dear Math Students,

Today I found the unknown number in this division equation by using a related multiplication. Is my calculation correct?

$$40 \div 5 = \boxed{} \qquad \boxed{9} \times 5 = 40$$

If not, please correct my work and tell me what I did wrong. How do you know my answer is wrong?

Your friend,
Puzzled Penguin

Write a response to Puzzled Penguin.

_____

_____

_____

Relate Division and Multiplication Equations with

Find the unknown numbers.

$$20 \div 5 = \boxed{} \qquad \boxed{} \times 5 = 20$$

$$20 \div 4 = \boxed{} \qquad \boxed{} \times 4 = 20$$

$$10 \div 5 = \boxed{} \qquad \boxed{} \times 5 = 10$$

$$10 \div 2 = \boxed{} \qquad \boxed{} \times 2 = 10$$

$$15 \div 5 = \boxed{} \qquad \boxed{} \times 5 = 15$$

$$15 \div 3 = \boxed{} \qquad \boxed{} \times 3 = 15$$

PATH to FLUENCY **Check Sheet 1: 5s and 2s**

5s Multiplications	5s Divisions	2s Multiplications	2s Divisions
2 × 5 = 10	30 / 5 = 6	4 × 2 = 8	8 / 2 = 4
5 • 6 = 30	5 ÷ 5 = 1	2 • 8 = 16	18 ÷ 2 = 9
5 * 9 = 45	15 / 5 = 3	1 * 2 = 2	2 / 2 = 1
4 × 5 = 20	50 ÷ 5 = 10	6 × 2 = 12	16 ÷ 2 = 8
5 • 7 = 35	20 / 5 = 4	2 • 9 = 18	4 / 2 = 2
10 * 5 = 50	10 ÷ 5 = 2	2 * 2 = 4	20 ÷ 2 = 10
1 × 5 = 5	35 / 5 = 7	3 × 2 = 6	10 / 2 = 5
5 • 3 = 15	40 ÷ 5 = 8	2 • 5 = 10	12 ÷ 2 = 6
8 * 5 = 40	25 / 5 = 5	10 * 2 = 20	6 / 2 = 3
5 × 5 = 25	45 / 5 = 9	2 × 7 = 14	14 / 2 = 7
5 • 8 = 40	20 ÷ 5 = 4	2 • 10 = 20	4 ÷ 2 = 2
7 * 5 = 35	15 / 5 = 3	9 * 2 = 18	2 / 2 = 1
5 × 4 = 20	30 ÷ 5 = 6	2 × 6 = 12	8 ÷ 2 = 4
6 • 5 = 30	25 / 5 = 5	8 • 2 = 16	6 / 2 = 3
5 * 1 = 5	10 ÷ 5 = 2	2 * 3 = 6	20 ÷ 2 = 10
5 × 10 = 50	45 / 5 = 9	2 × 2 = 4	14 / 2 = 7
9 • 5 = 45	35 ÷ 5 = 7	1 • 2 = 2	10 ÷ 2 = 5
5 * 2 = 10	50 ÷ 5 = 10	2 * 4 = 8	16 ÷ 2 = 8
3 × 5 = 15	40 / 5 = 8	5 × 2 = 10	12 / 2 = 6
5 • 5 = 25	5 ÷ 5 = 1	7 • 2 = 14	18 ÷ 2 = 9

© Houghton Mifflin Harcourt Publishing Company

30

Check Sheet 1: 5s and 2s

Name _____

PATH to FLUENCY **Use the Target**

×	0	1	2	3	4	5	6	7	8	9
0	0	0	0	0	0	0	0	0	0	0
1	0	1	2	3	4	5	6	7	8	9
2	0	2	4	6	8	10	12	14	16	18
3	0	3	6	9	12	15	18	21	24	27
4	0	4	8	12	16	20	24	28	32	36
5	0	5	10	15	20	25	30	35	40	45
6	0	6	12	18	24	30	36	42	48	54
7	0	7	14	21	28	35	42	49	56	63
8	0	8	16	24	32	40	48	56	64	72
9	0	9	18	27	36	45	54	63	72	81

1 Discuss how you can use the Target to find the product for 8 × 5.

2 Discuss how you can use the Target to practice division.

3 Practice using the Target.

4 When using the Target, how are multiplication and division alike? How are they different?

_____

_____

_____

_____

_____

_____

MATH TO FLUENCY Use the Target

0	0	0	0	0	0	0	0	0	0
0	1	2	3	4	5	6	7	8	9
0	2	4	6	8	10	12	14	16	18
0	3	6	9	12	15	18	21	24	27
0	4	8	12	16	20	24	28	32	36
0	5	10	15	20	25	30	35	40	45
0	6	12	18	24	30	36	42	48	54
0	7	14	21	28	35	42	49	56	63
0	8	16	24	32	40	48	56	64	72
0	9	18	27	36	45	54	63	72	81

1. Discuss how you can use the Target to find the product for 8 × 5.

2. Discuss how you can use the Target to practice division.

3. Practice using the Target.

4. When using the Target, how are multiplication and division alike? How are they different?

Write the correct answer.

1 5 × 3 = ☐

2 18 ÷ 2 = ☐

3 Complete the multiplication sentence.

5 × 6 = 6 × ☐

4 Andy uses 3 bananas in each of 5 loaves of banana bread he is baking. Write a multiplication expression to represent the total number of bananas Andy uses.

Show your work.

_____

5 Solve to find the unknown number in the equation.

5 × ☐ = 40

Unit 1 Big Idea 1

Name _____

Make a drawing. Write an equation. Solve.

1 Imaad has 5 bowls. He wants to serve 4 dumplings in each bowl. How many dumplings does he need in all?

_____

2 Marja arranges her toy cars so 7 toy cars are in each row. She makes 3 equal rows of toy cars. How many toy cars does Marja have?

_____

3 Noriko pastes stars on the first page of her book. She arranges the stars in 2 rows with 4 stars in each row. On the second page, she pastes 2 stars in a row. There are 4 rows of stars on the second page. How many stars are on each page?

_____

What's the Error?

Dear Math Students,

Today my teacher asked me to write a word problem that can be solved using the division 40 ÷ 10. Here is the problem I wrote:

Kim has 40 apples and puts 4 apples in each bag. How many bags does Kim use?

Is my problem correct? If not, please correct my work and tell me what I did wrong.

Your friend,
Puzzled Penguin

15 **Write an answer to the Puzzled Penguin.**

_____

_____

_____

_____

Write and Solve Problems with 10s

16 Write a word problem that can be solved using the multiplication 10 × 3. Then write a related division word problem.

_____

_____

_____

✔ **Check Understanding**

Give an example of a number that is a 10s count-by and explain how you know.

PATH to FLUENCY Check Sheet 2: 10s and 9s

10s Multiplications	10s Divisions	9s Multiplications	9s Divisions
$9 \times 10 = 90$	$100 / 10 = 10$	$3 \times 9 = 27$	$27 / 9 = 3$
$10 \cdot 3 = 30$	$50 \div 10 = 5$	$9 \cdot 7 = 63$	$9 \div 9 = 1$
$10 * 6 = 60$	$70 / 10 = 7$	$10 * 9 = 90$	$81 / 9 = 9$
$1 \times 10 = 10$	$40 \div 10 = 4$	$5 \times 9 = 45$	$45 \div 9 = 5$
$10 \cdot 4 = 40$	$80 / 10 = 8$	$9 \cdot 8 = 72$	$90 / 9 = 10$
$10 * 7 = 70$	$60 \div 10 = 6$	$9 * 1 = 9$	$36 \div 9 = 4$
$8 \times 10 = 80$	$10 / 10 = 1$	$2 \times 9 = 18$	$18 / 9 = 2$
$10 \cdot 10 = 100$	$20 \div 10 = 2$	$9 \cdot 9 = 81$	$63 \div 9 = 7$
$5 * 10 = 50$	$90 / 10 = 9$	$6 * 9 = 54$	$54 / 9 = 6$
$10 \times 2 = 20$	$30 / 10 = 3$	$9 \times 4 = 36$	$72 / 9 = 8$
$10 \cdot 5 = 50$	$80 \div 10 = 8$	$9 \cdot 5 = 45$	$27 \div 9 = 3$
$4 * 10 = 40$	$70 / 10 = 7$	$4 * 9 = 36$	$45 / 9 = 5$
$10 \times 1 = 10$	$100 \div 10 = 10$	$9 \times 1 = 9$	$63 \div 9 = 7$
$3 \cdot 10 = 30$	$90 / 10 = 9$	$3 \cdot 9 = 27$	$72 / 9 = 8$
$10 * 8 = 80$	$60 \div 10 = 6$	$9 * 8 = 72$	$54 \div 9 = 6$
$7 \times 10 = 70$	$30 / 10 = 3$	$7 \times 9 = 63$	$18 / 9 = 2$
$6 \cdot 10 = 60$	$10 \div 10 = 1$	$6 \cdot 9 = 54$	$90 \div 9 = 10$
$10 * 9 = 90$	$40 \div 10 = 4$	$9 * 9 = 81$	$9 \div 9 = 1$
$10 \times 10 = 100$	$20 / 10 = 2$	$10 \times 9 = 90$	$36 / 9 = 4$
$2 \cdot 10 = 20$	$50 \div 10 = 5$	$2 \cdot 9 = 18$	$81 \div 9 = 9$

Check Sheet 2: 10s and 9s

PATH to FLUENCY Check Sheet 3: 2s, 5s, 9s, and 10s

2s, 5s, 9s, 10s Multiplications	2s, 5s, 9s, 10s Multiplications	2s, 5s, 9s, 10s Divisions	2s, 5s, 9s, 10s Divisions
$2 \times 10 = 20$	$5 \times 10 = 50$	$18 / 2 = 9$	$36 / 9 = 4$
$10 \cdot 5 = 50$	$10 \cdot 9 = 90$	$50 \div 5 = 10$	$70 \div 10 = 7$
$9 * 6 = 54$	$4 * 10 = 40$	$72 / 9 = 8$	$18 / 2 = 9$
$7 \times 10 = 70$	$2 \times 9 = 18$	$60 \div 10 = 6$	$45 \div 5 = 9$
$2 \cdot 3 = 6$	$5 \cdot 3 = 15$	$12 / 2 = 6$	$45 / 9 = 5$
$5 * 7 = 35$	$6 * 9 = 54$	$30 \div 5 = 6$	$30 \div 10 = 3$
$9 \times 10 = 90$	$10 \times 3 = 30$	$18 / 9 = 2$	$6 / 2 = 3$
$6 \cdot 10 = 60$	$3 \cdot 2 = 6$	$50 \div 10 = 5$	$50 \div 5 = 10$
$8 * 2 = 16$	$5 * 8 = 40$	$14 / 2 = 7$	$27 / 9 = 3$
$5 \times 6 = 30$	$9 \times 9 = 81$	$25 / 5 = 5$	$70 / 10 = 7$
$9 \cdot 5 = 45$	$10 \cdot 4 = 40$	$81 \div 9 = 9$	$20 \div 2 = 10$
$8 * 10 = 80$	$9 * 2 = 18$	$20 / 10 = 2$	$45 / 5 = 9$
$2 \times 1 = 2$	$5 \times 1 = 5$	$8 \div 2 = 4$	$54 \div 9 = 6$
$3 \cdot 5 = 15$	$9 \cdot 6 = 54$	$45 / 5 = 9$	$80 / 10 = 8$
$4 * 9 = 36$	$10 * 1 = 10$	$63 \div 9 = 7$	$16 \div 2 = 8$
$3 \times 10 = 30$	$7 \times 2 = 14$	$30 / 10 = 3$	$15 / 5 = 3$
$2 \cdot 6 = 12$	$6 \cdot 5 = 30$	$10 \div 2 = 5$	$90 \div 9 = 10$
$4 * 5 = 20$	$8 * 9 = 72$	$40 \div 5 = 8$	$100 \div 10 = 10$
$9 \times 7 = 63$	$10 \times 6 = 60$	$9 / 9 = 1$	$12 / 2 = 6$
$1 \cdot 10 = 10$	$2 \cdot 8 = 16$	$50 \div 10 = 5$	$35 \div 5 = 7$

Write the correct answer.

1. $10 \cdot \boxed{} = 50$

2. $80 \div 10 = \boxed{}$

3. $2 \times \boxed{} = 16$

4. $4 \times 9 = \boxed{}$

5. $27 \div 9 = \boxed{}$

Complete the pattern below to show 9s multiplication.

1 $1 \times 9 = 10 - 1 = \boxed{}$

2 $2 \times 9 = 20 - 2 = \boxed{}$

3 $3 \times 9 = 30 - 3 = \boxed{}$

4 $4 \times 9 = 40 - \boxed{} = \boxed{}$

5 $5 \times 9 = \boxed{} - \boxed{} = \boxed{}$

6 $6 \times 9 = \boxed{} - \boxed{} = \boxed{}$

7 $7 \times 9 = \boxed{} - \boxed{} = \boxed{}$

8 $8 \times 9 = \boxed{} - \boxed{} = \boxed{}$

9 $9 \times 9 = \boxed{} - \boxed{} = \boxed{}$

10 $9 \times 10 = \boxed{} - \boxed{} = \boxed{}$

PATH to FLUENCY

Study Sheet B

4s

Count-bys	Mixed Up ×	Mixed Up ÷
1 × 4 = 4	4 × 4 = 16	12 ÷ 4 = 3
2 × 4 = 8	1 × 4 = 4	36 ÷ 4 = 9
3 × 4 = 12	7 × 4 = 28	24 ÷ 4 = 6
4 × 4 = 16	3 × 4 = 12	4 ÷ 4 = 1
5 × 4 = 20	9 × 4 = 36	20 ÷ 4 = 5
6 × 4 = 24	10 × 4 = 40	28 ÷ 4 = 7
7 × 4 = 28	2 × 4 = 8	8 ÷ 4 = 2
8 × 4 = 32	5 × 4 = 20	40 ÷ 4 = 10
9 × 4 = 36	8 × 4 = 32	32 ÷ 4 = 8
10 × 4 = 40	6 × 4 = 24	16 ÷ 4 = 4

1s

Count-bys	Mixed Up ×	Mixed Up ÷
1 × 1 = 1	5 × 1 = 5	10 ÷ 1 = 10
2 × 1 = 2	7 × 1 = 7	8 ÷ 1 = 8
3 × 1 = 3	10 × 1 = 10	4 ÷ 1 = 4
4 × 1 = 4	1 × 1 = 1	9 ÷ 1 = 9
5 × 1 = 5	8 × 1 = 8	6 ÷ 1 = 6
6 × 1 = 6	4 × 1 = 4	7 ÷ 1 = 7
7 × 1 = 7	9 × 1 = 9	1 ÷ 1 = 1
8 × 1 = 8	3 × 1 = 3	2 ÷ 1 = 2
9 × 1 = 9	2 × 1 = 2	5 ÷ 1 = 5
10 × 1 = 10	6 × 1 = 6	3 ÷ 1 = 3

3s

Count-bys	Mixed Up ×	Mixed Up ÷
1 × 3 = 3	5 × 3 = 15	27 ÷ 3 = 9
2 × 3 = 6	1 × 3 = 3	6 ÷ 3 = 2
3 × 3 = 9	8 × 3 = 24	18 ÷ 3 = 6
4 × 3 = 12	10 × 3 = 30	30 ÷ 3 = 10
5 × 3 = 15	3 × 3 = 9	9 ÷ 3 = 3
6 × 3 = 18	7 × 3 = 21	3 ÷ 3 = 1
7 × 3 = 21	9 × 3 = 27	12 ÷ 3 = 4
8 × 3 = 24	2 × 3 = 6	24 ÷ 3 = 8
9 × 3 = 27	4 × 3 = 12	15 ÷ 3 = 5
10 × 3 = 30	6 × 3 = 18	21 ÷ 3 = 7

0s

Count-bys	Mixed Up ×
1 × 0 = 0	3 × 0 = 0
2 × 0 = 0	10 × 0 = 0
3 × 0 = 0	5 × 0 = 0
4 × 0 = 0	8 × 0 = 0
5 × 0 = 0	7 × 0 = 0
6 × 0 = 0	2 × 0 = 0
7 × 0 = 0	9 × 0 = 0
8 × 0 = 0	6 × 0 = 0
9 × 0 = 0	1 × 0 = 0
10 × 0 = 0	4 × 0 = 0

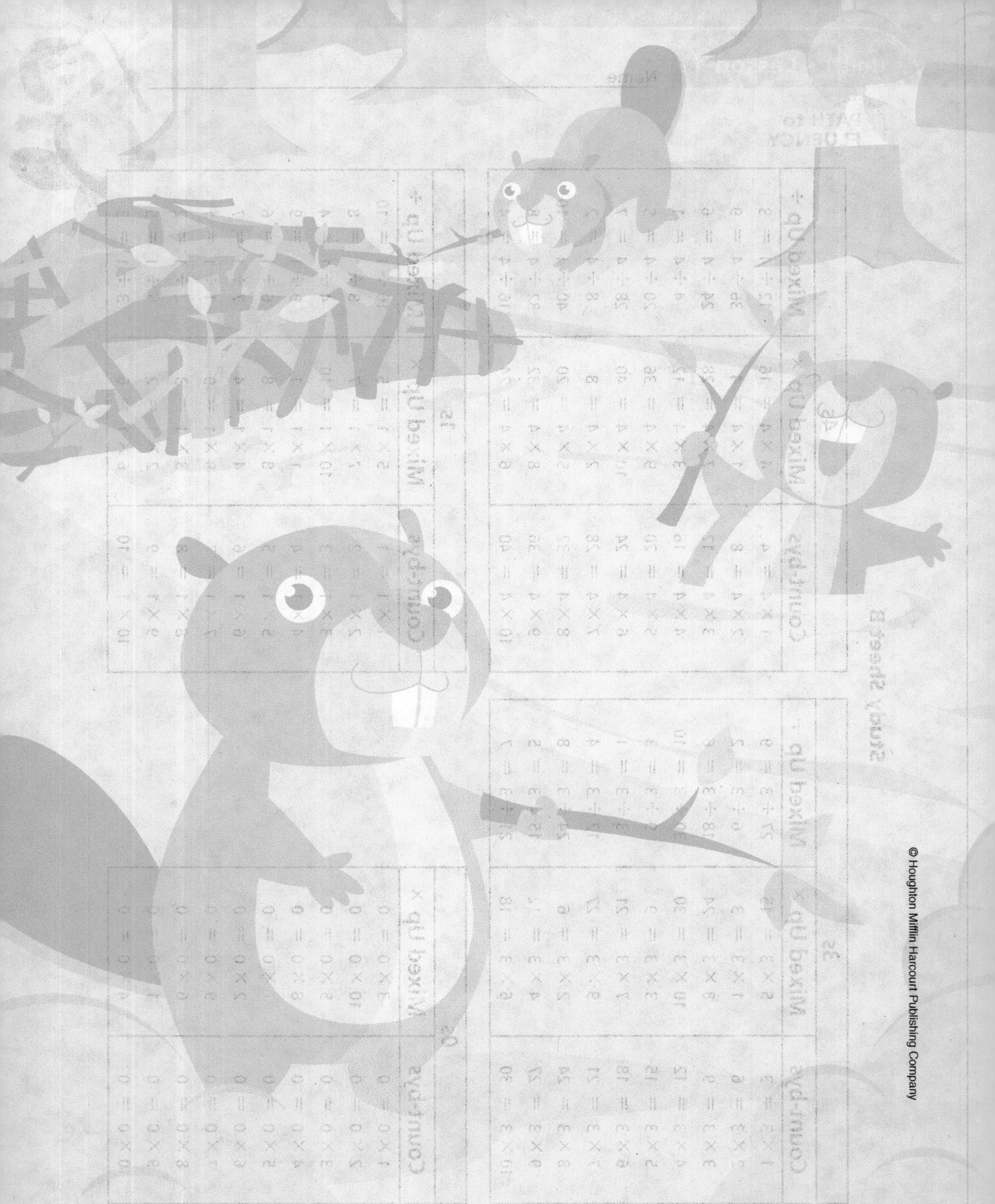

| 2×2 | $\begin{array}{r} 2 \\ \times 3 \end{array} \quad \begin{array}{r} 3 \\ \times 2 \end{array}$ | $\begin{array}{r} 2 \times 4 \\ 4 \times 2 \end{array}$ | $\begin{array}{r} 5 \\ \times 5 \end{array} \quad \begin{array}{r} 5 \\ \times 2 \end{array}$ |

| $\begin{array}{r} 2 \times 6 \\ 6 \times 2 \end{array}$ | $\begin{array}{r} 2 \\ \times 7 \end{array} \quad \begin{array}{r} 7 \\ \times 2 \end{array}$ | $\begin{array}{r} 2 \times 8 \\ 8 \times 2 \end{array}$ | $\begin{array}{r} 2 \\ \times 9 \end{array} \quad \begin{array}{r} 9 \\ \times 2 \end{array}$ |

Card 1

$$10 = 2 \times 5$$
$$10 = 5 \times 2$$

5 2
10 4
   6
   8
  10

5
2 | 10

Card 2

$$\begin{array}{r} 2 \\ \times\,4 \\ \hline 8 \end{array} \qquad \begin{array}{r} 4 \\ \times\,2 \\ \hline 8 \end{array}$$

2   4
4   8
6

2
4 | 8

Card 3

$$6 = 2 \times 3$$
$$6 = 3 \times 2$$

3 2
6 4
   6

3
2 | 6

Card 4

$$\begin{array}{r} 2 \\ \times\,2 \\ \hline 4 \end{array}$$

2
4

2
2 | 4

Card 5

$$18 = 2 \times 9$$
$$18 = 9 \times 2$$

9   2
18 4
    6
    8
   10

   12
   14
   16
   18

9
2 | 18

Card 6

$$\begin{array}{r} 2 \\ \times\,8 \\ \hline 16 \end{array} \qquad \begin{array}{r} 8 \\ \times\,2 \\ \hline 16 \end{array}$$

8   2
16 4
    6
    8
   10

   12
   14
   16

2
8 | 16

Card 7

$$14 = 2 \times 7$$
$$14 = 7 \times 2$$

7   2
14 4
    6
    8
   10

   12
   14

7
2 | 14

Card 8

$$\begin{array}{r} 2 \\ \times\,6 \\ \hline 12 \end{array} \qquad \begin{array}{r} 6 \\ \times\,2 \\ \hline 12 \end{array}$$

6   2
12 4
    6
    8
   10

   12

2
6 | 12

Multiplication Strategy Cards

3×3

$$\begin{array}{r} 4 \\ \times\ 4 \end{array} \qquad \times\ 3$$

$$3 \times 5$$
$$5 \times 3$$

$$\begin{array}{r} 6 \\ \times\ 6 \end{array} \qquad \times\ 3$$

3×7
7×3

$$\begin{array}{r} 8 \\ \times\ 8 \end{array} \qquad \times\ 3$$

3×9
9×3

$$\begin{array}{r} 4 \\ \times\ 4 \end{array}$$

Multiplication Strategy Cards

Card 1
18 = 3 × 6
18 = 6 × 3

6	3
12	6
18	9
	12
	15
	18

6
3 | 18

Card 2
3   5
× 5   × 3
15   15

5	3
10	6
15	9
	12
	15

3
5 | 15

Card 3
12 = 3 × 4
12 = 4 × 3

4	3
8	6
12	9
	12

4
3 | 12

Card 4
3
× 3
9

3
6
9

3
3 | 9

Card 5
16 = 4 × 4

4
8
12
16

4
4 | 16

Card 6
3   9
× 9   × 3
27   27

9	3
18	6
27	9
	12
	15
	18
	21
	24
	27

9
3 | 27

Card 7
24 = 3 × 8
24 = 8 × 3

8	3
16	6
24	9
	12
	15
	18
	21
	24

3
8 | 24

Card 8
3   7
× 7   × 3
21   21

7	3
14	6
21	9
	12
	15
	18
	21

7
3 | 21

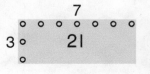

55D
Multiplication Strategy Cards

4×5	4	6	4×7	4	8
5×4	$\times 6$	$\times 4$	7×4	$\times 8$	$\times 4$

4×9	5	5×6	5	7
9×4	$\times 5$	6×5	$\times 7$	$\times 5$

Card 1

$32 = 4 \times 8$
$32 = 8 \times 4$

8	4
16	8
24	12
32	16
	20
	24
	28
	32

4

8 32

Card 2

4×7 7×4

4	7
$\times 7$	$\times 4$
28	28

7	4
14	8
21	12
28	16
	20
	24
	28

7

4 28

Card 3

$24 = 4 \times 6$
$24 = 6 \times 4$

6	4
12	8
18	12
24	16
	20
	24

4

6 24

Card 4

4×5 5×4

4	5
$\times 5$	$\times 4$
20	20

5	4
10	8
15	12
20	16
	20

5

4 20

Card 5

$35 = 5 \times 7$
$35 = 7 \times 5$

7	5
14	10
21	15
28	20
35	25
	30
	35

7

5 35

Card 6

5×6 6×5

5	6
$\times 6$	$\times 5$
30	30

6	5
12	10
18	15
24	20
30	25
	30

5

6 30

Card 7

$25 = 5 \times 5$

5
10
15
20
25

5

5 25

Card 8

4×9 9×4

4	9
$\times 9$	$\times 4$
36	36

9	4
18	8
27	12
36	16
	20
	24
	28
	32
	36

9

4 36

Multiplication Strategy Cards

5×8
8×5

5 9
$\times 9$ $\times 5$

6×6

6 7
$\times 7$ $\times 6$

6×8
8×6

6 9
$\times 9$ $\times 6$

7×7

7 8
$\times 8$ $\times 7$

Card 1

$42 = 7 \times 6$
$42 = 6 \times 7$

6	7
12	14
18	21
24	28
30	35
36	42
42	

7

6 **42**

Card 2

6
$\times 6$
36

6
12
18
24
30

36

6

6 **36**

Card 3

$45 = 9 \times 5$
$45 = 5 \times 9$

5	9
10	18
15	27
20	36
25	45
30	
35	
40	
45	

9

5 **45**

Card 4

5
$\times 5$
40

8
$\times 8$
40

5	8
10	16
15	24
20	32
25	40
30	
35	
40	

5

8 **40**

Card 5

$56 = 7 \times 8$
$56 = 8 \times 7$

8	7
16	14
24	21
32	28
40	35
48	42
56	49
	56

8

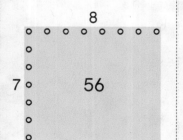

7 **56**

Card 6

7
$\times 7$
49

7
14
21
28
35

42
49

7

7 **49**

Card 7

$54 = 9 \times 6$
$54 = 6 \times 9$

6	9
12	18
18	27
24	36
30	45
36	54
42	
48	
54	

9

6 **54**

Card 8

6
$\times 8$
48

8
$\times 6$
48

8	6
16	12
24	18
32	24
40	30
48	36
	42
	48

8

6 **48**

7×9
9×7

8
× 8

9×8
8×9

9
× 9

Card 1

$81 = 9 \times 9$

9
18
27
36
45

54
63
72
81

9

9 81

Card 2

9×8 8×9

$\begin{array}{r} 9 \\ \times 8 \\ \hline 72 \end{array}$ $\begin{array}{r} 8 \\ \times 9 \\ \hline 72 \end{array}$

8   9
16   18
24   27
32   36
40   45

48   54
56   63
64   72
72

9

8 72

Card 3

$64 = 8 \times 8$

8
16
24
32
40

48
56
64

8

8 64

Card 4

7×9 9×7

$\begin{array}{r} 7 \\ \times 9 \\ \hline 63 \end{array}$ $\begin{array}{r} 9 \\ \times 7 \\ \hline 63 \end{array}$

9   7
18   14
27   21
36   28
45   35

54   42
63   49
       56
       63

9

7 63

$2\overline{)4}$	$2\overline{)6}$	$2\overline{)8}$	$2\overline{)10}$
$4 \div 2$	$6 \div 2$	$8 \div 2$	$10 \div 2$

$2\overline{)12}$	$2\overline{)14}$	$2\overline{)16}$	$2\overline{)18}$
$12 \div 2$	$14 \div 2$	$16 \div 2$	$18 \div 2$

Top row:

5
2)10   5)10
2   5
4   10
6
8
10

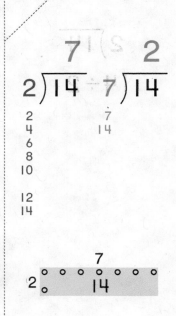

5
2 ∘∘∘∘∘ 10

4
2)8   4)8
2   4
4   8
6
8

4
2 ∘∘∘∘ 8

3
2)6   3)6
2   3
4   6
6

3
2 ∘∘∘ 6

2
2)4
2
4

2
2 ∘∘ 4

Bottom row:

9
2)18   9)18
2   9
4   18
6
8
10

12
14
16
18

9
2 ∘∘∘∘∘∘∘∘∘ 18

8
2)16   8)16
2   8
4   16
6
8
10

12
14
16

8
2 ∘∘∘∘∘∘∘∘ 16

7
2)14   7)14
2   7
4   14
6
8
10

12
14

7
2 ∘∘∘∘∘∘∘ 14

6
2)12   6)12
2   6
4   12
6
8
10

12

6
2 ∘∘∘∘∘∘ 12

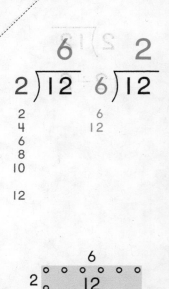

$3\overline{)6}$

$6 \div 3 = 2$

$4\overline{)8}$

$8 \div 4 = 2$

$5\overline{)10}$

$10 \div 5 = 2$

$6\overline{)12}$

$12 \div 6 = 2$

$7\overline{)14}$

$14 \div 7 = 2$

$8\overline{)16}$

$16 \div 8 = 2$

$9\overline{)18}$

$18 \div 9 = 2$

$3\overline{)9}$

$9 \div 3 = 3$

Row 1

Card 1

2
6)12 — 6 2)12

6
12

2
4
6
8
10
12

2
6 ○ 12

Card 2

2
5)10 — 5 2)10

5
10

2
4
6
8
10

2
5 ○ 10

Card 3

2
4)8 — 4 2)8

4
8

2
4
6
8

2
4 ○ 8

Card 4

2
3)6 — 3 2)6

3
6

2
4
6

2
3 ○ 6

Row 2

Card 5

3
3)9

3
6
9

3
3 ○ 9

Card 6

2
9)18 — 9 2)18

9
18

2
4
6
8
10

12
14
16
18

2
9 ○ 18

Card 7

2
8)16 — 8 2)16

8
16

2
4
6
8
10

12
14
16

2
8 ○ 16

Card 8

2
7)14 — 7 2)14

7
14

2
4
6
8
10

12
14

2
7 ○ 14

$$3\overline{)12}$$
$$12 \div 3 = 4$$

$$3\overline{)15}$$
$$15 \div 3 = 5$$

$$3\overline{)18}$$
$$18 \div 3 = 6$$

$$3\overline{)21}$$
$$21 \div 3 = 7$$

$$3\overline{)24}$$
$$24 \div 3 = 8$$

$$3\overline{)27}$$
$$27 \div 3 = 9$$

$$4\overline{)12}$$
$$12 \div 4 = 3$$

$$5\overline{)15}$$
$$15 \div 5 = 3$$

Card 1

$3\overline{)21}$ $7\overline{)21}$

3	7
6	14
9	21
12	
15	
18	
21	

7
3 • 21

Card 2

$3\overline{)18}$ $6\overline{)18}$

3	6
6	12
9	18
12	
15	
18	

6
3 • 18

Card 3

$3\overline{)15}$ $5\overline{)15}$

3	5
6	10
9	15
12	
15	

5
3 • 15

Card 4

$3\overline{)12}$ $4\overline{)12}$

3	4
6	8
9	12
12	

4
3 • 12

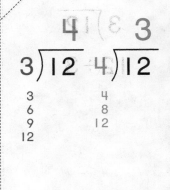

Card 5

$5\overline{)15}$ $3\overline{)15}$

5	3
10	6
15	9
	12
	15

3
5 • 15

Card 6

$4\overline{)12}$ $3\overline{)12}$

4	3
8	6
12	9
	12

3
4 • 12

Card 7

$3\overline{)27}$ $9\overline{)27}$

3	9
6	18
9	27
12	
15	
18	
21	
24	
27	

9
3 • 27

Card 8

$3\overline{)24}$ $8\overline{)24}$

3	8
6	16
9	24
12	
15	
18	
21	
24	

8
3 • 24

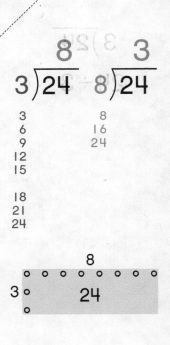

$6\overline{)18}$	$7\overline{)21}$	$8\overline{)24}$	$9\overline{)27}$
$18 \div 6$	$21 \div 7$	$24 \div 8$	$27 \div 9$

$4\overline{)16}$	$4\overline{)20}$	$4\overline{)24}$	$4\overline{)28}$
$16 \div 4$	$20 \div 4$	$24 \div 4$	$28 \div 4$

Division Strategy Cards

3 9)27   **9** 3)27

9	3
18	6
27	9
	12
	15
	18
	21
	24
	27

3
9 o 27

3 8)24   **8** 3)24

8	3
16	6
24	9
	12
	15
	18
	21
	24

3
8 o 24

3 7)21   **7** 3)21

7	3
14	6
21	9
	12
	15
	18
	21

3
7 o 21

3 6)18   **6** 3)18

6	3
12	6
18	9
	12
	15
	18

3
6 o 18

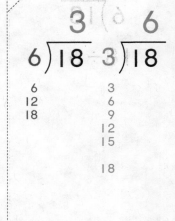

7 4)28   **4** 7)28

4	7
8	14
12	21
16	28
20	
24	
28	

7
4 o 28

6 4)24   **4** 6)24

4	6
8	12
12	18
16	24
20	
24	

6
4 o 24

5 4)20   **4** 5)20

4	5
8	10
12	15
16	20
20	

5
4 o 20

4 4)16

4
8
12
16

4
4 o 16

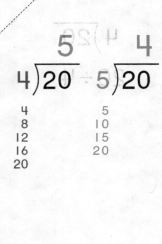

Division Strategy Cards

$4\overline{)32}$	$4\overline{)36}$	$5\overline{)20}$	$6\overline{)24}$
$32 \div 4$	$36 \div 4$	$20 \div 5$	$24 \div 6$

$7\overline{)28}$	$8\overline{)32}$	$9\overline{)36}$	$5\overline{)25}$
$28 \div 7$	$32 \div 8$	$36 \div 9$	$25 \div 5$

UNIT 1 LESSON 11
© Houghton Mifflin Harcourt Publishing Company

Division Strategy Cards

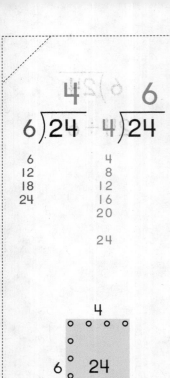
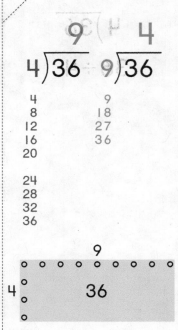
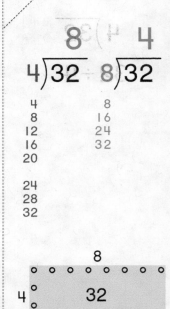

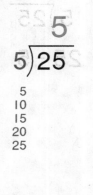
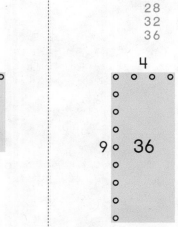
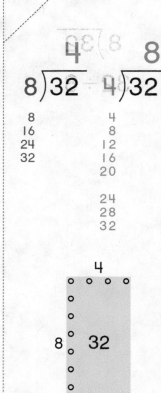
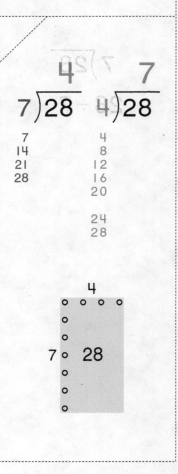

Division Strategy Cards

$5 \overline{)30}$

$30 \div 5$

$5 \overline{)35}$

$35 \div 5$

$5 \overline{)40}$

$40 \div 5$

$5 \overline{)45}$

$45 \div 5$

$6 \overline{)30}$

$30 \div 6$

$7 \overline{)35}$

$35 \div 7$

$8 \overline{)40}$

$40 \div 8$

$9 \overline{)45}$

$45 \div 9$

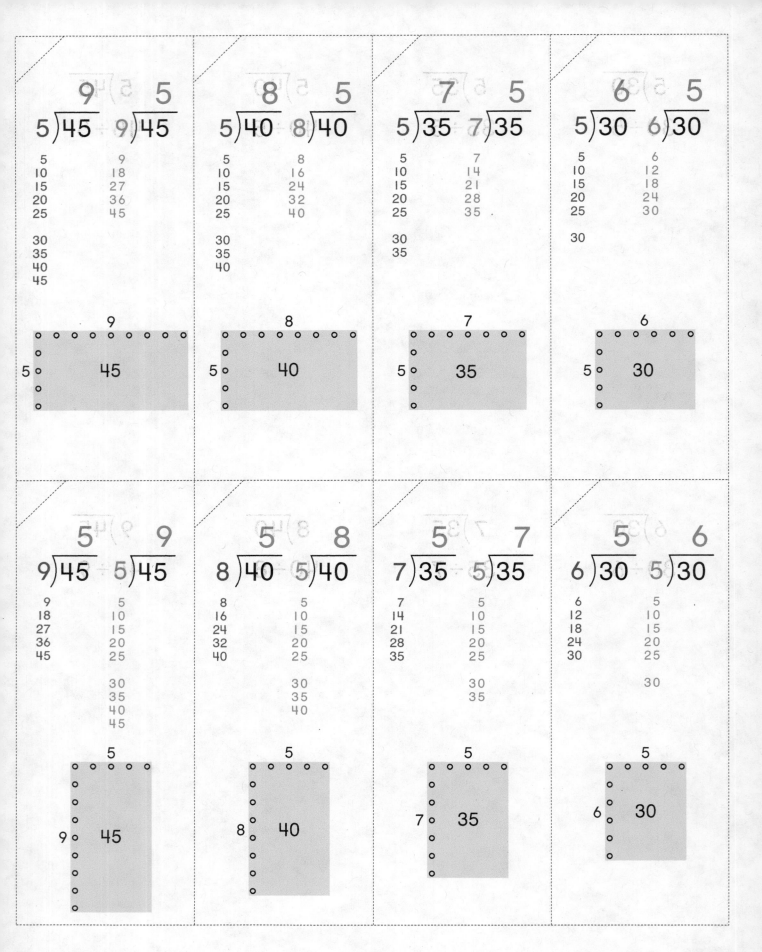

$6 \overline{)36}$

$36 \div 6$

$6 \overline{)42}$

$42 \div 6$

$6 \overline{)48}$

$48 \div 6$

$6 \overline{)54}$

$54 \div 6$

$7 \overline{)42}$

$42 \div 7$

$8 \overline{)48}$

$48 \div 8$

$9 \overline{)54}$

$54 \div 9$

$7 \overline{)49}$

$49 \div 7$

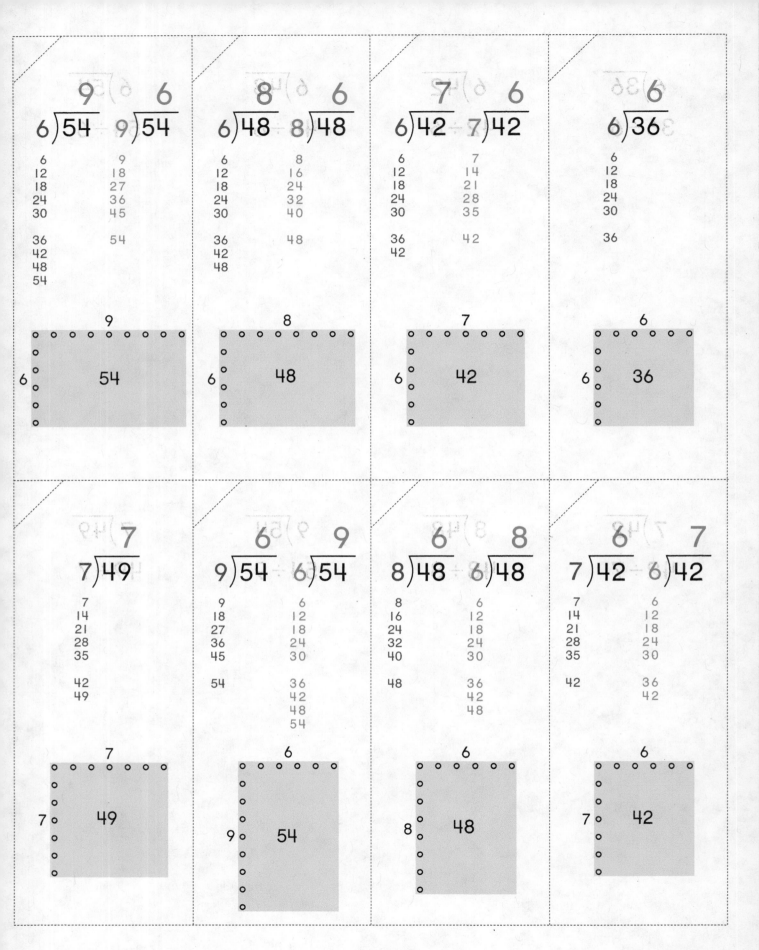

UNIT 1 LESSON 11
© Houghton Mifflin Harcourt Publishing Company

Division Strategy Cards

$7\overline{)56}$	$7\overline{)63}$	$8\overline{)56}$	$9\overline{)63}$
$56 \div 7$	$63 \div 7$	$56 \div 8$	$63 \div 9$

$8\overline{)64}$	$8\overline{)72}$	$9\overline{)72}$	$9\overline{)81}$
$64 \div 8$	$72 \div 8$	$72 \div 9$	$81 \div 9$

UNIT 1 LESSON 11
© Houghton Mifflin Harcourt Publishing Company

Division Strategy Cards

Card 1

$9\overline{)63}$ = 7 $7\overline{)63}$ = 9

9	7
18	14
27	21
36	28
45	35
54	42
63	49
	56
	63

7 · 9 → 63

Card 2

$8\overline{)56}$ = 7 $7\overline{)56}$ = 8

8	7
16	14
24	21
32	28
40	35
48	42
56	49
	56

7 · 8 → 56

Card 3

$7\overline{)63}$ = 9 $9\overline{)63}$ = 7

7	9
14	18
21	27
28	36
35	45
42	54
49	63
56	
63	

9 · 7 → 63

Card 4

$7\overline{)56}$ = 8 $8\overline{)56}$ = 7

7	8
14	16
21	24
28	32
35	40
42	48
49	56
56	

8 · 7 → 56

Card 5

$9\overline{)81}$ = 9

9
18
27
36
45
54
63
72
81

9 · 9 → 81

Card 6

$9\overline{)72}$ = 8 $8\overline{)72}$ = 9

9	8
18	16
27	24
36	32
45	40
54	48
63	56
72	64
	72

8 · 9 → 72

Card 7

$8\overline{)72}$ = 9 $9\overline{)72}$ = 8

8	9
16	18
24	27
32	36
40	45
48	54
56	63
64	72
72	

9 · 8 → 72

Card 8

$8\overline{)64}$ = 8

8
16
24
32
40
48
56
64

8 · 8 → 64

Name _____

PATH to FLUENCY **Find the Area**

The **area** of a rectangle is the number of **square units** that fit inside of it.

First, write a multiplication equation to represent the area of each rectangle. Then shade a whole number of rows in each rectangle. Write a multiplication to represent the area of the shaded rectangle and the area of the unshaded rectangle. Then write an addition equation to represent the area of the entire rectangle.

 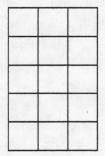   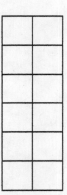   

_____   _____   _____

_____   _____   _____

_____   _____   _____

Make a rectangle drawing to represent each problem. Then give the product.

4 $5 \times 3 =$ _____   **5** $7 * 2 =$ _____   **6** $2 \cdot 9 =$ _____

Find the Area

VOCABULARY
area
square units

5 × 3 = _____   7 × 2 = _____   2 × 9 = _____

PATH to FLUENCY   Check Sheet 4: 3s and 4s

3s Multiplications	3s Divisions	4s Multiplications	4s Divisions
8 × 3 = 24	9 / 3 = 3	1 × 4 = 4	40 / 4 = 10
3 • 2 = 6	21 ÷ 3 = 7	4 • 5 = 20	12 ÷ 4 = 3
3 * 5 = 15	27 / 3 = 9	8 * 4 = 32	24 / 4 = 6
10 × 3 = 30	3 ÷ 3 = 1	3 × 4 = 12	8 ÷ 4 = 2
3 • 3 = 9	18 / 3 = 6	4 • 6 = 24	4 / 4 = 1
3 * 6 = 18	12 ÷ 3 = 4	4 * 9 = 36	28 ÷ 4 = 7
7 × 3 = 21	30 / 3 = 10	10 × 4 = 40	32 / 4 = 8
3 • 9 = 27	6 ÷ 3 = 2	4 • 7 = 28	16 ÷ 4 = 4
4 * 3 = 12	24 / 3 = 8	4 * 4 = 16	36 / 4 = 9
3 × 1 = 3	15 / 3 = 5	2 × 4 = 8	20 / 4 = 5
3 • 4 = 12	21 ÷ 3 = 7	4 • 3 = 12	4 ÷ 4 = 1
3 * 3 = 9	3 / 3 = 1	4 * 2 = 8	32 / 4 = 8
3 × 10 = 30	9 ÷ 3 = 3	9 × 4 = 36	8 ÷ 4 = 2
2 • 3 = 6	27 / 3 = 9	1 • 4 = 4	16 / 4 = 4
3 * 7 = 21	30 ÷ 3 = 10	4 * 6 = 24	36 ÷ 4 = 9
6 × 3 = 18	18 / 3 = 6	5 × 4 = 20	12 / 4 = 3
5 • 3 = 15	6 ÷ 3 = 2	4 • 4 = 16	40 ÷ 4 = 10
3 * 8 = 24	15 ÷ 3 = 5	7 * 4 = 28	20 ÷ 4 = 5
9 × 3 = 27	12 / 3 = 4	8 × 4 = 32	24 / 4 = 6
2 • 3 = 6	24 ÷ 3 = 8	10 • 4 = 40	28 ÷ 4 = 7

58

Check Sheet 4: 3s and 4s

Name _____

What's the Error?

Dear Math Students,

Today I had to find 8 × 4. I didn't know the answer,
but I figured it out by combining two multiplications
I did know:

$$5 \times 2 = 10$$
$$\underline{3 \times 2 = 6}$$
$$8 \times 4 = 16$$

Is my answer right? If not, please correct my work
and tell me why it is wrong.

Your friend,
The Puzzled Penguin

11 **Write an answer to the Puzzled Penguin.**

_____

_____

_____

Make Sense of Problems

Write an equation and solve the problem.

12 Galen has 20 pictures to place in his book. If he
puts 4 pictures on each page, how many pages
will he fill?

_____

13 Emery arranged tiles in an array with 4 columns
and 7 rows. How many tiles were in the array?

_____

✓ **Check Understanding**
Draw a picture to show how you can use the answers
to 5 × 4 and 3 × 4 to find 8 × 4.

PATH to FLUENCY Play *Solve the Stack*

Read the rules for playing *Solve the Stack*. Then play the game with your group.

Rules for *Solve the Stack*

Number of players: 2–4

What you will need: 1 set of Multiplication and Division Strategy Cards

1. Shuffle the cards. Place them exercise side up in the center of the table.

2. Players take turns. On each turn, a player finds the answer to the multiplication or division on the top card and then turns the card over to check the answer.

3. If a player's answer is correct, he or she takes the card. If it is incorrect, the card is placed at the bottom of the stack.

4. Play ends when there are no more cards in the stack. The player with the most cards wins.

$7)\overline{56}$

$56 \div 7$

PATH to FLUENCY Play *High Card Wins*

Read the rules for playing *High Card Wins*. Then play the game with your partner.

Rules for *High Card Wins*

Number of players: 2

What you will need: 1 set of Multiplication and Division Strategy Cards for 2s, 3s, 4s, 5s, 9s

1. Shuffle the cards. Deal all the cards evenly between the two players.

2. Players put their stacks in front of them, exercise side up.

3. Each player takes the top card from his or her stack and puts it exercise side up in the center of the table.

4. Each player says the multiplication or division answer and then turns the card over to check. Then players do one of the following:

   • If one player says the wrong answer, the other player takes both cards and puts them at the bottom of his or her pile.

   • If both players say the wrong answer, both players take back their cards and put them at the bottom of their piles.

   • If both players say the correct answer, the player with the higher product or quotient takes both cards and puts them at the bottom of his or her pile. If the products or quotients are the same, the players set the cards aside and play another round. The winner of the next round takes all the cards.

5. Play continues until one player has all the cards.

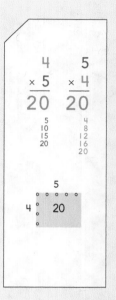

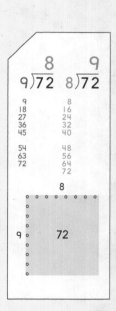

PRACTICE/
PROFICIENCY

Play High Card Wins

Name _____

Write an equation and solve the problem.

Show your work.

1 A three-story apartment building has a total of 24 apartments. There are the same number of apartments on each floor. How many apartments are there on one floor?

_____

2 Marcus puts shoes on 5 horses at his family's farm. How many horseshoes does Marcus put on the horses altogether?

_____

3 The 14 players on the basketball team line up in 2 equal rows to practice passing. How many players are there in each row?

_____

4 Marla uses 4 cups of chicken stock for some soup she is cooking. There are 8 ounces in each cup. How many ounces of chicken stock does Marla use?

_____

5 Show the area of this rectangle in square units.

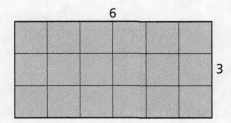

_____

Name _____

Complete.

1 Rashawn knows the multiplications 6 × 4 and 2 × 4. How can he use their products to find 8 × 4?

_____

2 Ruben puts 4 buttons on each puppet. He used 20 buttons for 5 puppets. He needs to put buttons on 3 more puppets. How many buttons does he need for all 8 puppets? Explain.

_____

_____

3 What multiplication can you use to find 21 ÷ 3?

_____

4 Find the area of the large rectangle. Explain.

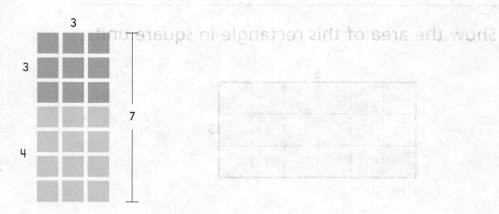

_____

_____

PATH to FLUENCY **Check Sheet 5: 1s and 0s**

1s Multiplications	1s Divisions	0s Multiplications
$1 \times 4 = 4$	$10 / 1 = 10$	$4 \times 0 = 0$
$5 \cdot 1 = 5$	$5 \div 1 = 5$	$2 \cdot 0 = 0$
$7 * 1 = 7$	$7 / 1 = 7$	$0 * 8 = 0$
$1 \times 8 = 8$	$9 \div 1 = 9$	$0 \times 5 = 0$
$1 \cdot 6 = 6$	$3 / 1 = 3$	$6 \cdot 0 = 0$
$10 * 1 = 10$	$10 \div 1 = 10$	$0 * 7 = 0$
$1 \times 9 = 9$	$2 / 1 = 2$	$0 \times 2 = 0$
$3 \cdot 1 = 3$	$8 \div 1 = 8$	$0 \cdot 9 = 0$
$1 * 2 = 2$	$6 / 1 = 6$	$10 * 0 = 0$
$1 \times 1 = 1$	$9 / 1 = 9$	$1 \times 0 = 0$
$8 \cdot 1 = 8$	$1 \div 1 = 1$	$0 \cdot 6 = 0$
$1 * 7 = 7$	$5 / 1 = 5$	$9 * 0 = 0$
$1 \times 5 = 5$	$3 \div 1 = 3$	$0 \times 4 = 0$
$6 \cdot 1 = 6$	$4 / 1 = 4$	$3 \cdot 0 = 0$
$1 * 1 = 1$	$2 \div 1 = 2$	$0 * 3 = 0$
$1 \times 10 = 10$	$8 / 1 = 8$	$8 \times 0 = 0$
$9 \cdot 1 = 9$	$4 \div 1 = 4$	$0 \cdot 10 = 0$
$4 * 1 = 4$	$7 \div 1 = 7$	$0 * 1 = 0$
$2 \times 1 = 2$	$1 / 1 = 1$	$5 \times 0 = 0$
$1 \cdot 3 = 3$	$6 \div 1 = 6$	$7 \cdot 0 = 0$

Name _____

PATH to FLUENCY Check Sheet 6: Mixed 3s, 4s, 0s, and 1s

3s, 4s, 0s, 1s Multiplications	3s, 4s, 0s, 1s Multiplications	3s, 4s, 1s Divisions	3s, 4s, 1s Divisions
$5 \times 3 = 15$	$0 \times 5 = 0$	$18 / 3 = 6$	$4 / 1 = 4$
$6 \cdot 4 = 24$	$10 \cdot 1 = 10$	$20 \div 4 = 5$	$21 \div 3 = 7$
$9 * 0 = 0$	$6 * 3 = 18$	$1 / 1 = 1$	$16 / 4 = 4$
$7 \times 1 = 7$	$2 \times 4 = 8$	$21 \div 3 = 7$	$9 \div 1 = 9$
$3 \cdot 3 = 9$	$5 \cdot 0 = 0$	$12 / 4 = 3$	$15 / 3 = 5$
$4 * 7 = 28$	$1 * 2 = 2$	$5 \div 1 = 5$	$8 \div 4 = 2$
$0 \times 10 = 0$	$10 \times 3 = 30$	$15 / 3 = 5$	$5 / 1 = 5$
$1 \cdot 6 = 6$	$5 \cdot 4 = 20$	$24 \div 4 = 6$	$30 \div 3 = 10$
$3 * 4 = 12$	$0 * 8 = 0$	$7 / 1 = 7$	$12 / 4 = 3$
$5 \times 4 = 20$	$9 \times 1 = 9$	$12 / 3 = 4$	$8 / 1 = 8$
$0 \cdot 5 = 0$	$10 \cdot 3 = 30$	$36 \div 4 = 9$	$27 \div 3 = 9$
$9 * 1 = 9$	$9 * 4 = 36$	$6 / 1 = 6$	$40 / 4 = 10$
$2 \times 3 = 6$	$1 \times 0 = 0$	$12 \div 3 = 4$	$4 \div 1 = 4$
$3 \cdot 4 = 12$	$1 \cdot 6 = 6$	$16 / 4 = 4$	$9 / 3 = 3$
$0 * 9 = 0$	$3 * 6 = 18$	$7 \div 1 = 7$	$16 \div 4 = 4$
$1 \times 5 = 5$	$7 \times 4 = 28$	$9 / 3 = 3$	$10 / 1 = 10$
$2 \cdot 3 = 6$	$6 \cdot 0 = 0$	$8 \div 4 = 2$	$9 \div 3 = 3$
$4 * 4 = 16$	$8 * 1 = 8$	$2 \div 1 = 2$	$20 \div 4 = 5$
$9 \times 0 = 0$	$3 \times 9 = 27$	$6 / 3 = 2$	$6 / 1 = 6$
$1 \cdot 1 = 1$	$1 \cdot 4 = 4$	$32 \div 4 = 8$	$24 \div 3 = 8$

PATH to FLUENCY Play *Multiplication Three-in-a-Row*

Read the rules for playing *Multiplication Three-in-a-Row*. Then play the game with a partner.

Rules for *Multiplication Three-in-a-Row*

Number of players: 2

What You Will Need: A set of Multiplication Strategy Cards, *Three-in-a-Row* Game Grids for each player (see page 83)

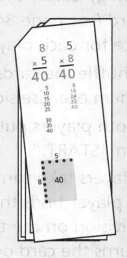

1. Each player looks through the cards and writes any nine of the products in the squares of a Game Grid. A player may write the same product more than once.

2. Shuffle the cards and place them exercise side up in the center of the table.

3. Players take turns. On each turn, a player finds the answer to the multiplication on the top card and then turns the card over to check the answer.

4. If the answer is correct, the player looks to see if the product is on the game grid. If it is, the player puts an X through that grid square. If the answer is wrong, or if the product is not on the grid, the player does not mark anything. The player then puts the card problem side up on the bottom of the stack.

5. The first player to mark three squares in a row (horizontally, vertically, or diagonally) wins.

© Houghton Mifflin Harcourt Publishing Company

Name _____

Play *Division Race*

Read the rules for playing *Division Race*. Then play the game with a partner.

Rules for *Division Race*

Number of players: 2

What You Will Need: a set of Division Strategy Cards, the *Division Race* game board (see page 84), a different game piece for each player

1. Shuffle the cards and then place them exercise side up on the table.

2. Both players put their game pieces on "START."

3. Players take turns. On each turn, a player finds the answer to the division on the top card and then turns the card over to check the answer.

4. If the answer is correct, the player moves *forward* that number of spaces. If a player's answer is wrong, the player moves *back* a number of spaces equal to the correct answer. Players cannot move back beyond the "START" square. The player puts the card on the bottom of the stack.

5. If a player lands on a space with special instructions, he or she should follow those instructions.

6. The game ends when everyone lands on or passes the "End" square.

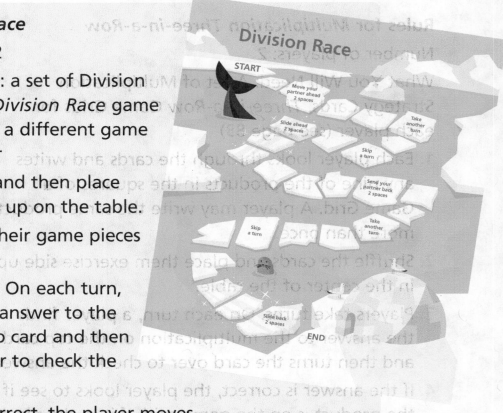

Name

83

Three-in-a-Row Game Grids

Division Race

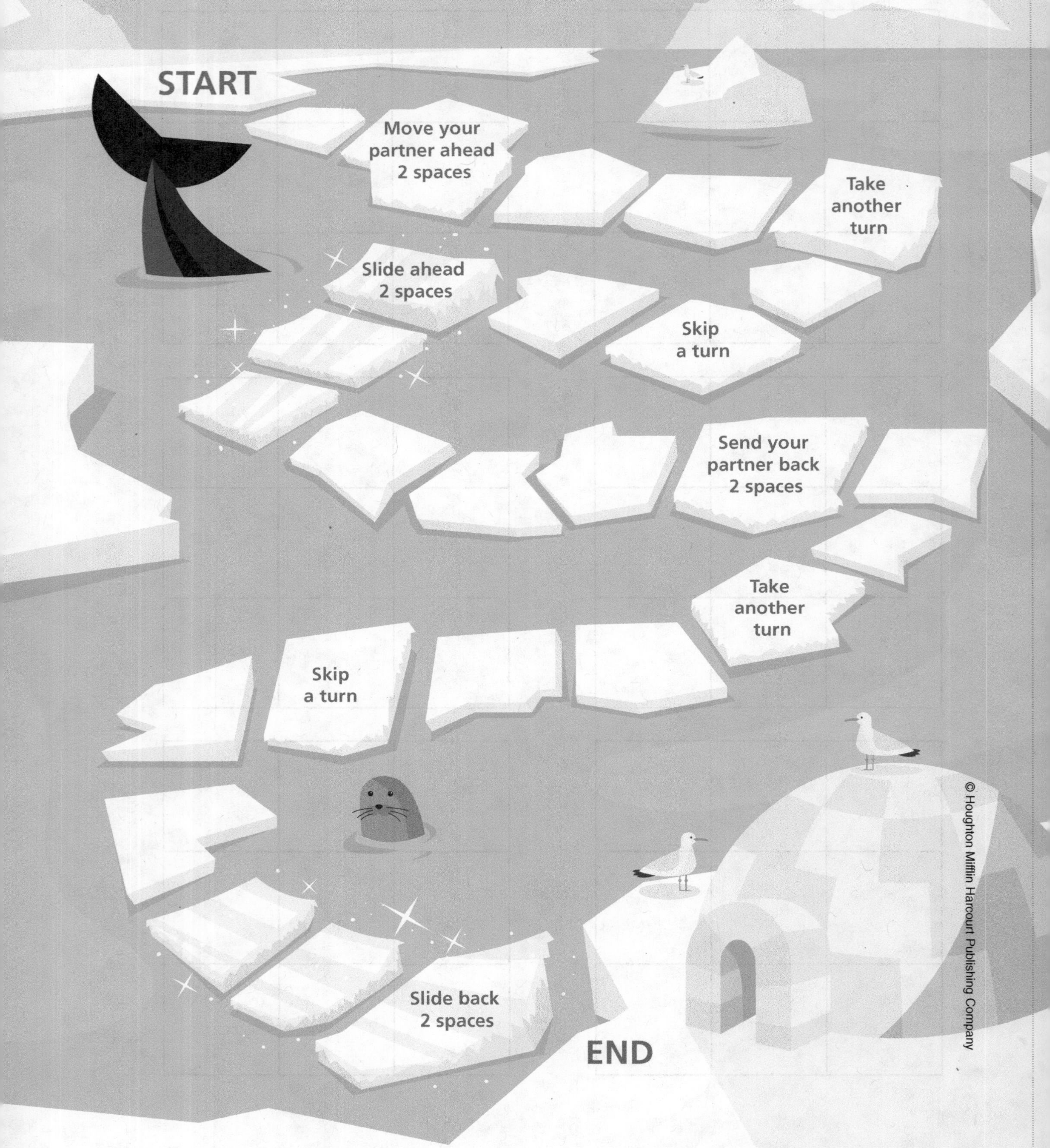

START

Move your partner ahead 2 spaces

Take another turn

Slide ahead 2 spaces

Skip a turn

Send your partner back 2 spaces

Take another turn

Skip a turn

Slide back 2 spaces

END

PATH to FLUENCY Dashes 1–4

Complete each Dash. Check your answers on page 89.

Dash 1 2s and 5s Multiplications	Dash 2 2s and 5s Divisions	Dash 3 9s and 10s Multiplications	Dash 4 9s and 10s Divisions
a. $2 \times 6 =$ ___	a. $18 / 2 =$ ___	a. $9 \times 10 =$ ___	a. $100 / 10 =$ ___
b. $9 * 5 =$ ___	b. $25 \div 5 =$ ___	b. $10 * 3 =$ ___	b. $9 \div 9 =$ ___
c. $7 \cdot 2 =$ ___	c. $8 / 2 =$ ___	c. $1 \cdot 9 =$ ___	c. $30 / 10 =$ ___
d. $5 \times 8 =$ ___	d. $45 \div 5 =$ ___	d. $2 \times 10 =$ ___	d. $81 \div 9 =$ ___
e. $2 * 4 =$ ___	e. $16 / 2 =$ ___	e. $9 * 9 =$ ___	e. $70 / 10 =$ ___
f. $3 \cdot 5 =$ ___	f. $20 \div 5 =$ ___	f. $10 \cdot 6 =$ ___	f. $45 \div 9 =$ ___
g. $1 \times 2 =$ ___	g. $4 / 2 =$ ___	g. $4 \times 9 =$ ___	g. $10 / 10 =$ ___
h. $5 * 7 =$ ___	h. $40 \div 5 =$ ___	h. $10 \times 10 =$ ___	h. $54 \div 9 =$ ___
i. $2 \cdot 9 =$ ___	i. $20 / 2 =$ ___	i. $9 * 2 =$ ___	i. $50 / 10 =$ ___
j. $4 \times 5 =$ ___	j. $35 \div 5 =$ ___	j. $1 \cdot 10 =$ ___	j. $27 \div 9 =$ ___
k. $5 * 2 =$ ___	k. $6 / 2 =$ ___	k. $7 \times 9 =$ ___	k. $20 / 10 =$ ___
l. $5 \cdot 1 =$ ___	l. $15 \div 5 =$ ___	l. $10 * 5 =$ ___	l. $72 \div 9 =$ ___
m. $2 \times 2 =$ ___	m. $14 / 2 =$ ___	m. $9 \cdot 8 =$ ___	m. $40 / 10 =$ ___
n. $10 \times 5 =$ ___	n. $5 \div 5 =$ ___	n. $7 \times 10 =$ ___	n. $18 \div 9 =$ ___
o. $10 * 2 =$ ___	o. $10 / 2 =$ ___	o. $3 * 9 =$ ___	o. $60 / 10 =$ ___
p. $5 \cdot 6 =$ ___	p. $10 \div 5 =$ ___	p. $10 \cdot 4 =$ ___	p. $90 \div 9 =$ ___
q. $2 \times 3 =$ ___	q. $6 / 2 =$ ___	q. $9 \times 5 =$ ___	q. $90 / 10 =$ ___
r. $5 * 5 =$ ___	r. $30 \div 5 =$ ___	r. $8 * 10 =$ ___	r. $63 \div 9 =$ ___
s. $8 \cdot 2 =$ ___	s. $2 / 2 =$ ___	s. $6 \cdot 9 =$ ___	s. $80 / 10 =$ ___
t. $6 \times 5 =$ ___	t. $45 \div 5 =$ ___	t. $10 \times 9 =$ ___	t. $36 \div 9 =$ ___

Name _____

PATH to FLUENCY Dashes 5–8

Complete each Dash. Check your answers on page 89.

Dash 5 3s and 4s Multiplications	Dash 6 3s and 4s Divisions	Dash 7 0s and 1s Multiplications	Dash 8 1s and $n \div n$ Divisions
a. $3 \times 9 = $ ___	a. $12 / 4 = $ ___	a. $0 \times 6 = $ ___	a. $9 / 9 = $ ___
b. $4 * 2 = $ ___	b. $20 \div 4 = $ ___	b. $1 * 4 = $ ___	b. $8 \div 1 = $ ___
c. $6 \cdot 3 = $ ___	c. $21 / 3 = $ ___	c. $4 \cdot 0 = $ ___	c. $7 / 7 = $ ___
d. $10 \times 4 = $ ___	d. $16 \div 4 = $ ___	d. $8 \times 1 = $ ___	d. $6 \div 1 = $ ___
e. $3 * 1 = $ ___	e. $9 / 3 = $ ___	e. $0 * 2 = $ ___	e. $1 / 1 = $ ___
f. $4 \cdot 1 = $ ___	f. $32 \div 4 = $ ___	f. $1 \cdot 3 = $ ___	f. $4 \div 1 = $ ___
g. $10 \times 3 = $ ___	g. $24 / 4 = $ ___	g. $9 \times 0 = $ ___	g. $2 / 2 = $ ___
h. $5 * 4 = $ ___	h. $18 \div 3 = $ ___	h. $2 * 1 = $ ___	h. $2 \div 1 = $ ___
i. $3 \cdot 3 = $ ___	i. $40 / 4 = $ ___	i. $0 \cdot 8 = $ ___	i. $8 / 8 = $ ___
j. $4 \times 4 = $ ___	j. $12 \div 3 = $ ___	j. $1 \times 10 = $ ___	j. $9 \div 1 = $ ___
k. $8 * 3 = $ ___	k. $6 / 3 = $ ___	k. $7 * 0 = $ ___	k. $3 / 3 = $ ___
l. $7 \cdot 4 = $ ___	l. $28 \div 4 = $ ___	l. $1 \cdot 1 = $ ___	l. $5 \div 1 = $ ___
m. $3 \times 2 = $ ___	m. $24 / 3 = $ ___	m. $0 \times 0 = $ ___	m. $5 / 5 = $ ___
n. $4 * 9 = $ ___	n. $20 \div 4 = $ ___	n. $5 * 1 = $ ___	n. $10 / 10 = $ ___
o. $7 \cdot 3 = $ ___	o. $27 / 3 = $ ___	o. $1 \cdot 0 = $ ___	o. $7 \div 1 = $ ___
p. $3 \times 4 = $ ___	p. $15 \div 3 = $ ___	p. $1 \times 6 = $ ___	p. $4 / 4 = $ ___
q. $3 * 5 = $ ___	q. $27 / 3 = $ ___	q. $5 * 0 = $ ___	q. $10 \div 1 = $ ___
r. $4 \cdot 6 = $ ___	r. $36 \div 4 = $ ___	r. $0 \cdot 3 = $ ___	r. $6 / 6 = $ ___
s. $4 \times 3 = $ ___	s. $8 / 4 = $ ___	s. $7 \times 1 = $ ___	s. $3 \div 1 = $ ___
t. $8 * 4 = $ ___	t. $40 \div 4 = $ ___	t. $1 * 9 = $ ___	t. $1 / 1 = $ ___

Name _____

PATH to FLUENCY **Dashes 9–12**

Complete each Dash. Check your answers on page 90.

Dash 9 2s, 5s, 9s, 10s Multiplications	Dash 10 2s, 5s, 9s, 10s Divisions	Dash 11 3s, 4s, 0s, 1s Multiplications	Dash 12 3s, 4s, 1s Divisions
a. $4 \times 5 = $ ____	a. $8 / 2 = $ ____	a. $3 \times 0 = $ ____	a. $12 / 4 = $ ____
b. $10 \cdot 3 = $ ____	b. $50 \div 10 = $ ____	b. $4 \cdot 6 = $ ____	b. $5 \div 1 = $ ____
c. $8 * 9 = $ ____	c. $15 / 5 = $ ____	c. $9 * 1 = $ ____	c. $21 / 3 = $ ____
d. $6 \times 2 = $ ____	d. $63 \div 9 = $ ____	d. $3 \times 3 = $ ____	d. $1 \div 1 = $ ____
e. $5 \cdot 7 = $ ____	e. $90 / 10 = $ ____	e. $8 \cdot 4 = $ ____	e. $16 / 4 = $ ____
f. $10 * 5 = $ ____	f. $90 \div 9 = $ ____	f. $0 * 5 = $ ____	f. $9 \div 3 = $ ____
g. $8 \times 2 = $ ____	g. $35 / 5 = $ ____	g. $1 \times 6 = $ ____	g. $32 / 4 = $ ____
h. $6 \cdot 10 = $ ____	h. $14 \div 2 = $ ____	h. $4 \cdot 3 = $ ____	h. $8 \div 1 = $ ____
i. $9 * 3 = $ ____	i. $27 / 9 = $ ____	i. $7 * 4 = $ ____	i. $24 / 4 = $ ____
j. $2 \times 9 = $ ____	j. $45 / 5 = $ ____	j. $3 \times 7 = $ ____	j. $18 / 3 = $ ____
k. $5 \cdot 8 = $ ____	k. $10 \div 10 = $ ____	k. $0 \cdot 1 = $ ____	k. $10 \div 1 = $ ____
l. $10 * 7 = $ ____	l. $25 / 5 = $ ____	l. $10 * 1 = $ ____	l. $40 / 4 = $ ____
m. $5 \times 5 = $ ____	m. $54 \div 9 = $ ____	m. $4 \times 4 = $ ____	m. $12 \div 3 = $ ____
n. $1 \cdot 5 = $ ____	n. $6 / 2 = $ ____	n. $9 \cdot 3 = $ ____	n. $6 / 3 = $ ____
o. $9 * 6 = $ ____	o. $72 \div 9 = $ ____	o. $8 * 0 = $ ____	o. $4 \div 4 = $ ____
p. $10 \times 10 = $ ____	p. $40 / 5 = $ ____	p. $5 \times 4 = $ ____	p. $7 / 1 = $ ____
q. $4 \cdot 2 = $ ____	q. $80 \div 10 = $ ____	q. $1 \cdot 6 = $ ____	q. $28 \div 4 = $ ____
r. $10 * 8 = $ ____	r. $18 \div 2 = $ ____	r. $3 * 8 = $ ____	r. $24 \div 3 = $ ____
s. $3 \times 9 = $ ____	s. $36 / 9 = $ ____	s. $4 \times 9 = $ ____	s. $20 / 4 = $ ____
t. $9 \cdot 9 = $ ____	t. $30 \div 5 = $ ____	t. $0 \cdot 4 = $ ____	t. $27 \div 3 = $ ____

Name _____

PATH to FLUENCY Dashes 9A–12A

Complete each Dash. Check your answers on page 90.

Dash 9A 2s, 5s, 9s, 10s Multiplications	**Dash 10A** 2s, 5s, 9s, 10s Divisions	**Dash 11A** 3s, 4s, 0s, 1s Multiplications	**Dash 12A** 3s, 4s, 1s Divisions
a. $9 \times 9 =$ ___	a. $30 / 5 =$ ___	a. $0 \times 4 =$ ___	a. $10 / 1 =$ ___
b. $4 * 5 =$ ___	b. $18 \div 2 =$ ___	b. $4 * 9 =$ ___	b. $40 \div 4 =$ ___
c. $10 \cdot 3 =$ ___	c. $40 / 5 =$ ___	c. $3 \cdot 8 =$ ___	c. $12 / 3 =$ ___
d. $3 \times 9 =$ ___	d. $6 \div 2 =$ ___	d. $3 \times 0 =$ ___	d. $6 \div 3 =$ ___
e. $10 * 8 =$ ___	e. $25 / 5 =$ ___	e. $4 * 6 =$ ___	e. $4 / 4 =$ ___
f. $6 \cdot 2 =$ ___	f. $45 \div 5 =$ ___	f. $9 \cdot 1 =$ ___	f. $7 \div 1 =$ ___
g. $8 \times 9 =$ ___	g. $14 / 2 =$ ___	g. $3 \times 3 =$ ___	g. $28 / 4 =$ ___
h. $4 * 2 =$ ___	h. $90 \div 9 =$ ___	h. $8 * 4 =$ ___	h. $24 \div 3 =$ ___
i. $10 \cdot 10 =$ ___	i. $63 / 9 =$ ___	i. $0 \cdot 5 =$ ___	i. $20 / 4 =$ ___
j. $9 \times 6 =$ ___	j. $50 \div 10 =$ ___	j. $1 \times 6 =$ ___	j. $27 \div 3 =$ ___
k. $5 * 7 =$ ___	k. $8 / 2 =$ ___	k. $5 * 4 =$ ___	k. $12 / 4 =$ ___
l. $10 \cdot 5 =$ ___	l. $15 \div 5 =$ ___	l. $8 \cdot 0 =$ ___	l. $5 \div 1 =$ ___
m. $8 \times 2 =$ ___	m. $90 / 10 =$ ___	m. $9 \times 3 =$ ___	m. $21 / 3 =$ ___
n. $6 * 10 =$ ___	n. $35 \div 5 =$ ___	n. $4 * 4 =$ ___	n. $1 \div 1 =$ ___
o. $2 * 9 =$ ___	o. $27 / 9 =$ ___	o. $10 \cdot 1 =$ ___	o. $16 / 4 =$ ___
p. $9 \cdot 6 =$ ___	p. $10 \div 10 =$ ___	p. $4 \times 3 =$ ___	p. $9 \div 3 =$ ___
q. $1 \times 5 =$ ___	q. $54 / 9 =$ ___	q. $7 * 4 =$ ___	q. $32 / 4 =$ ___
r. $5 * 5 =$ ___	r. $72 \div 9 =$ ___	r. $3 \cdot 7 =$ ___	r. $8 \div 1 =$ ___
s. $10 \cdot 7 =$ ___	s. $80 / 10 =$ ___	s. $0 \times 1 =$ ___	s. $24 / 4 =$ ___
t. $5 \times 8 =$ ___	t. $36 \div 9 =$ ___	t. $10 * 1 =$ ___	t. $18 \div 3 =$ ___

88

Name

PATH to FLUENCY Answers to Dashes 1–8

Use this sheet to check your answers to the Dashes on pages 85 and 86.

Dash 1 2s and 5s ×	Dash 2 2s and 5s ÷	Dash 3 9s and 10s ×	Dash 4 9s and 10s ÷	Dash 5 3s and 4s ×	Dash 6 3s and 4s ÷	Dash 7 0s and 1s ×	Dash 8 1s and $n \div n$ ÷
a. 12	a. 9	a. 90	a. 10	a. 27	a. 3	a. 0	a. 1
b. 45	b. 5	b. 30	b. 1	b. 8	b. 5	b. 4	b. 8
c. 14	c. 4	c. 9	c. 3	c. 18	c. 7	c. 0	c. 1
d. 40	d. 9	d. 20	d. 9	d. 40	d. 4	d. 8	d. 6
e. 8	e. 8	e. 81	e. 7	e. 3	e. 3	e. 0	e. 1
f. 15	f. 4	f. 60	f. 5	f. 4	f. 8	f. 3	f. 4
g. 2	g. 2	g. 36	g. 1	g. 30	g. 6	g. 0	g. 1
h. 35	h. 8	h. 100	h. 6	h. 20	h. 6	h. 2	h. 2
i. 18	i. 10	i. 18	i. 5	i. 9	i. 10	i. 0	i. 1
j. 20	j. 7	j. 10	j. 3	j. 16	j. 4	j. 10	j. 9
k. 10	k. 3	k. 63	k. 2	k. 24	k. 2	k. 0	k. 1
l. 5	l. 3	l. 50	l. 8	l. 28	l. 7	l. 1	l. 5
m. 4	m. 7	m. 72	m. 4	m. 6	m. 8	m. 0	m. 1
n. 50	n. 1	n. 70	n. 2	n. 36	n. 5	n. 5	n. 1
o. 20	o. 5	o. 27	o. 6	o. 21	o. 9	o. 0	o. 7
p. 30	p. 2	p. 40	p. 10	p. 12	p. 5	p. 6	p. 1
q. 6	q. 3	q. 45	q. 9	q. 15	q. 9	q. 0	q. 10
r. 25	r. 6	r. 80	r. 7	r. 24	r. 9	r. 0	r. 1
s. 16	s. 1	s. 54	s. 8	s. 12	s. 2	s. 7	s. 3
t. 30	t. 9	t. 90	t. 4	t. 32	t. 10	t. 9	t. 1

Name _____

PATH to FLUENCY Answers to Dashes 9–12, 9A–12A

Use this sheet to check your answers to the Dashes on pages 87 and 88.

Dash 9 ×	Dash 10 ÷	Dash 11 ×	Dash 12 ÷	Dash 9A ×	Dash 10A ÷	Dash 11A ×	Dash 12A ÷
a. 20	a. 4	a. 0	a. 3	a. 81	a. 6	a. 0	a. 10
b. 30	b. 5	b. 24	b. 5	b. 20	b. 9	b. 36	b. 10
c. 72	c. 3	c. 9	c. 7	c. 30	c. 8	c. 24	c. 4
d. 12	d. 7	d. 9	d. 1	d. 27	d. 3	d. 0	d. 2
e. 35	e. 9	e. 32	e. 4	e. 80	e. 5	e. 24	e. 1
f. 50	f. 10	f. 0	f. 3	f. 12	f. 9	f. 9	f. 7
g. 16	g. 7	g. 6	g. 8	g. 72	g. 7	g. 9	g. 7
h. 60	h. 7	h. 12	h. 8	h. 8	h. 10	h. 32	h. 8
i. 27	i. 3	i. 28	i. 6	i. 100	i. 7	i. 0	i. 5
j. 18	j. 9	j. 21	j. 6	j. 54	j. 5	j. 6	j. 9
k. 40	k. 1	k. 0	k. 10	k. 35	k. 4	k. 20	k. 3
l. 70	l. 5	l. 10	l. 10	l. 50	l. 3	l. 0	l. 5
m. 25	m. 6	m. 16	m. 4	m. 16	m. 9	m. 27	m. 7
n. 5	n. 3	n. 27	n. 2	n. 60	n. 7	n. 16	n. 1
o. 54	o. 8	o. 0	o. 1	o. 18	o. 3	o. 10	o. 4
p. 100	p. 8	p. 20	p. 7	p. 54	p. 1	p. 12	p. 3
q. 8	q. 8	q. 6	q. 7	q. 5	q. 6	q. 28	q. 8
r. 80	r. 9	r. 24	r. 8	r. 25	r. 8	r. 21	r. 8
s. 27	s. 4	s. 36	s. 5	s. 70	s. 8	s. 0	s. 6
t. 81	t. 6	t. 0	t. 9	t. 40	t. 4	t. 10	t. 6

(PATH to FLUENCY) **What is Your Hobby?**

Carina asked some third graders, "What is your hobby?"
The answers are shown under the photos.

Dancing
Four third graders
said dancing.

Photography
Eight more than
dancing
said photography.

Reading
Six less than
photography said
reading.

Games
Eight third graders
said games.

3 **Use the information above to complete the chart below.**

| What is Your Hobby? ||
Hobby	Number of Students
Dancing	
Photography	
Games	
Reading	

4 **Use the chart to complete the pictograph below.**

Hobbies	
Dancing	
Photography	
Games	
Reading	

Each ☐ stands for 2 third graders.

5 **How many third graders answered Carina's question?**

_____

Write an equation and solve the problem.

Show your work.

1 Mrs. Andrews divides 45 milliliters of water equally into 9 test tubes for her science class. How many milliliters of water does she place in each test tube?

_____

_____

2 The chorus members singing at a school concert stand in 3 rows, with 9 members in each row. How many chorus members are there altogether?

_____

_____

3 The 32 students on a field trip are organized into groups of 4 for a tour. How many groups of students are there?

_____

_____

Solve.

4 Susan arranges her model cars in 6 rows, with 3 cars in each row. How else can Susan arrange her model cars in equal rows?

_____

_____

5 Philip bakes 8 muffins and gives each of his friends 1 muffin. He has no muffins left over. To how many of his friends does Philip give a muffin?

_____

Name _____

Add.

1 1 + 6 = ☐

2 3 + 8 = ☐

3 8 + 5 = ☐

4 5 + 3 = ☐

5 2 + 8 = ☐

6 3 + 9 = ☐

7 4 + 5 = ☐

8 6 + 7 = ☐

9 5 + 9 = ☐

10
```
   7
+  5
```

11
```
   6
+  9
```

12
```
   8
+  0
```

13
```
   9
+  7
```

14
```
   8
+  6
```

15
```
   7
+  8
```

1 Write a multiplication equation for the array.

_____

2 Write the numbers that complete the pattern.

6	7	8	9	72	81

$$4 \times 9 = 36$$

$$5 \times 9 = 45$$

$$\square \times 9 = 54$$

$$7 \times \square = 63$$

$$8 \times 9 = \square$$

3 Read the problem. Choose the type of problem it is.
Then write an equation to solve the problem.

Pala is drawing tulips on 9 posters. She draws
4 tulips on each poster. How many tulips
does Pala draw on the posters?

The type of problem is
array multiplication
array division
equal groups multiplication
.

Equation: _____

_____ tulips

4 Draw a line to match the equation on the left with the
unknown number on the right.

$\frac{45}{5} = \blacksquare$ •　　• 0

$9 \times \blacksquare = 0$ •　　• 5

$\blacksquare \times 3 = 15$ •　　• 8

$\blacksquare \div 3 = 7$ •　　• 9

$72 \div \blacksquare = 9$ •　　• 14

$7 \times 2 = \blacksquare$ •　　• 21

5 Write the number that completes the multiplication equation.

$$6 \times 4 = \boxed{} \times 6$$

$$7 \times 3 = (4 + 3) \times \boxed{}$$

$$5 \times (2 \times 4) = (\boxed{} \times \boxed{}) \times 4$$

6 Sydney wants to find the area of the large rectangle by adding the areas of the two small rectangles.

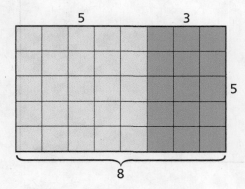

For numbers 6a–6d, choose Yes or No to tell whether or not Sydney could use the expression to find the area of the large rectangle.

6a. $(8 \times 5) + (5 \times 5)$ ○ Yes   ○ No

6b. $25 + 15$ ○ Yes   ○ No

6c. $(5 \times 5) + (3 \times 5)$ ○ Yes   ○ No

6d. $(5 \times 5) + (5 \times 3)$ ○ Yes   ○ No

7 Look at the rectangle drawing.

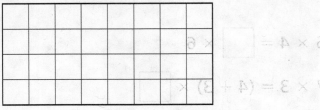

Part A

Write a word problem that can be solved using the drawing.

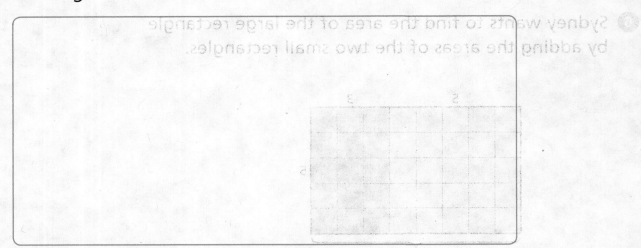

Part B

Solve the problem. Explain how to use the rectangle drawing to check your answer.

© Houghton Mifflin Harcourt Publishing Company

8 Select the situation which could be represented by the multiplication expression 5×7. Mark all that apply.

Ⓐ total number of stamps on 5 pages with 7 stamps on each page

Ⓑ total number of stamps when there are 5 stamps on one page and 7 stamps on another page

Ⓒ 5 stamps divided evenly onto 7 pages

Ⓓ 5 more stamps than on a page with 7 stamps

Make a drawing for the problem. Then write an equation and solve it.

9 The 28 desks in Mr. Becker's class are arranged in 7 equal rows. How many desks are in each row?

10 Michelle's bookcase has 3 shelves. It holds 9 books on each shelf. How many books will fit in the bookcase?

11 Rami counts 6 birds sitting on each of 5 different wires. How many birds does Rami count?

12 Use properties of multiplication to solve.

12a. $9 \times 6 = \boxed{} \times 9$

12b. $\boxed{} \times 10 = 10$

12c. $\boxed{} \times 2 = 0$

12d. $(3 \times \boxed{}) \times 5 = 3 \times (4 \times 5)$

13 Chloe buys 10 balloons for her sisters. She gives 5 balloons to each sister and has none left.

Part A

How many sisters does Chloe have? Write an equation and solve the problem.

Equation: _____

_____ sisters

Part B

Solve the problem in a different way. Tell how the ways are alike and different.

Make Travel Plans

A group of 40 students is going to a science museum. Some parents have offered to drive the students. The table below shows the vehicles they can use.

Type of Vehicle	Number of Students the Vehicle Can Hold	Number of Vehicles Available
Small Car	2	3
Large Car	3	10
Crossover	4	4
Minivan	5	4
SUV	6	5

1 Plan two different ways the 40 students can ride to the museum. For each plan, be sure all the students have a ride. Describe the plan with words, pictures, equations, or a table. Explain which plan is better and tell why.

2 Plan a way to use the least number of vehicles. Describe the plan with words, pictures, equations, or a table. Explain why the plan uses the least number of vehicles.

3 If there is another trip, different parents will drive. Will that change the least number of cars that are needed? Explain your answer and show how you know.

4 How would you change your strategy for planning the trip if each vehicle needs to have an adult other than the driver?

Dear Family:

In this unit, students learn multiplications and divisions for 6s, 7s, and 8s, while continuing to practice the rest of the basic multiplications and divisions covered in Unit 1.

Although students practice all the 6s, 7s, and 8s multiplications, they really have only six new multiplications to learn: 6×6, 6×7, 6×8, 7×7, 7×8, and 8×8. The lessons for these multiplications focus on strategies for finding the products using multiplications they know.

This unit also focuses on word problems. Students are presented with a variety of one-step and two-step word problems.

Here is an example of a two-step problem:

> A roller coaster has 7 cars. Each car has 4 seats. If there were 3 empty seats, how many people were on the roller coaster?

Students use the language and context of each problem to determine which operation or operations—multiplication, division, addition, or subtraction—they must use to solve it. Students use a variety of methods to solve two-step word problems.

Please continue to help your child get faster on multiplications and divisions. Use all of the practice materials that your child has brought home. Your support is crucial to your child's learning.

Please contact me if you have any questions or comments.

Thank you.

Sincerely,
Your child's teacher

Estimada familia:

En esta unidad los estudiantes aprenden las multiplicaciones y divisiones con el 6, el 7 y el 8, mientras siguen practicando las demás multiplicaciones y divisiones que se presentaron en la Unidad 1.

Aunque los estudiantes practican todas las multiplicaciones con el 6, el 7 y el 8, en realidad sólo tienen que aprender seis multiplicaciones nuevas: 6×6, 6×7, 6×8, 7×7, 7×8 y 8×8. Las lecciones acerca de estas multiplicaciones se centran en estrategias para hallar los productos usando multiplicaciones que ya se conocen.

Esta unidad también se centra en problemas verbales. A los estudiantes se les presenta una variedad de problemas de uno y de dos pasos.

> Este es un ejemplo de un problema de dos pasos:
> Una montaña rusa tiene 7 carros. Cada carro tiene 7 asientos. Si hay 3 asientos vacíos. Cuántas personas había en la montaña rusa?

Los estudiantes aprovechan el lenguaje y el contexto de cada problema para determinar qué operación u operaciones deben usar para resolverlo: multiplicación, división, suma o resta. Los estudiantes usan una variedad de métodos para resolver problemas de dos pasos.

Por favor continúe ayudando a su niño a practicar las multiplicaciones y las divisiones. Use todos los materiales de práctica que su niño ha llevado a casa. Su apoyo es importante para el aprendizaje de su niño.

Si tiene alguna duda o pregunta, por favor comuníquese conmigo.

Atentamente,
El maestro de su niño

expression

Order of Operations

square number

A combination of numbers, variables, and/or operation signs. An expression does not have an equal sign.

Examples:

$4 + 7 \qquad a - 3$

A set of rules that state the order in which the operations in an expression should be done.

STEP 1: Perform operations inside parentheses first.

STEP 2: Multiply and divide from left to right.

STEP 3: Add and subtract from left to right.

The product of a whole number and itself.

Example:

$$3 \times 3 = 9$$

square number

© Houghton Mifflin Harcourt Publishing Company

Name _____

PATH to FLUENCY

Study Sheet C

6s

Count-bys	Mixed Up ×	Mixed Up ÷
1 × 6 = 6	10 × 6 = 60	54 ÷ 6 = 9
2 × 6 = 12	8 × 6 = 48	30 ÷ 6 = 5
3 × 6 = 18	2 × 6 = 12	12 ÷ 6 = 2
4 × 6 = 24	6 × 6 = 36	60 ÷ 6 = 10
5 × 6 = 30	4 × 6 = 24	48 ÷ 6 = 8
6 × 6 = 36	1 × 6 = 6	36 ÷ 6 = 6
7 × 6 = 42	9 × 6 = 54	6 ÷ 6 = 1
8 × 6 = 48	3 × 6 = 18	42 ÷ 6 = 7
9 × 6 = 54	7 × 6 = 42	18 ÷ 6 = 3
10 × 6 = 60	5 × 6 = 30	24 ÷ 6 = 4

7s

Count-bys	Mixed Up ×	Mixed Up ÷
1 × 7 = 7	6 × 7 = 42	70 ÷ 7 = 10
2 × 7 = 14	8 × 7 = 56	14 ÷ 7 = 2
3 × 7 = 21	5 × 7 = 35	28 ÷ 7 = 4
4 × 7 = 28	9 × 7 = 63	56 ÷ 7 = 8
5 × 7 = 35	4 × 7 = 28	42 ÷ 7 = 6
6 × 7 = 42	10 × 7 = 70	63 ÷ 7 = 9
7 × 7 = 49	3 × 7 = 21	21 ÷ 7 = 3
8 × 7 = 56	1 × 7 = 7	49 ÷ 7 = 7
9 × 7 = 63	7 × 7 = 49	7 ÷ 7 = 1
10 × 7 = 70	2 × 7 = 14	35 ÷ 7 = 5

8s

Count-bys	Mixed Up ×	Mixed Up ÷
1 × 8 = 8	6 × 8 = 48	16 ÷ 8 = 2
2 × 8 = 16	10 × 8 = 80	40 ÷ 8 = 5
3 × 8 = 24	7 × 8 = 56	72 ÷ 8 = 9
4 × 8 = 32	2 × 8 = 16	32 ÷ 8 = 4
5 × 8 = 40	4 × 8 = 32	8 ÷ 8 = 1
6 × 8 = 48	8 × 8 = 64	80 ÷ 8 = 10
7 × 8 = 56	5 × 8 = 40	64 ÷ 8 = 8
8 × 8 = 64	9 × 8 = 72	24 ÷ 8 = 3
9 × 8 = 72	3 × 8 = 24	56 ÷ 8 = 7
10 × 8 = 80	1 × 8 = 8	48 ÷ 8 = 6

Squares

Count-bys	Mixed Up ×	Mixed Up ÷
1 × 1 = 1	3 × 3 = 9	25 ÷ 5 = 5
2 × 2 = 4	9 × 9 = 81	4 ÷ 2 = 2
3 × 3 = 9	4 × 4 = 16	81 ÷ 9 = 9
4 × 4 = 16	6 × 6 = 36	9 ÷ 3 = 3
5 × 5 = 25	2 × 2 = 4	36 ÷ 6 = 6
6 × 6 = 36	7 × 7 = 49	100 ÷ 10 = 10
7 × 7 = 49	10 × 10 = 100	16 ÷ 4 = 4
8 × 8 = 64	1 × 1 = 1	49 ÷ 7 = 7
9 × 9 = 81	5 × 5 = 25	1 ÷ 1 = 1
10 × 10 = 100	8 × 8 = 64	64 ÷ 8 = 8

Name

PATH to FLUENCY Unknown Number Puzzles

Complete each Unknown Number puzzle.

1

×	5	2	
	30		48
4		8	32
	45		72

2

×		3	
6	30		42
4			28
	40	24	56

3

×	4		8
9		81	
	12		24
	20	45	40

4

×		3	
	60		20
6	36		
	18	9	6

5

×	8		2
7		28	
	16	8	
	32	16	8

6

×	9		
8		56	24
	54	42	18
5			15

7

×	8		7
8		40	
	32	20	28
	24	15	

8

×	3	4	
	27	36	81
7			63
			18

9

×			10
8	48	16	
7	42	14	
		36	60

Tiling and Multiplying to Find Area

Use inch tiles to find the area. Then label the side lengths and find the area using multiplication.

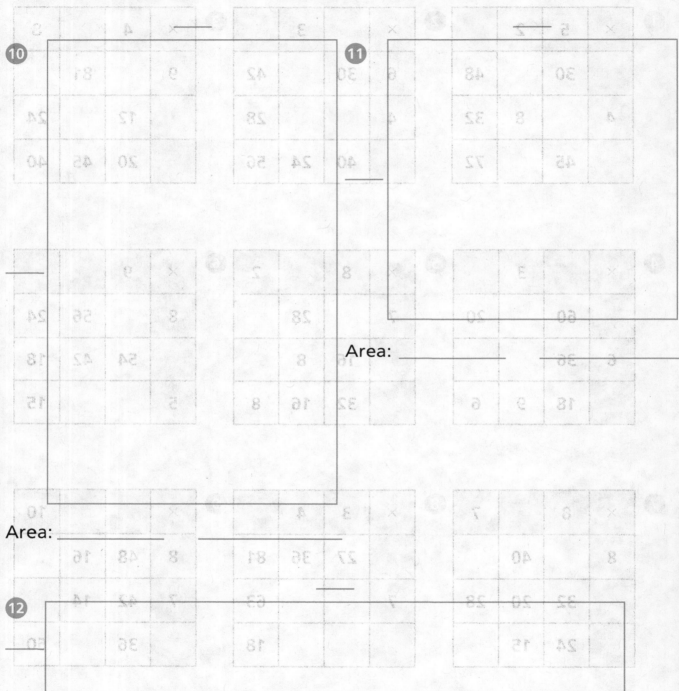

Area: _____

Area: _____

Area: _____

112

Solve Area Word Problems

PATH to FLUENCY Check Sheet 7: 6s and 8s

6s Multiplications	6s Divisions	8s Multiplications	8s Divisions
$10 \times 6 = 60$	$24 / 6 = 4$	$2 \times 8 = 16$	$72 / 8 = 9$
$6 \cdot 4 = 24$	$48 \div 6 = 8$	$8 \cdot 10 = 80$	$16 \div 8 = 2$
$6 * 7 = 42$	$60 / 6 = 10$	$3 * 8 = 24$	$40 / 8 = 5$
$2 \times 6 = 12$	$12 \div 6 = 2$	$9 \times 8 = 72$	$8 \div 8 = 1$
$6 \cdot 5 = 30$	$42 / 6 = 7$	$8 \cdot 4 = 32$	$80 / 8 = 10$
$6 * 8 = 48$	$30 \div 6 = 5$	$8 * 7 = 56$	$48 \div 8 = 6$
$9 \times 6 = 54$	$6 / 6 = 1$	$5 \times 8 = 40$	$56 / 8 = 7$
$6 \cdot 1 = 6$	$18 \div 6 = 3$	$8 \cdot 6 = 48$	$24 \div 8 = 3$
$6 * 6 = 36$	$54 / 6 = 9$	$1 * 8 = 8$	$64 / 8 = 8$
$6 \times 3 = 18$	$36 / 6 = 6$	$8 \times 8 = 64$	$32 / 8 = 4$
$6 \cdot 6 = 36$	$48 \div 6 = 8$	$4 \cdot 8 = 32$	$80 \div 8 = 10$
$5 * 6 = 30$	$12 / 6 = 2$	$6 * 8 = 48$	$56 / 8 = 7$
$6 \times 2 = 12$	$24 \div 6 = 4$	$8 \times 3 = 24$	$8 \div 8 = 1$
$4 \cdot 6 = 24$	$60 / 6 = 10$	$7 \cdot 8 = 56$	$24 / 8 = 3$
$6 * 9 = 54$	$6 \div 6 = 1$	$8 * 2 = 16$	$64 \div 8 = 8$
$8 \times 6 = 48$	$42 / 6 = 7$	$8 \times 9 = 72$	$16 / 8 = 2$
$7 \cdot 6 = 42$	$18 \div 6 = 3$	$8 \cdot 1 = 8$	$72 \div 8 = 9$
$6 * 10 = 60$	$36 \div 6 = 6$	$8 * 8 = 64$	$32 \div 8 = 4$
$1 \times 6 = 6$	$30 / 6 = 5$	$10 \times 8 = 80$	$40 / 8 = 5$
$4 \cdot 6 = 24$	$54 \div 6 = 9$	$5 \cdot 8 = 40$	$48 \div 8 = 6$

© Houghton Mifflin Harcourt Publishing Company

Check Sheet 7: 6s and 8s

Identify the Type and Choose the Operation

Solve. Then circle what type of problem it is and what operation you use.

1 Students in Mr. Till's class hung their paintings on the wall. They made 6 rows, with 5 paintings in each row. How many paintings did the students hang?

_____

Circle one: array   equal groups   area
Circle one: multiplication   division

2 Write your own problem that is the same type as Problem 1. _____

_____

3 There are 8 goldfish in each tank at the pet store. If there are 56 goldfish in all, how many tanks are there?

_____

Circle one: array   equal groups   area
Circle one: multiplication   division

4 Write your own problem that is the same type as Problem 3. _____

_____

5 Pierre built a rectangular pen for his rabbits. The pen is 4 feet wide and 6 feet long. What is the area of the pen? _____

Circle one: array   equal groups   area
Circle one: multiplication   division

119

PATH to FLUENCY Identify the Type and Choose the Operation (continued)

6 Write your own problem that is the same type as Problem 5. _____

_____

_____

7 Paulo arranged 72 baseball cards in rows and columns. If there were 9 rows, into how many columns did he arrange the cards?

Circle one: array   equal groups   area
Circle one: multiplication   division

8 Write your own problem that is the same type as Problem 7. _____

_____

_____

9 The store sells bottles of juice in six-packs. Mr. Lee bought 9 six-packs for a picnic. How many bottles did he buy? _____

Circle one: array   equal groups   area
Circle one: multiplication   division

10 Write your own problem that is the same type as Problem 9. _____

_____

_____

11 **Math Journal** Write an area multiplication problem. Draw a fast array to solve it.

120 Write Word Problems and Equations

Name _____

What's the Error?

Dear Math Students,

Today my teacher asked me to find the answer to 8 × 6. Here is what I wrote:

8 × 6 = 14

Is my answer correct? If not, please correct my work and tell me what I did wrong.

Your friend,
Puzzled Penguin

12 Write an answer to the Puzzled Penguin.

_____

_____

Write and Solve Equations

Write an equation and solve the problem.

13 A large box of crayons holds 60 crayons. There are 10 crayons in each row. How many rows are there?

_____

_____

14 A sign covers 12 square feet. The sign is 4 feet long. How wide is the sign?

_____

_____

15 There are 28 students working on a project. There are 7 groups with an equal number of students in each group. How many students are in each group?

_____

_____

16 Amanda had 15 bracelets. She gave the same number of bracelets to 3 friends. How many bracelets did she give to each friend?

_____

_____

121   Write Word Problems and Equations

PATH to FLUENCY Check Sheet 8: 7s and Squares

7s Multiplications	7s Divisions	Squares Multiplications	Squares Divisions
$4 \times 7 = 28$	$14 / 7 = 2$	$8 \times 8 = 64$	$81 / 9 = 9$
$7 \cdot 2 = 14$	$28 \div 7 = 4$	$10 \cdot 10 = 100$	$4 \div 2 = 2$
$7 * 8 = 56$	$70 / 7 = 10$	$3 * 3 = 9$	$25 / 5 = 5$
$7 \times 7 = 49$	$56 \div 7 = 8$	$9 \times 9 = 81$	$1 \div 1 = 1$
$7 \cdot 1 = 7$	$42 / 7 = 6$	$4 \cdot 4 = 16$	$100 / 10 = 10$
$7 * 10 = 70$	$63 \div 7 = 9$	$7 * 7 = 49$	$36 \div 6 = 6$
$3 \times 7 = 21$	$7 / 7 = 1$	$5 \times 5 = 25$	$49 / 7 = 7$
$7 \cdot 6 = 42$	$49 \div 7 = 7$	$6 \cdot 6 = 36$	$9 \div 3 = 3$
$5 * 7 = 35$	$21 / 7 = 3$	$1 * 1 = 1$	$64 / 8 = 8$
$7 \times 9 = 63$	$35 / 7 = 5$	$5 * 5 = 25$	$16 / 4 = 4$
$7 \cdot 4 = 28$	$7 \div 7 = 1$	$1 \cdot 1 = 1$	$100 \div 10 = 10$
$9 * 7 = 63$	$63 / 7 = 9$	$3 \cdot 3 = 9$	$49 / 7 = 7$
$2 \times 7 = 14$	$14 \div 7 = 2$	$10 \times 10 = 100$	$1 \div 1 = 1$
$7 \cdot 5 = 35$	$70 / 7 = 10$	$4 \times 4 = 16$	$9 / 3 = 3$
$8 * 7 = 56$	$21 \div 7 = 3$	$9 * 9 = 81$	$64 \div 8 = 8$
$7 \times 3 = 21$	$49 / 7 = 7$	$2 \times 2 = 4$	$4 / 2 = 2$
$6 \cdot 7 = 42$	$28 \div 7 = 4$	$6 * 6 = 36$	$81 \div 9 = 9$
$10 * 7 = 70$	$56 \div 7 = 8$	$7 \times 7 = 49$	$16 \div 4 = 4$
$1 \times 7 = 7$	$35 / 7 = 5$	$5 \cdot 5 = 25$	$25 / 5 = 5$
$7 \cdot 7 = 49$	$42 \div 7 = 6$	$8 \cdot 8 = 64$	$36 \div 6 = 6$

© Houghton Mifflin Harcourt Publishing Company

Look for Patterns

VOCABULARY
square numbers

11 List the products in Exercises 1–10 in order.
Discuss the patterns you see with your class.

The numbers you listed in Exercise 11 are called **square numbers** because they are the areas of squares with whole-number lengths of sides. A square number is the product of a whole number and itself. So, if n is a whole number, $n \times n$ is a square number.

Patterns on the Multiplication Table

12 In the table on the right, circle the products that are square numbers. Discuss the patterns you see with your class.

X	1	2	3	4	5	6	7	8	9	10
1	1	2	3	4	5	6	7	8	9	10
2	2	4	6	8	10	12	14	16	18	20
3	3	6	9	12	15	18	21	24	27	30
4	4	8	12	16	20	24	28	32	36	40
5	5	10	15	20	25	30	35	40	45	50
6	6	12	18	24	30	36	42	48	54	60
7	7	14	21	28	35	42	49	56	63	70
8	8	16	24	32	40	48	56	64	72	80
9	9	18	27	36	45	54	63	72	81	90
10	10	20	30	40	50	60	70	80	90	100

✔ **Check Understanding**

Complete the sentence.

The number _____ is a square number because _____

PATH to FLUENCY **Check Sheet 9: 6s, 7s, and 8s**

6s, 7s, and 8s Multiplications	6s, 7s, and 8s Multiplications	6s, 7s, and 8s Divisions	6s, 7s, and 8s Divisions
$1 \times 6 = 6$	$0 \times 8 = 0$	$24 / 6 = 4$	$54 / 6 = 9$
$6 \cdot 7 = 42$	$6 \cdot 2 = 12$	$21 \div 7 = 3$	$24 \div 8 = 3$
$3 * 8 = 24$	$4 * 7 = 28$	$16 / 8 = 2$	$14 / 7 = 2$
$6 \times 2 = 12$	$8 \times 3 = 24$	$24 \div 8 = 3$	$32 \div 8 = 4$
$7 \cdot 5 = 35$	$5 \cdot 6 = 30$	$14 / 7 = 2$	$18 / 6 = 3$
$8 * 4 = 32$	$7 * 2 = 14$	$30 \div 6 = 5$	$56 \div 7 = 8$
$6 \times 6 = 36$	$3 \times 8 = 24$	$35 / 7 = 5$	$40 / 8 = 5$
$8 \cdot 7 = 56$	$6 \cdot 4 = 24$	$24 \div 8 = 3$	$35 \div 7 = 5$
$9 * 8 = 72$	$0 * 7 = 0$	$18 / 6 = 3$	$12 / 6 = 2$
$6 \times 10 = 60$	$8 \times 1 = 8$	$12 / 6 = 2$	$21 / 7 = 3$
$7 \cdot 1 = 7$	$8 \cdot 6 = 48$	$42 \div 7 = 6$	$16 \div 8 = 2$
$8 * 3 = 24$	$7 * 9 = 63$	$56 / 8 = 7$	$42 / 6 = 7$
$5 \times 6 = 30$	$10 \times 8 = 80$	$49 \div 7 = 7$	$80 \div 8 = 10$
$4 \cdot 7 = 28$	$6 \cdot 10 = 60$	$16 / 8 = 2$	$36 / 6 = 6$
$2 * 8 = 16$	$3 * 7 = 21$	$60 \div 6 = 10$	$7 \div 7 = 1$
$7 \times 7 = 49$	$8 \times 4 = 32$	$54 / 6 = 9$	$64 / 8 = 8$
$7 \cdot 6 = 42$	$6 \cdot 5 = 30$	$8 \div 8 = 1$	$24 \div 6 = 4$
$8 * 8 = 64$	$7 * 4 = 28$	$28 \div 7 = 4$	$21 \div 7 = 3$
$9 \times 6 = 54$	$8 \times 8 = 64$	$72 / 8 = 9$	$49 / 7 = 7$
$10 \cdot 7 = 70$	$6 \cdot 9 = 54$	$56 \div 7 = 8$	$24 \div 8 = 3$

Name _____

PATH to FLUENCY Check Sheet 10: 0s–10s

0s–10s Multiplications	0s–10s Multiplications	0s–10s Divisions	0s–10s Divisions
$9 \times 0 = 0$	$9 \times 4 = 36$	$9 / 1 = 9$	$90 / 10 = 9$
$1 \cdot 1 = 1$	$5 \cdot 9 = 45$	$12 \div 3 = 4$	$64 \div 8 = 8$
$2 * 3 = 6$	$6 * 10 = 60$	$14 / 2 = 7$	$15 / 5 = 3$
$1 \times 3 = 3$	$7 \times 3 = 21$	$20 \div 4 = 5$	$12 \div 6 = 2$
$5 \cdot 4 = 20$	$5 \cdot 3 = 15$	$10 / 5 = 2$	$14 / 7 = 2$
$7 * 5 = 35$	$4 * 1 = 4$	$48 \div 8 = 6$	$45 \div 9 = 5$
$6 \times 9 = 54$	$7 \times 5 = 35$	$35 / 7 = 5$	$8 / 1 = 8$
$4 \cdot 7 = 28$	$6 \cdot 3 = 18$	$60 \div 6 = 10$	$30 \div 3 = 10$
$1 * 8 = 8$	$8 * 7 = 56$	$81 / 9 = 9$	$16 / 4 = 4$
$9 \times 8 = 72$	$5 \times 8 = 40$	$20 / 10 = 2$	$8 / 2 = 4$
$2 \cdot 10 = 20$	$9 \cdot 9 = 81$	$16 \div 2 = 8$	$80 \div 10 = 8$
$0 * 7 = 0$	$9 * 10 = 90$	$30 / 5 = 6$	$36 / 4 = 9$
$4 \times 1 = 4$	$0 \times 0 = 0$	$49 \div 7 = 7$	$25 \div 5 = 5$
$2 \cdot 4 = 8$	$1 \cdot 0 = 0$	$60 / 6 = 10$	$42 / 7 = 6$
$10 * 3 = 30$	$1 * 6 = 6$	$30 \div 3 = 10$	$36 \div 6 = 6$
$8 \times 4 = 32$	$7 \times 2 = 14$	$8 / 1 = 8$	$90 / 9 = 10$
$5 \cdot 8 = 40$	$6 \cdot 3 = 18$	$16 \div 4 = 4$	$24 \div 8 = 3$
$4 * 6 = 24$	$4 * 5 = 20$	$16 \div 8 = 2$	$6 \div 2 = 3$
$7 \times 6 = 42$	$6 \times 6 = 36$	$40 / 10 = 4$	$9 / 3 = 3$
$1 \cdot 8 = 8$	$10 \cdot 7 = 70$	$36 \div 9 = 4$	$1 \div 1 = 1$

Name _____

Play Quotient Match and Division Blockout

PATH to FLUENCY

Read the rules for playing a game.
Then play the game.

Rules for Quotient Match

Number of players: 2 or 3

What each player will need: Division Strategy Cards for 6s, 7s, and 8s

1. Shuffle the cards. Put the division cards, sides without answers, face up on the table in 6 rows of 4.

2. Players take turns. On each turn, a player chooses three cards that he or she thinks have the same quotient and turns them over.

3. If all three cards do have the same quotient the player takes them. If the cards do not have the same quotient, the player turns them back over so the without answers side is up.

4. Play continues until no cards remain.

Rules for Division Blockout

Number of players: 3

What each player will need: *Blockout* Game Board (TRB M70), Division Strategy Cards for 6s, 7s, and 8s

1. Players do not write anything on the game board. The first row is for 6s, the second row for 7s, and the third row for 8s, as indicated in the gray column on the left.

2. Each player shuffles his or her Division Strategy Cards for 6s, 7s, 8s, making sure the division sides without answers are face up.

3. Repeat Steps 2, 3, and 4 above. This time players will place the Strategy Cards in the appropriate row to indicate whether the unknown factor is 6, 7, or 8.

131
Play Quotient Match and Division Blockout

PATH to FLUENCY Play Multiplication Blockout

Read the rules for playing *Multiplication Blockout*. Then play the game.

Rules for *Multiplication Block Out*

Number of players: 3

What each player will need: *Blockout* Game Board (TRB M70), Multiplication Strategy Cards for 6s, 7s, and 8s

1. Players choose any 5 factors from 2–9 and write them in any order in the gray spaces at the top of the game board. The players then write the products in the large white spaces. The result will be a scrambled multiplication table.

2. Once the table is complete, players cut off the gray row and gray column that show the factors so that only the products are showing. This will be the game board.

3. Each player shuffles his or her Multiplication Strategy Cards for 6s, 7s, and 8s, making sure the multiplication sides without answers are facing up.

4. One player says, "Go!" and everyone quickly places their Strategy Cards on the game board spaces showing the corresponding products. When a player's game board is completely filled, he or she calls out, "Blockout!"

5. Everyone stops and checks the player's work. If all the cards are placed correctly, that player is the winner. If the player has made a mistake, he or she sits out and waits for the next player to call out, "Blockout!"

Name _____

PATH to FLUENCY Complete a Multiplication Table

1 Look at the factors to complete the Multiplication Table. Leave blanks for the products you do not know.

×	1	2	3	4	5	6	7	8	9	10
1										
2										
3										
4										
5										
6										
7										
8										
9										
10										

2 Write the multiplications you need to practice.

_____

_____

_____

_____

_____

Name

PATH to FLUENCY Scrambled Multiplication Tables

Complete each table.

A

×										
	6	30	54	60	42	24	18	12	48	36
	2	10	18	20	14	8	6	4	16	12
	10	50	90	100	70	40	30	20	80	60
	8	40	72	80	56	32	24	16	64	48
	5	25	45	50	35	20	15	10	40	30
	1	5	9	10	7	4	3	2	8	6
	9	45	81	90	63	36	27	18	72	54
	4	20	36	40	28	16	12	8	32	24
	7	35	63	70	49	28	21	14	56	42
	3	15	27	30	21	12	9	6	24	18

B

×										
	27	6	24	21	18	15	12	9	3	
	36	8	32	28	24		16	12	4	40
	9	2	8	7	6	5	4	3	1	10
	18	4	16	14		10	8	6	2	20
		14	56	49	42		28	21	7	
	72		64	56	48	40	32	24	8	80
	45	10	40		30	25	20	15	5	
	54	12	48	42	36	30	24	18	6	60
	90		80	70	60		40	30	10	100
	81	18	72		54	45	36	27	9	

C

×										
	100		20		70	50		90		10
	50	15		20	35		30		40	5
	10	3		4	7		6	9		1
		9		12	21	15		27	24	
		6	4	8			12	18	16	2
		12	8	16	28	20		36	32	
	90	27	18	36	63	45	54		72	
		18	12	24		30	36	54	48	6
		21		28	49		42		56	7
		24		32	56	40		72	64	8

D

×										
	48		42	12	36		18	6		30
	56	28		14		70	21		63	35
			70		60			10		50
		20	35		30		15	5	45	
	32			8		40			36	
	8	4		2			3	1		5
		8	14		12		6		18	10
	64		56		48	80	24	8		40
	72	36		18			27		81	
	24		21		18	30		3	27	

✔ **Check Understanding**

Complete the sentences.

The numbers in the blue boxes are _____.

The numbers in the white boxes are _____.

PATH to FLUENCY Dashes 13–16

Complete each Dash. Check your answers on page 141.

Dash 13 6s and 8s Multiplications	Dash 14 6s and 8s Divisions	Dash 15 7s and 8s Multiplications	Dash 16 7s and 8s Divisions
a. $6 \times 9 = $ _____	a. $72 / 8 = $ _____	a. $7 \times 3 = $ _____	a. $63 / 7 = $ _____
b. $8 * 2 = $ _____	b. $12 \div 6 = $ _____	b. $8 * 5 = $ _____	b. $80 \div 8 = $ _____
c. $4 \cdot 6 = $ _____	c. $16 / 8 = $ _____	c. $2 \cdot 7 = $ _____	c. $14 / 7 = $ _____
d. $7 \times 8 = $ _____	d. $24 \div 6 = $ _____	d. $1 \times 8 = $ _____	d. $16 \div 8 = $ _____
e. $6 * 1 = $ _____	e. $8 / 8 = $ _____	e. $7 * 9 = $ _____	e. $7 / 7 = $ _____
f. $8 \cdot 9 = $ _____	f. $6 \div 6 = $ _____	f. $8 \cdot 4 = $ _____	f. $48 \div 8 = $ _____
g. $3 \times 6 = $ _____	g. $40 / 8 = $ _____	g. $4 \times 7 = $ _____	g. $35 / 7 = $ _____
h. $4 * 8 = $ _____	h. $42 \div 6 = $ _____	h. $7 * 8 = $ _____	h. $32 \div 8 = $ _____
i. $6 \cdot 8 = $ _____	i. $24 / 8 = $ _____	i. $7 \cdot 1 = $ _____	i. $21 / 7 = $ _____
j. $8 \times 1 = $ _____	j. $18 \div 6 = $ _____	j. $8 \times 2 = $ _____	j. $8 \div 8 = $ _____
k. $2 * 6 = $ _____	k. $48 / 8 = $ _____	k. $5 * 7 = $ _____	k. $28 / 7 = $ _____
l. $3 \cdot 8 = $ _____	l. $48 \div 6 = $ _____	l. $9 \cdot 8 = $ _____	l. $40 \div 8 = $ _____
m. $6 \times 5 = $ _____	m. $64 / 8 = $ _____	m. $7 \times 6 = $ _____	m. $49 / 7 = $ _____
n. $8 * 8 = $ _____	n. $42 \div 6 = $ _____	n. $8 * 3 = $ _____	n. $72 \div 8 = $ _____
o. $6 \cdot 6 = $ _____	o. $56 / 8 = $ _____	o. $7 \cdot 7 = $ _____	o. $42 / 7 = $ _____
p. $5 \times 8 = $ _____	p. $30 \div 6 = $ _____	p. $8 \times 8 = $ _____	p. $24 \div 8 = $ _____
q. $6 * 7 = $ _____	q. $32 / 8 = $ _____	q. $7 * 0 = $ _____	q. $56 / 7 = $ _____
r. $8 \times 0 = $ _____	r. $54 \div 6 = $ _____	r. $6 \cdot 8 = $ _____	r. $64 \div 8 = $ _____
s. $0 * 6 = $ _____	s. $80 / 8 = $ _____	s. $8 \times 0 = $ _____	s. $70 / 7 = $ _____
t. $6 \cdot 10 = $ _____	t. $60 \div 6 = $ _____	t. $7 * 10 = $ _____	t. $56 \div 8 = $ _____

PATH to FLUENCY Dashes 17–20

Complete each Dash. Check your answers on page 141.

Dash 17 6s and 7s Multiplications	Dash 18 6s and 7s Divisions	Dash 19 6s, 7s, 8s Multiplications	Dash 20 6s, 7s, 8s Divisions
a. $6 \times 6 =$ _____	a. $70 / 7 =$ _____	a. $7 \times 7 =$ _____	a. $21 / 7 =$ _____
b. $7 * 7 =$ _____	b. $60 \div 6 =$ _____	b. $6 \cdot 3 =$ _____	b. $16 \div 8 =$ _____
c. $3 \cdot 6 =$ _____	c. $28 / 7 =$ _____	c. $8 * 6 =$ _____	c. $54 / 6 =$ _____
d. $8 \times 7 =$ _____	d. $30 \div 6 =$ _____	d. $6 \times 6 =$ _____	d. $48 \div 8 =$ _____
e. $6 * 1 =$ _____	e. $42 / 7 =$ _____	e. $7 \cdot 6 =$ _____	e. $64 / 8 =$ _____
f. $7 \cdot 2 =$ _____	f. $24 \div 6 =$ _____	f. $4 * 7 =$ _____	f. $42 \div 6 =$ _____
g. $9 \times 6 =$ _____	g. $35 / 7 =$ _____	g. $9 \times 7 =$ _____	g. $56 / 7 =$ _____
h. $9 * 7 =$ _____	h. $12 \div 6 =$ _____	h. $6 \cdot 9 =$ _____	h. $72 \div 8 =$ _____
i. $6 \cdot 8 =$ _____	i. $7 / 7 =$ _____	i. $6 * 4 =$ _____	i. $18 / 6 =$ _____
j. $7 \times 3 =$ _____	j. $36 \div 6 =$ _____	j. $8 \times 8 =$ _____	j. $28 / 7 =$ _____
k. $7 * 6 =$ _____	k. $21 / 7 =$ _____	k. $7 \cdot 3 =$ _____	k. $56 \div 8 =$ _____
l. $1 \cdot 7 =$ _____	l. $48 \div 6 =$ _____	l. $8 * 7 =$ _____	l. $30 / 6 =$ _____
m. $6 \times 2 =$ _____	m. $63 / 7 =$ _____	m. $6 \times 7 =$ _____	m. $63 \div 7 =$ _____
n. $7 * 5 =$ _____	n. $6 \div 6 =$ _____	n. $3 \cdot 6 =$ _____	n. $32 / 8 =$ _____
o. $4 \cdot 6 =$ _____	o. $56 / 7 =$ _____	o. $2 * 7 =$ _____	o. $48 \div 6 =$ _____
p. $6 \times 7 =$ _____	p. $18 \div 6 =$ _____	p. $9 \times 8 =$ _____	p. $49 / 7 =$ _____
q. $6 * 5 =$ _____	q. $49 / 7 =$ _____	q. $5 \cdot 6 =$ _____	q. $36 \div 6 =$ _____
r. $7 \cdot 4 =$ _____	r. $42 \div 6 =$ _____	r. $7 * 8 =$ _____	r. $24 \div 8 =$ _____
s. $6 \times 10 =$ _____	s. $14 / 7 =$ _____	s. $3 \times 7 =$ _____	s. $42 / 7 =$ _____
t. $7 \times 10 =$ _____	t. $54 \div 6 =$ _____	t. $9 \cdot 6 =$ _____	t. $24 \div 6 =$ _____

PATH to FLUENCY Dashes 9B–12B

Complete each multiplication and division Dash.
Check your answers on page 142.

Dash 9B 2s, 5s, 9s, 10s Multiplications	Dash 10B 2s, 5s, 9s, 10s Divisions	Dash 11B 0s, 1s, 3s, 4s Multiplications	Dash 12B 1s, 3s, 4s Divisions
a. $6 \times 2 =$ _____	a. $18 / 2 =$ _____	a. $7 \times 1 =$ _____	a. $2 / 1 =$ _____
b. $9 \bullet 4 =$ _____	b. $25 \div 5 =$ _____	b. $0 \bullet 6 =$ _____	b. $28 \div 4 =$ _____
c. $8 * 5 =$ _____	c. $70 / 10 =$ _____	c. $4 * 4 =$ _____	c. $3 / 3 =$ _____
d. $1 \times 10 =$ _____	d. $54 \div 9 =$ _____	d. $7 \times 3 =$ _____	d. $1 \div 1 =$ _____
e. $2 \bullet 7 =$ _____	e. $50 / 5 =$ _____	e. $3 \bullet 1 =$ _____	e. $40 / 4 =$ _____
f. $9 * 9 =$ _____	f. $81 \div 9 =$ _____	f. $4 * 7 =$ _____	f. $21 \div 3 =$ _____
g. $5 \times 6 =$ _____	g. $8 / 2 =$ _____	g. $9 \times 0 =$ _____	g. $5 / 1 =$ _____
h. $10 \bullet 4 =$ _____	h. $90 \div 10 =$ _____	h. $1 \bullet 1 =$ _____	h. $16 \div 4 =$ _____
i. $7 * 5 =$ _____	i. $35 / 5 =$ _____	i. $3 * 4 =$ _____	i. $15 / 3 =$ _____
j. $8 \times 2 =$ _____	j. $27 / 9 =$ _____	j. $4 \times 9 =$ _____	j. $6 / 1 =$ _____
k. $10 \bullet 10 =$ _____	k. $2 \div 2 =$ _____	k. $8 \bullet 1 =$ _____	k. $12 \div 4 =$ _____
l. $5 * 3 =$ _____	l. $36 / 9 =$ _____	l. $3 * 3 =$ _____	l. $27 / 3 =$ _____
m. $9 \times 7 =$ _____	m. $45 \div 5 =$ _____	m. $0 \times 4 =$ _____	m. $9 \div 1 =$ _____
n. $9 \bullet 2 =$ _____	n. $14 / 2 =$ _____	n. $10 \bullet 3 =$ _____	n. $8 / 4 =$ _____
o. $5 * 5 =$ _____	o. $20 \div 10 =$ _____	o. $6 * 4 =$ _____	o. $12 \div 3 =$ _____
p. $6 \times 9 =$ _____	p. $9 / 9 =$ _____	p. $1 \times 4 =$ _____	p. $3 / 1 =$ _____
q. $5 \bullet 2 =$ _____	q. $20 \div 5 =$ _____	q. $3 \bullet 6 =$ _____	q. $36 \div 4 =$ _____
r. $9 * 5 =$ _____	r. $45 \div 9 =$ _____	r. $4 * 8 =$ _____	r. $6 \div 3 =$ _____
s. $8 \times 10 =$ _____	s. $5 / 5 =$ _____	s. $7 \times 0 =$ _____	s. $4 / 1 =$ _____
t. $5 \bullet 10 =$ _____	t. $4 \div 2 =$ _____	t. $5 \bullet 3 =$ _____	t. $4 \div 4 =$ _____

Name

PATH to FLUENCY Dashes 9C–12C

Complete each Dash. Check your answers on page 142.

Dash 9C 2s, 5 ,9s, 10s Multiplications	Dash 10C 2s, 5, 9s, 10s Divisions	Dash 11C 0s, 1s ,3s, 4s Multiplications	Dash 12C 1s, 3s, 4s Divisions
a. $5 \times 8 =$ ___	a. $36 \div 9 =$ ___	a. $0 \times 7 =$ ___	a. $4 / 1 =$ ___
b. $9 * 9 =$ ___	b. $30 / 5 =$ ___	b. $1 * 4 =$ ___	b. $15 \div 3 =$ ___
c. $10 \cdot 7 =$ ___	c. $18 \div 2 =$ ___	c. $3 \cdot 6 =$ ___	c. $24 / 4 =$ ___
d. $4 \times 5 =$ ___	d. $80 / 10 =$ ___	d. $4 \times 9 =$ ___	d. $9 \div 1 =$ ___
e. $5 * 5 =$ ___	e. $40 \div 5 =$ ___	e. $8 * 0 =$ ___	e. $21 / 3 =$ ___
f. $10 \cdot 3 =$ ___	f. $72 / 9 =$ ___	f. $7 * 1 =$ ___	f. $12 \div 4 =$ ___
g. $1 \times 5 =$ ___	g. $6 \div 2 =$ ___	g. $4 \cdot 3 =$ ___	g. $5 / 1 =$ ___
h. $3 * 9 =$ ___	h. $54 / 9 =$ ___	h. $4 \times 4 =$ ___	h. $3 \div 3 =$ ___
i. $9 \cdot 6 =$ ___	i. $25 \div 5 =$ ___	i. $0 * 5 =$ ___	i. $32 / 4 =$ ___
j. $10 \times 8 =$ ___	j. $10 / 10 =$ ___	j. $1 \cdot 6 =$ ___	j. $2 \div 1 =$ ___
k. $2 * 9 =$ ___	k. $45 \div 5 =$ ___	k. $3 \times 2 =$ ___	k. $18 / 3 =$ ___
l. $6 \cdot 2 =$ ___	l. $27 / 9 =$ ___	l. $4 * 7 =$ ___	l. $36 \div 4 =$ ___
m. $6 \times 10 =$ ___	m. $14 \div 2 =$ ___	m. $1 \cdot 0 =$ ___	m. $7 / 1 =$ ___
n. $8 * 9 =$ ___	n. $35 / 5 =$ ___	n. $2 \times 1 =$ ___	n. $24 \div 3 =$ ___
o. $8 \cdot 2 =$ ___	o. $90 \div 9 =$ ___	o. $9 * 3 =$ ___	o. $4 / 4 =$ ___
p. $4 \times 2 =$ ___	p. $90 / 10 =$ ___	p. $2 \cdot 4 =$ ___	p. $6 \div 1 =$ ___
q. $10 * 5 =$ ___	q. $63 \div 9 =$ ___	q. $0 \times 3 =$ ___	q. $12 / 3 =$ ___
r. $10 \cdot 10 =$ ___	r. $15 / 5 =$ ___	r. $1 * 1 =$ ___	r. $20 \div 4 =$ ___
s. $9 \times 6 =$ ___	s. $50 \div 10 =$ ___	s. $3 \cdot 9 =$ ___	s. $8 / 1 =$ ___
t. $5 * 7 =$ ___	t. $8 / 2 =$ ___	t. $4 \times 5 =$ ___	t. $27 \div 3 =$ ___

Name _____

PATH to FLUENCY Answers to Dashes 13–20

Use this sheet to check your answers to the Dashes on pages 137 and 138.

Dash 13 ×	Dash 14 ÷	Dash 15 ×	Dash 16 ÷	Dash 17 ×	Dash 18 ÷	Dash 19 ×	Dash 20 ×
a. 54	a. 9	a. 21	a. 9	a. 36	a. 10	a. 49	a. 3
b. 16	b. 2	b. 40	b. 10	b. 49	b. 10	b. 18	b. 2
c. 24	c. 2	c. 14	c. 2	c. 18	c. 4	c. 48	c. 9
d. 56	d. 4	d. 8	d. 2	d. 56	d. 5	d. 36	d. 6
e. 6	e. 1	e. 63	e. 1	e. 6	e. 6	e. 42	e. 8
f. 72	f. 1	f. 32	f. 6	f. 14	f. 4	f. 28	f. 7
g. 18	g. 5	g. 28	g. 5	g. 54	g. 5	g. 63	g. 8
h. 32	h. 7	h. 56	h. 4	h. 63	h. 2	h. 54	h. 9
i. 48	i. 3	i. 7	i. 3	i. 48	i. 1	i. 24	i. 3
j. 8	j. 3	j. 16	j. 1	j. 21	j. 6	j. 64	j. 4
k. 12	k. 6	k. 35	k. 4	k. 42	k. 3	k. 21	k. 7
l. 24	l. 8	l. 72	l. 5	l. 7	l. 8	l. 56	l. 5
m. 30	m. 8	m. 42	m. 7	m. 12	m. 9	m. 42	m. 9
n. 64	n. 7	n. 24	n. 9	n. 35	n. 1	n. 18	n. 4
o. 36	o. 7	o. 49	o. 6	o. 24	o. 8	o. 14	o. 8
p. 40	p. 5	p. 64	p. 3	p. 42	p. 3	p. 72	p. 7
q. 42	q. 4	q. 0	q. 8	q. 30	q. 7	q. 30	q. 6
r. 0	r. 9	r. 48	r. 8	r. 28	r. 7	r. 56	r. 3
s. 0	s. 10	s. 0	s. 10	s. 60	s. 2	s. 21	s. 6
t. 60	t. 10	t. 70	t. 7	t. 70	t. 9	t. 54	t. 4

PATH to FLUENCY Answers to Dashes 9B–12B, 9C–12C

Use this sheet to check your answers to the Dashes on pages 139 and 140.

Dash 9B ×	Dash 10B ÷	Dash 11B ×	Dash 12B ÷	Dash 9C ×	Dash 10C ÷	Dash 11C ×	Dash 12C ÷
a. 12	a. 9	a. 7	a. 2	a. 40	a. 4	a. 0	a. 4
b. 36	b. 5	b. 0	b. 7	b. 81	b. 6	b. 4	b. 5
c. 40	c. 7	c. 16	c. 1	c. 70	c. 9	c. 18	c. 6
d. 10	d. 6	d. 21	d. 1	d. 20	d. 8	d. 36	d. 9
e. 14	e. 10	e. 3	e. 10	e. 25	e. 8	e. 0	e. 7
f. 81	f. 9	f. 28	f. 7	f. 30	f. 8	f. 7	f. 3
g. 30	g. 4	g. 0	g. 5	g. 5	g. 3	g. 12	g. 5
h. 40	h. 9	h. 1	h. 4	h. 27	h. 6	h. 16	h. 1
i. 35	i. 7	i. 12	i. 5	i. 54	i. 5	i. 0	i. 8
j. 16	j. 3	j. 36	j. 6	j. 80	j. 1	j. 6	j. 2
k. 100	k. 1	k. 8	k. 3	k. 18	k. 9	k. 6	k. 6
l. 15	l. 4	l. 9	l. 9	l. 12	l. 3	l. 28	l. 9
m. 63	m. 9	m. 0	m. 9	m. 60	m. 7	m. 0	m. 7
n. 18	n. 7	n. 30	n. 2	n. 72	n. 7	n. 2	n. 8
o. 25	o. 2	o. 24	o. 4	o. 16	o. 10	o. 27	o. 1
p. 54	p. 1	p. 4	p. 3	p. 8	p. 9	p. 8	p. 6
q. 10	q. 4	q. 18	q. 9	q. 50	q. 7	q. 0	q. 4
r. 45	r. 5	r. 32	r. 2	r. 100	r. 3	r. 1	r. 5
s. 80	s. 1	s. 0	s. 4	s. 54	s. 5	s. 27	s. 8
t. 50	t. 2	t. 15	t. 1	t. 35	t. 4	t. 20	t. 9

Name _____

Write an equation and solve the problem. *Show your work.*

1 The area of the rectangle shown is
42 square inches. What is the value of *n*?

Area = 42
square inches   6 inches

n

_____

2 There are 81 bottles of apple juice to be equally
shared among 9 people. How many bottles will
each of those 9 people receive?

_____

Solve.

3 7 × ▢ = 56

▢ = _____

4 9 × 9 = ▢

▢ = _____

5 Jaewon arranges his stamps in 6 equal rows. If
he has 48 stamps, how many stamps will be in
each row?

_____

Unit 2 Big Idea 1

Name _____

Write an equation and solve the problem.   *Show your work.*

1 There are 7 rows of 9 mango trees in an orchard. How many mango trees are there in all?

_____

2 A carrot seed needs about 8 weeks to become a carrot. How many days is that?

_____

3 It takes a little more than 63 days for pea seeds to become peas that you can eat. How many weeks are 63 days?

_____

4 During harvest season each 24-hour day is split into 3 equal shifts. How long is each shift?

_____

5 Hal packs 6 boxes of oranges. Each box weighs 6 pounds. How much do the boxes weigh in all?

_____

What's the Error?

Dear Math Students,

Today I found the answer to 6 + 3 x 2.
Here is how I found the answer.

6 + 3 x 2

9 x 2 = 18

Is my answer correct? If not, please correct my
work and tell me what I did wrong.

Your friend,
Puzzled Penguin

9 Write an answer to the Puzzled Penguin.

_____

_____

_____

Find the answer.

10 4 + 3 × 5 = _____

11 10 ÷ 2 + 3 = _____

12 12 − 9 ÷ 3 = _____

13 3 × 5 − 2 = _____

14 (4 + 3) × 5 = _____

15 10 ÷ (2 + 3) = _____

16 (12 − 9) ÷ 3 = _____

17 3 × (5 − 2) = _____

PATH to FLUENCY **Dashes 21–22, 19A–20A**

Complete each Dash. Check your answers on page 161.

Dash 21 2s, 3s, 4s, 5s, 9s Multiplications	Dash 22 2s, 3s, 4s, 5s, 9s Divisions	Dash 19A 6s, 7s, 8s Multiplications	Dash 20A 6s, 7s, 8s Divisions
a. 6 × 3 = ____	a. 16 / 4 = ____	a. 9 × 6 = ____	a. 24 ÷ 6 = ____
b. 4 • 7 = ____	b. 54 ÷ 9 = ____	b. 7 * 7 = ____	b. 21 / 7 = ____
c. 8 * 2 = ____	c. 4 / 2 = ____	c. 3 • 7 = ____	c. 42 ÷ 7 = ____
d. 5 × 3 = ____	d. 28 ÷ 4 = ____	d. 6 × 3 = ____	d. 16 / 8 = ____
e. 4 • 4 = ____	e. 25 / 5 = ____	e. 7 * 8 = ____	e. 24 ÷ 8 = ____
f. 3 • 9 = ____	f. 21 ÷ 3 = ____	f. 8 • 6 = ____	f. 54 / 6 = ____
g. 9 × 9 = ____	g. 40 / 4 = ____	g. 5 × 6 = ____	g. 36 ÷ 6 = ____
h. 8 • 9 = ____	h. 81 ÷ 9 = ____	h. 6 * 6 = ____	h. 48 / 8 = ____
i. 6 * 4 = ____	i. 35 / 5 = ____	i. 9 • 8 = ____	i. 49 ÷ 7 = ____
j. 3 × 3 = ____	j. 12 / 3 = ____	j. 7 × 6 = ____	j. 64 / 8 = ____
k. 2 • 7 = ____	k. 2 ÷ 2 = ____	k. 2 * 7 = ____	k. 48 ÷ 6 = ____
l. 8 • 5 = ____	l. 63 / 9 = ____	l. 4 • 7 = ____	l. 42 / 6 = ____
m. 4 × 9 = ____	m. 36 ÷ 4 = ____	m. 3 × 6 = ____	m. 32 ÷ 8 = ____
n. 9 • 5 = ____	n. 18 / 2 = ____	n. 9 * 7 = ____	n. 56 / 7 = ____
o. 7 * 3 = ____	o. 9 ÷ 3 = ____	o. 6 • 7 = ____	o. 63 ÷ 7 = ____
p. 2 × 2 = ____	p. 36 / 9 = ____	p. 6 × 9 = ____	p. 72 / 8 = ____
q. 8 • 4 = ____	q. 40 ÷ 5 = ____	q. 8 * 7 = ____	q. 30 ÷ 6 = ____
r. 5 * 1 = ____	r. 12 ÷ 4 = ____	r. 6 • 4 = ____	r. 18 / 6 = ____
s. 5 × 5 = ____	s. 9 / 9 = ____	s. 7 × 3 = ____	s. 56 ÷ 8 = ____
t. 6 • 9 = ____	t. 14 ÷ 2 = ____	t. 8 * 8 = ____	t. 28 / 7 = ____

Name _____

PATH to FLUENCY Dashes 21A–22A, 19B–20B

Complete each Dash. Check your answers on page 161.

Dash 21A **2s, 3s, 4s, 5s, 9s** **Multiplications**	**Dash 22A** **2s, 3s, 4s, 5s, 9s** **Divisions**	**Dash 19B** **6s, 7s, 8s** **Multiplications**	**Dash 20B** **6s, 7s, 8s** **Divisions**
a. $6 \times 9 =$ _____	a. $14 \div 2 =$ _____	a. $6 \times 2 =$ _____	a. $36 \div 6 =$ _____
b. $6 * 3 =$ _____	b. $16 / 4 =$ _____	b. $7 * 7 =$ _____	b. $63 / 7 =$ _____
c. $4 \cdot 7 =$ _____	c. $9 \div 9 =$ _____	c. $8 \cdot 5 =$ _____	c. $24 \div 8 =$ _____
d. $5 \times 5 =$ _____	d. $54 / 9 =$ _____	d. $4 \times 6 =$ _____	d. $18 / 6 =$ _____
e. $8 * 2 =$ _____	e. $12 \div 4 =$ _____	e. $3 * 7 =$ _____	e. $28 \div 7 =$ _____
f. $5 \cdot 1 =$ _____	f. $4 / 2 =$ _____	f. $1 \cdot 8 =$ _____	f. $48 / 8 =$ _____
g. $5 \times 3 =$ _____	g. $40 \div 5 =$ _____	g. $6 \times 9 =$ _____	g. $54 \div 6 =$ _____
h. $8 * 4 =$ _____	h. $28 / 4 =$ _____	h. $7 * 5 =$ _____	h. $42 / 7 =$ _____
i. $4 \cdot 4 =$ _____	i. $36 \div 9 =$ _____	i. $8 \cdot 3 =$ _____	i. $72 \div 8 =$ _____
j. $2 \times 2 =$ _____	j. $25 / 5 =$ _____	j. $4 \times 6 =$ _____	j. $6 / 6 =$ _____
k. $3 * 9 =$ _____	k. $9 \div 3 =$ _____	k. $9 * 7 =$ _____	k. $14 \div 7 =$ _____
l. $7 \cdot 3 =$ _____	l. $21 / 3 =$ _____	l. $8 \cdot 8 =$ _____	l. $56 / 8 =$ _____
m. $9 \times 9 =$ _____	m. $18 \div 2 =$ _____	m. $6 \times 1 =$ _____	m. $12 \div 6 =$ _____
n. $9 * 5 =$ _____	n. $40 / 4 =$ _____	n. $7 * 4 =$ _____	n. $7 / 7 =$ _____
o. $8 \cdot 9 =$ _____	o. $36 \div 4 =$ _____	o. $8 \cdot 6 =$ _____	o. $16 \div 8 =$ _____
p. $4 \times 9 =$ _____	p. $81 / 9 =$ _____	p. $7 \times 6 =$ _____	p. $30 / 6 =$ _____
q. $6 * 4 =$ _____	q. $63 \div 9 =$ _____	q. $2 * 7 =$ _____	q. $56 \div 7 =$ _____
r. $8 \cdot 5 =$ _____	r. $35 / 5 =$ _____	r. $9 \cdot 8 =$ _____	r. $8 / 8 =$ _____
s. $2 \times 7 =$ _____	s. $12 \div 3 =$ _____	s. $6 \times 5 =$ _____	s. $48 \div 6 =$ _____
t. $3 * 3 =$ _____	t. $2 / 2 =$ _____	t. $7 * 6 =$ _____	t. $21 / 7 =$ _____

Name

PATH to FLUENCY Dashes 21B–22B, 19C–20C

Complete each Dash. Check your answers on page 162.

Dash 21B 2s, 3s, 4s, 5s, 9s Multiplications	Dash 22B 2s, 3s, 4s, 5s, 9s Divisions	Dash 19C 6s, 7s, 8s Multiplications	Dash 20C 6s, 7s, 8s Divisions
a. $2 \times 3 =$	a. $8 \div 2 =$	a. $6 \times 8 =$	a. $54 \div 6 =$
b. $3 * 8 =$	b. $18 / 3 =$	b. $7 * 3 =$	b. $49 / 7 =$
c. $4 \cdot 4 =$	c. $12 \div 4 =$	c. $8 \cdot 6 =$	c. $24 \div 8 =$
d. $5 \times 6 =$	d. $25 / 5 =$	d. $2 \times 6 =$	d. $6 / 6 =$
e. $9 * 8 =$	e. $63 \div 9 =$	e. $8 * 7 =$	e. $35 \div 7 =$
f. $9 \cdot 2 =$	f. $16 / 2 =$	f. $9 \cdot 8 =$	f. $72 / 8 =$
g. $3 \times 3 =$	g. $3 \div 3 =$	g. $6 \times 4 =$	g. $18 \div 6 =$
h. $4 * 2 =$	h. $28 / 4 =$	h. $7 * 1 =$	h. $28 / 7 =$
i. $9 \cdot 5 =$	i. $45 \div 5 =$	i. $8 \cdot 3 =$	i. $8 \div 8 =$
j. $9 \times 4 =$	j. $27 / 9 =$	j. $5 \times 6 =$	j. $30 / 6 =$
k. $2 * 7 =$	k. $12 \div 2 =$	k. $9 * 7 =$	k. $21 \div 7 =$
l. $3 \cdot 5 =$	l. $12 / 3 =$	l. $4 \cdot 8 =$	l. $40 / 8 =$
m. $4 \times 8 =$	m. $20 \div 4 =$	m. $6 \times 6 =$	m. $42 \div 6 =$
n. $5 * 3 =$	n. $40 / 5 =$	n. $7 * 5 =$	n. $63 / 7 =$
o. $9 \cdot 6 =$	o. $54 \div 9 =$	o. $8 \cdot 8 =$	o. $32 \div 8 =$
p. $2 \times 8 =$	p. $2 / 2 =$	p. $1 \times 6 =$	p. $36 / 6 =$
q. $3 * 7 =$	q. $9 \div 3 =$	q. $2 * 7 =$	q. $14 \div 7 =$
r. $4 \cdot 1 =$	r. $36 / 4 =$	r. $5 \cdot 8 =$	r. $56 / 8 =$
s. $5 \times 8 =$	s. $15 \div 5 =$	s. $6 \times 9 =$	s. $24 \div 6 =$
t. $9 * 9 =$	t. $9 / 9 =$	t. $7 * 7 =$	t. $42 / 7 =$

159

Name

PATH to FLUENCY Dashes 21C–22C, 19D–20D

Complete each Dash. Check your answers on page 162.

Dash 21C 2s, 3s, 4s, 5s, 9s Multiplications	Dash 22C 2s, 3s, 4s, 5s, 9s Divisions	Dash 19D 6s, 7s, 8s Multiplications	Dash 20D 6s, 7s, 8s Divisions
a. $2 \times 9 =$ ____	a. $8 \div 2 =$ ____	a. $6 \times 9 =$ ____	a. $18 / 6 =$ ____
b. $3 * 7 =$ ____	b. $6 / 3 =$ ____	b. $7 * 6 =$ ____	b. $42 \div 7 =$ ____
c. $4 \cdot 5 =$ ____	c. $4 \div 4 =$ ____	c. $8 \cdot 2 =$ ____	c. $32 / 8 =$ ____
d. $5 \times 3 =$ ____	d. $20 / 5 =$ ____	d. $3 \times 6 =$ ____	d. $54 \div 6 =$ ____
e. $9 * 1 =$ ____	e. $63 \div 9 =$ ____	e. $4 * 7 =$ ____	e. $49 / 7 =$ ____
f. $1 \cdot 2 =$ ____	f. $16 / 2 =$ ____	f. $9 \cdot 8 =$ ____	f. $8 / 8 =$ ____
g. $4 \times 3 =$ ____	g. $15 \div 3 =$ ____	g. $6 \times 6 =$ ____	g. $30 \div 6 =$ ____
h. $4 * 1 =$ ____	h. $32 / 4 =$ ____	h. $7 * 2 =$ ____	h. $35 / 7 =$ ____
i. $7 \cdot 5 =$ ____	i. $30 \div 5 =$ ____	i. $8 \cdot 1 =$ ____	i. $48 \div 8 =$ ____
j. $9 \times 9 =$ ____	j. $45 / 9 =$ ____	j. $2 \times 6 =$ ____	j. $24 / 6 =$ ____
k. $2 * 3 =$ ____	k. $2 \div 2 =$ ____	k. $8 * 7 =$ ____	k. $14 \div 7 =$ ____
l. $3 \cdot 8 =$ ____	l. $21 / 3 =$ ____	l. $3 \cdot 8 =$ ____	l. $56 / 8 =$ ____
m. $4 \times 4 =$ ____	m. $12 \div 4 =$ ____	m. $6 \times 4 =$ ____	m. $6 \div 6 =$ ____
n. $5 * 2 =$ ____	n. $10 / 5 =$ ____	n. $7 * 5 =$ ____	n. $21 / 7 =$ ____
o. $9 \cdot 6 =$ ____	o. $9 \div 9 =$ ____	o. $8 \cdot 8 =$ ____	o. $40 \div 8 =$ ____
p. $6 \times 2 =$ ____	p. $12 / 2 =$ ____	p. $1 \times 6 =$ ____	p. $48 / 6 =$ ____
q. $9 * 3 =$ ____	q. $27 \div 3 =$ ____	q. $3 * 7 =$ ____	q. $56 \div 7 =$ ____
r. $6 \cdot 4 =$ ____	r. $20 / 4 =$ ____	r. $4 \cdot 8 =$ ____	r. $64 / 8 =$ ____
s. $5 \times 5 =$ ____	s. $40 \div 8 =$ ____	s. $6 \times 7 =$ ____	s. $36 \div 6 =$ ____
t. $3 * 9 =$ ____	t. $81 / 9 =$ ____	t. $7 * 7 =$ ____	t. $7 / 7 =$ ____

© Houghton Mifflin Harcourt Publishing Company

Name _____

Answers to Dashes 21–22, 19A–22A, 19B–20B

Use this sheet to check your answers to the Dashes on pages 157 and 158.

Dash 21 ×	Dash 22 ÷	Dash 19A ×	Dash 20A ÷	Dash 21A ×	Dash 22A ÷	Dash 19B ×	Dash 20B ÷
a. 18	a. 4	a. 54	a. 4	a. 54	a. 7	a. 12	a. 6
b. 28	b. 6	b. 49	b. 3	b. 18	b. 4	b. 49	b. 9
c. 16	c. 2	c. 21	c. 6	c. 28	c. 1	c. 40	c. 3
d. 15	d. 7	d. 18	d. 2	d. 25	d. 6	d. 24	d. 3
e. 16	e. 5	e. 56	e. 3	e. 16	e. 3	e. 21	e. 4
f. 27	f. 7	f. 48	f. 9	f. 5	f. 2	f. 8	f. 6
g. 81	g. 10	g. 30	g. 6	g. 15	g. 8	g. 54	g. 9
h. 72	h. 9	h. 36	h. 6	h. 32	h. 7	h. 35	h. 6
i. 24	i. 7	i. 72	i. 7	i. 16	i. 4	i. 24	i. 9
j. 9	j. 4	j. 42	j. 8	j. 4	j. 5	j. 24	j. 1
k. 14	k. 1	k. 14	k. 8	k. 27	k. 3	k. 63	k. 2
l. 40	l. 7	l. 28	l. 7	l. 21	l. 7	l. 64	l. 7
m. 36	m. 9	m. 18	m. 4	m. 81	m. 9	m. 6	m. 2
n. 45	n. 9	n. 63	n. 8	n. 45	n. 10	n. 28	n. 1
o. 21	o. 3	o. 42	o. 9	o. 72	o. 9	o. 48	o. 2
p. 4	p. 4	p. 54	p. 9	p. 36	p. 9	p. 42	p. 5
q. 32	q. 8	q. 56	q. 5	q. 24	q. 7	q. 14	q. 8
r. 5	r. 3	r. 24	r. 3	r. 40	r. 7	r. 72	r. 1
s. 25	s. 1	s. 21	s. 7	s. 14	s. 4	s. 30	s. 8
t. 54	t. 7	t. 64	t. 4	t. 9	t. 1	t. 42	t. 3

161

Name

Answers to Dashes 21B–22B, 19C–22C, 19D–20D

Use this sheet to check your answers to the Dashes on pages 159 and 160.

Dash 21B ×	Dash 22B ÷	Dash 19C ×	Dash 20C ÷	Dash 21C ×	Dash 22C ÷	Dash 19D ×	Dash 20D ÷
a. 6	a. 4	a. 48	a. 9	a. 18	a. 4	a. 54	a. 3
b. 24	b. 6	b. 21	b. 7	b. 21	b. 2	b. 42	b. 6
c. 16	c. 3	c. 48	c. 3	c. 20	c. 1	c. 16	c. 4
d. 30	d. 5	d. 12	d. 1	d. 15	d. 4	d. 18	d. 9
e. 72	e. 7	e. 56	e. 5	e. 9	e. 7	e. 28	e. 7
f. 18	f. 8	f. 72	f. 9	f. 2	f. 8	f. 72	f. 1
g. 9	g. 1	g. 24	g. 3	g. 12	g. 5	g. 36	g. 5
h. 8	h. 7	h. 7	h. 4	h. 4	h. 8	h. 14	h. 5
i. 45	i. 9	i. 24	i. 1	i. 35	i. 6	i. 8	i. 6
j. 36	j. 3	j. 30	j. 5	j. 81	j. 5	j. 12	j. 4
k. 14	k. 6	k. 63	k. 3	k. 6	k. 1	k. 56	k. 2
l. 15	l. 4	l. 32	l. 5	l. 24	l. 7	l. 24	l. 7
m. 32	m. 5	m. 36	m. 7	m. 16	m. 3	m. 24	m. 1
n. 15	n. 8	n. 35	n. 9	n. 10	n. 2	n. 35	n. 3
o. 54	o. 6	o. 64	o. 4	o. 54	o. 1	o. 64	o. 5
p. 16	p. 1	p. 6	p. 6	p. 12	p. 6	p. 6	p. 8
q. 21	q. 3	q. 14	q. 2	q. 27	q. 9	q. 21	q. 8
r. 4	r. 9	r. 40	r. 7	r. 24	r. 5	r. 32	r. 8
s. 40	s. 3	s. 54	s. 4	s. 25	s. 5	s. 42	s. 6
t. 81	t. 1	t. 49	t. 6	t. 27	t. 9	t. 49	t. 1

Name _____

PATH to FLUENCY What's My Rule?

A function table is a table of ordered pairs. For every input number, there is only one output number. The rule describes what to do to the input number to get the output number.

Write the rule and then complete the function table.

6 Rule: _____

Input	Output
7	42
8	____
____	54
6	36
4	24
5	____

7 Rule: _____

Input	Output
81	9
45	5
72	____
____	7
27	____
54	6

8 Rule: _____

Input	Output
21	7
27	9
____	6
15	____
____	8
9	3

9 Rule: _____

Input	Output
5	25
____	40
9	____
3	15
7	35
____	20

✓ Check Understanding

Explain how you chose the rule for the table in Exercise 9.

164

Play Multiplication and Division Games

PATH to FLUENCY · Play *Division Three-in-a-Row*

Rules for *Division Three-in-a-Row*

Number of players: 2
What You Will Need: Product Cards, one
Three-in-a-Row Game Grid for each player

1. Players write a number in each of the
   squares on their game grids. They may
   use only numbers from 1 to 9, but they
   may use the same number more than once.

2. Shuffle the cards. Place them division side
   up in a stack in the center of the table.

3. Players take turns. On each turn, a player
   completes the division on the top card
   and then partners check the answer.

4. For a correct answer, if the quotient is on
   the game grid, the player puts an X
   through that grid square. If the answer
   is wrong, or if the quotient is not on the
   grid, the player doesn't mark anything.
   The player puts the card division
   side up on the bottom of the stack.

5. The first player to mark three squares
   in a row (horizontally, vertically, or
   diagonally) wins.

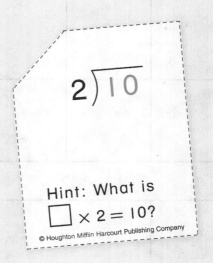

Name _____

2×2	$2 \cdot 3$	$2 * 4$	2×5
Hint: What is $3 \cdot 2$? <small>© Houghton Mifflin Harcourt Publishing Company</small>	Hint: What is $4 * 2$? <small>© Houghton Mifflin Harcourt Publishing Company</small>	Hint: What is 5×2? <small>© Houghton Mifflin Harcourt Publishing Company</small>	
2×6	$2 \cdot 7$	$2 * 8$	2×9
Hint: What is 6×2? <small>© Houghton Mifflin Harcourt Publishing Company</small>	Hint: What is $7 \cdot 2$? <small>© Houghton Mifflin Harcourt Publishing Company</small>	Hint: What is $8 * 2$? <small>© Houghton Mifflin Harcourt Publishing Company</small>	Hint: What is 9×2? <small>© Houghton Mifflin Harcourt Publishing Company</small>
5×2	$5 \cdot 3$	$5 * 4$	5×5
Hint: What is 2×5? <small>© Houghton Mifflin Harcourt Publishing Company</small>	Hint: What is $3 \cdot 5$? <small>© Houghton Mifflin Harcourt Publishing Company</small>	Hint: What is $4 * 5$? <small>© Houghton Mifflin Harcourt Publishing Company</small>	
5×6	$5 \cdot 7$	$5 * 8$	5×9
Hint: What is 6×5? <small>© Houghton Mifflin Harcourt Publishing Company</small>	Hint: What is $7 \cdot 5$? <small>© Houghton Mifflin Harcourt Publishing Company</small>	Hint: What is $8 * 5$? <small>© Houghton Mifflin Harcourt Publishing Company</small>	Hint: What is 9×5? <small>© Houghton Mifflin Harcourt Publishing Company</small>

$2{\overline{\smash{)}10}}$

Hint: What is
$\square \times 2 = 10$?

$2{\overline{\smash{)}8}}$

Hint: What is
$\square \times 2 = 8$?

$2{\overline{\smash{)}6}}$

Hint: What is
$\square \times 2 = 6$?

$2{\overline{\smash{)}4}}$

Hint: What is
$\square \times 2 = 4$?

$2{\overline{\smash{)}18}}$

Hint: What is
$\square \times 2 = 18$?

$2{\overline{\smash{)}16}}$

Hint: What is
$\square \times 2 = 16$?

$2{\overline{\smash{)}14}}$

Hint: What is
$\square \times 2 = 14$?

$2{\overline{\smash{)}12}}$

Hint: What is
$\square \times 2 = 12$?

$5{\overline{\smash{)}25}}$

Hint: What is
$\square \times 5 = 25$?

$5{\overline{\smash{)}20}}$

Hint: What is
$\square \times 5 = 20$?

$5{\overline{\smash{)}15}}$

Hint: What is
$\square \times 5 = 15$?

$5{\overline{\smash{)}10}}$

Hint: What is
$\square \times 5 = 10$?

$5{\overline{\smash{)}45}}$

Hint: What is
$\square \times 5 = 45$?

$5{\overline{\smash{)}40}}$

Hint: What is
$\square \times 5 = 40$?

$5{\overline{\smash{)}35}}$

Hint: What is
$\square \times 5 = 35$?

$5{\overline{\smash{)}30}}$

Hint: What is
$\square \times 5 = 30$?

9×2

$9 \cdot 3$

$9 * 4$

9×5

Hint:
What is 2×9?
© Houghton Mifflin Harcourt Publishing Company

Hint:
What is $3 \cdot 9$?
© Houghton Mifflin Harcourt Publishing Company

Hint:
What is $4 * 9$?
© Houghton Mifflin Harcourt Publishing Company

Hint:
What is 5×9?
© Houghton Mifflin Harcourt Publishing Company

9×6

$9 \cdot 7$

$9 * 8$

9×9

Hint:
What is 6×9?
© Houghton Mifflin Harcourt Publishing Company

Hint:
What is $7 \cdot 9$?
© Houghton Mifflin Harcourt Publishing Company

Hint:
What is $8 * 9$?
© Houghton Mifflin Harcourt Publishing Company

© Houghton Mifflin Harcourt Publishing Company

$\times$

$\bullet$

$*$

$\times$

$\times$

$\bullet$

$*$

$\times$

You can write any numbers on the last 8 cards. Use them to practice difficult problems or if you lose a card.

$9 \overline{)45}$ $9 \overline{)36}$ $9 \overline{)27}$ $9 \overline{)18}$

Hint: What is
$\square \times 9 = 45?$

Hint: What is
$\square \times 9 = 36?$

Hint: What is
$\square \times 9 = 27?$

Hint: What is
$\square \times 9 = 18?$

$9 \overline{)81}$ $9 \overline{)72}$ $9 \overline{)63}$ $9 \overline{)54}$

Hint: What is
$\square \times 9 = 81?$

Hint: What is
$\square \times 9 = 72?$

Hint: What is
$\square \times 9 = 63?$

Hint: What is
$\square \times 9 = 54?$

You can write any numbers on the last 8 cards. Use them to practice difficult problems or if you lose a card.

3×2	$3 \cdot 3$	$3 * 4$	3×5
Hint: What is 2×3?	Hint: What is	Hint: What is $4 * 3$?	Hint: What is 5×3?
© Houghton Mifflin Harcourt Publishing Company	© Houghton Mifflin Harcourt Publishing Company	© Houghton Mifflin Harcourt Publishing Company	© Houghton Mifflin Harcourt Publishing Company
3×6	$3 \cdot 7$	$3 * 8$	3×9
Hint: What is 6×3?	Hint: What is $7 \cdot 3$?	Hint: What is $8 * 3$?	Hint: What is 9×3?
© Houghton Mifflin Harcourt Publishing Company	© Houghton Mifflin Harcourt Publishing Company	© Houghton Mifflin Harcourt Publishing Company	© Houghton Mifflin Harcourt Publishing Company
4×2	$4 \cdot 3$	$4 * 4$	4×5
Hint: What is 2×4?	Hint: What is $3 \cdot 4$?	Hint: What is	Hint: What is 5×4?
© Houghton Mifflin Harcourt Publishing Company	© Houghton Mifflin Harcourt Publishing Company	© Houghton Mifflin Harcourt Publishing Company	© Houghton Mifflin Harcourt Publishing Company
4×6	$4 \cdot 7$	$4 * 8$	4×9
Hint: What is 6×4?	Hint: What is $7 \cdot 4$?	Hint: What is $8 * 4$?	Hint: What is 9×4?
© Houghton Mifflin Harcourt Publishing Company	© Houghton Mifflin Harcourt Publishing Company	© Houghton Mifflin Harcourt Publishing Company	© Houghton Mifflin Harcourt Publishing Company

© Houghton Mifflin Harcourt Publishing Company

$3 \overline{)15}$

Hint: What is
□ × 3 = 15?
© Houghton Mifflin Harcourt Publishing Company

$3 \overline{)12}$

Hint: What is
□ × 3 = 12?
© Houghton Mifflin Harcourt Publishing Company

$3 \overline{)9}$

Hint: What is
□ × 3 = 9?
© Houghton Mifflin Harcourt Publishing Company

$3 \overline{)6}$

Hint: What is
□ × 3 = 6?
© Houghton Mifflin Harcourt Publishing Company

$3 \overline{)27}$

Hint: What is
□ × 3 = 27?
© Houghton Mifflin Harcourt Publishing Company

$3 \overline{)24}$

Hint: What is
□ × 3 = 24?
© Houghton Mifflin Harcourt Publishing Company

$3 \overline{)21}$

Hint: What is
□ × 3 = 21?
© Houghton Mifflin Harcourt Publishing Company

$3 \overline{)18}$

Hint: What is
□ × 3 = 18?
© Houghton Mifflin Harcourt Publishing Company

$4 \overline{)20}$

Hint: What is
□ × 4 = 20?
© Houghton Mifflin Harcourt Publishing Company

$4 \overline{)16}$

Hint: What is
□ × 4 = 16?
© Houghton Mifflin Harcourt Publishing Company

$4 \overline{)12}$

Hint: What is
□ × 4 = 12?
© Houghton Mifflin Harcourt Publishing Company

$4 \overline{)8}$

Hint: What is
□ × 4 = 8?
© Houghton Mifflin Harcourt Publishing Company

$4 \overline{)36}$

Hint: What is
□ × 4 = 36?
© Houghton Mifflin Harcourt Publishing Company

$4 \overline{)32}$

Hint: What is
□ × 4 = 32?
© Houghton Mifflin Harcourt Publishing Company

$4 \overline{)28}$

Hint: What is
□ × 4 = 28?
© Houghton Mifflin Harcourt Publishing Company

$4 \overline{)24}$

Hint: What is
□ × 4 = 24?
© Houghton Mifflin Harcourt Publishing Company

6×2	$6 \cdot 3$	$6 * 4$	6×5
Hint: What is 2×6?	Hint: What is $3 \cdot 6$?	Hint: What is $4 * 6$?	Hint: What is 5×6?

6×6	$6 \cdot 7$	$6 * 8$	6×9
	Hint: What is $7 \cdot 6$?	Hint: What is $8 * 6$?	Hint: What is 9×6?

7×2	$7 \cdot 3$	$7 * 4$	7×5
Hint: What is 2×7?	Hint: What is $3 \cdot 7$?	Hint: What is $4 * 7$?	Hint: What is 5×7?

7×6	$7 \cdot 7$	$7 * 8$	7×9
Hint: What is 6×7?	Hint: What is	Hint: What is $8 * 7$?	Hint: What is 9×7?

$6 \overline{)30}$

Hint: What is
$\square \times 6 = 30$?

$6 \overline{)24}$

Hint: What is
$\square \times 6 = 24$?

$6 \overline{)18}$

Hint: What is
$\square \times 6 = 18$?

$6 \overline{)12}$

Hint: What is
$\square \times 6 = 12$?

$6 \overline{)54}$

Hint: What is
$\square \times 6 = 54$?

$6 \overline{)48}$

Hint: What is
$\square \times 6 = 48$?

$6 \overline{)42}$

Hint: What is
$\square \times 6 = 42$?

$6 \overline{)36}$

Hint: What is
$\square \times 6 = 36$?

$7 \overline{)35}$

Hint: What is
$\square \times 7 = 35$?

$7 \overline{)28}$

Hint: What is
$\square \times 7 = 28$?

$7 \overline{)21}$

Hint: What is
$\square \times 7 = 21$?

$7 \overline{)14}$

Hint: What is
$\square \times 7 = 14$?

$7 \overline{)63}$

Hint: What is
$\square \times 7 = 63$?

$7 \overline{)56}$

Hint: What is
$\square \times 7 = 56$?

$7 \overline{)49}$

Hint: What is
$\square \times 7 = 49$?

$7 \overline{)42}$

Hint: What is
$\square \times 7 = 42$?

8×2	$8 \cdot 3$	$8 * 4$	8×5

Hint: What is 2×8?
© Houghton Mifflin Harcourt Publishing Company

Hint: What is $3 \cdot 8$?
© Houghton Mifflin Harcourt Publishing Company

Hint: What is $4 * 8$?
© Houghton Mifflin Harcourt Publishing Company

Hint: What is 5×8?
© Houghton Mifflin Harcourt Publishing Company

8×6	$8 \cdot 7$	$8 * 8$	8×9

Hint: What is 6×8?
© Houghton Mifflin Harcourt Publishing Company

Hint: What is $7 \cdot 8$?
© Houghton Mifflin Harcourt Publishing Company

© Houghton Mifflin Harcourt Publishing Company

Hint: What is 9×8?
© Houghton Mifflin Harcourt Publishing Company

$\times$ $\bullet$ $*$ $\times$

$\times$ $\bullet$ $*$ $\times$

You can write any numbers on the last 8 cards. Use them to practice difficult problems or if you lose a card.

$8 \overline{)40}$ $8 \overline{)32}$ $8 \overline{)24}$ $8 \overline{)16}$

Hint: What is $\square \times 8 = 40?$

Hint: What is $\square \times 8 = 32?$

Hint: What is $\square \times 8 = 24?$

Hint: What is $\square \times 8 = 16?$

$8 \overline{)72}$ $8 \overline{)64}$ $8 \overline{)56}$ $8 \overline{)48}$

Hint: What is $\square \times 8 = 72?$

Hint: What is $\square \times 8 = 64?$

Hint: What is $\square \times 8 = 56?$

Hint: What is $\square \times 8 = 48?$

You can write any numbers on the last 8 cards. Use them to practice difficult problems or if you lose a card.

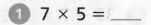

Diagnostic Checkup for Basic Multiplication

1. 7 × 5 = _____   2. 2 × 3 = _____   3. 9 × 9 = _____   4. 9 × 6 = _____

5. 6 × 2 = _____   6. 3 × 0 = _____   7. 3 × 4 = _____   8. 6 × 8 = _____

9. 5 × 9 = _____   10. 3 × 3 = _____   11. 2 × 9 = _____   12. 5 × 7 = _____

13. 6 × 10 = _____   14. 4 × 1 = _____   15. 6 × 4 = _____   16. 4 × 8 = _____

17. 5 × 2 = _____   18. 1 × 3 = _____   19. 3 × 9 = _____   20. 7 × 6 = _____

21. 7 × 2 = _____   22. 9 × 0 = _____   23. 8 × 9 = _____   24. 8 × 7 = _____

25. 8 × 10 = _____   26. 6 × 3 = _____   27. 4 × 4 = _____   28. 3 × 8 = _____

29. 5 × 5 = _____   30. 6 × 0 = _____   31. 7 × 9 = _____   32. 6 × 6 = _____

33. 9 × 2 = _____   34. 8 × 3 = _____   35. 5 × 4 = _____   36. 7 × 7 = _____

37. 5 × 10 = _____   38. 5 × 1 = _____   39. 10 × 9 = _____   40. 5 × 6 = _____

41. 6 × 5 = _____   42. 9 × 3 = _____   43. 4 × 2 = _____   44. 7 × 8 = _____

45. 8 × 2 = _____   46. 5 × 0 = _____   47. 4 × 9 = _____   48. 6 × 7 = _____

49. 9 × 5 = _____   50. 6 × 1 = _____   51. 7 × 4 = _____   52. 9 × 8 = _____

53. 4 × 10 = _____   54. 5 × 3 = _____   55. 6 × 9 = _____   56. 8 × 6 = _____

57. 8 × 5 = _____   58. 8 × 0 = _____   59. 8 × 4 = _____   60. 4 × 7 = _____

61. 3 × 5 = _____   62. 7 × 3 = _____   63. 5 × 9 = _____   64. 3 × 6 = _____

65. 7 × 10 = _____   66. 8 × 1 = _____   67. 0 × 4 = _____   68. 9 × 7 = _____

69. 4 × 5 = _____   70. 4 × 3 = _____   71. 1 × 9 = _____   72. 8 × 8 = _____

Name _____

PATH to FLUENCY Diagnostic Checkup for Basic Division

1 $12 \div 2 =$ _____

2 $8 \div 1 =$ _____

3 $36 \div 9 =$ _____

4 $35 \div 7 =$ _____

5 $20 \div 5 =$ _____

6 $24 \div 3 =$ _____

7 $12 \div 4 =$ _____

8 $6 \div 6 =$ _____

9 $6 \div 2 =$ _____

10 $3 \div 3 =$ _____

11 $18 \div 9 =$ _____

12 $63 \div 7 =$ _____

13 $20 \div 10 =$ _____

14 $0 \div 1 =$ _____

15 $40 \div 4 =$ _____

16 $48 \div 8 =$ _____

17 $18 \div 2 =$ _____

18 $6 \div 3 =$ _____

19 $8 \div 4 =$ _____

20 $36 \div 6 =$ _____

21 $8 \div 2 =$ _____

22 $9 \div 1 =$ _____

23 $9 \div 9 =$ _____

24 $56 \div 7 =$ _____

25 $40 \div 5 =$ _____

26 $9 \div 3 =$ _____

27 $36 \div 4 =$ _____

28 $56 \div 8 =$ _____

29 $80 \div 10 =$ _____

30 $7 \div 1 =$ _____

31 $45 \div 9 =$ _____

32 $48 \div 6 =$ _____

33 $5 \div 5 =$ _____

34 $30 \div 3 =$ _____

35 $16 \div 4 =$ _____

36 $72 \div 8 =$ _____

37 $10 \div 2 =$ _____

38 $1 \div 1 =$ _____

39 $54 \div 9 =$ _____

40 $21 \div 7 =$ _____

41 $25 \div 5 =$ _____

42 $15 \div 3 =$ _____

43 $32 \div 4 =$ _____

44 $24 \div 8 =$ _____

45 $90 \div 10 =$ _____

46 $18 \div 3 =$ _____

47 $63 \div 9 =$ _____

48 $54 \div 6 =$ _____

49 $45 \div 5 =$ _____

50 $6 \div 1 =$ _____

51 $20 \div 4 =$ _____

52 $49 \div 7 =$ _____

53 $15 \div 5 =$ _____

54 $0 \div 3 =$ _____

55 $28 \div 4 =$ _____

56 $30 \div 6 =$ _____

57 $16 \div 2 =$ _____

58 $21 \div 3 =$ _____

59 $81 \div 9 =$ _____

60 $64 \div 8 =$ _____

61 $30 \div 5 =$ _____

62 $12 \div 3 =$ _____

63 $27 \div 9 =$ _____

64 $42 \div 7 =$ _____

65 $40 \div 10 =$ _____

66 $10 \div 1 =$ _____

67 $24 \div 4 =$ _____

68 $18 \div 6 =$ _____

69 $35 \div 5 =$ _____

70 $27 \div 3 =$ _____

71 $72 \div 9 =$ _____

72 $42 \div 6 =$ _____

Name _____

Favorite Zoo Animals

The students in third grade took a field trip to a zoo. The students were asked to name their favorite zoo animal. The pictograph below shows the animals the students chose.

Favorite Zoo Animal

Bear	☺ ☺ ☺ ☺ ☺ ☺ ☺
Elephant	☺ ☺ ☺ ☺ ☺ ☺ ☺ ☺
Giraffe	☺ ☺ ☺ ☺
Gorilla	☺ ☺ ☺ ☺ ☺ ☺
Lion	☺ ☺

Each ☺ stands for 7 students.

3 Use the information in the pictograph to complete the chart to show the number of students that chose each zoo animal.

Favorite Zoo Animal

Zoo Animal	Number of Students
Bear	
Elephant	
Giraffe	
Gorilla	
Lion	

Solve.

4 If 63 students chose a zebra as their favorite zoo animal, how many symbols would you use to show that on the pictograph?

_____

Name _____

Solve.

① $6 + 8 \div 4 =$ ■

■ $=$ _____

② $3 \times 40 =$ ■

■ $=$ _____

Write an equation and solve the problem.

Show your work.

③ The pet shop had 8 cages of mice, with 4 mice in each cage. 5 mice escaped. How many mice were left in cages?

_____

④ Ingrid baked 47 cookies, but 5 were burned and thrown away. The rest were shared equally among 6 people. How many cookies did each person get?

_____

⑤ Maria had $4. Then she earned $7 each day for 8 days. How much money does she have now?

_____

Name _____

Subtract.

1 8 − 6 = ☐

2 6 − 4 = ☐

3 5 − 5 = ☐

4 11 − 6 = ☐

5 12 − 8 = ☐

6 10 − 1 = ☐

7 13 − 8 = ☐

8 14 − 7 = ☐

9 15 − 9 = ☐

10
$$\begin{array}{r} 17 \\ -\ 8 \\ \hline \end{array}$$

11
$$\begin{array}{r} 12 \\ -\ 6 \\ \hline \end{array}$$

12
$$\begin{array}{r} 15 \\ -\ 7 \\ \hline \end{array}$$

13
$$\begin{array}{r} 19 \\ -\ 9 \\ \hline \end{array}$$

14
$$\begin{array}{r} 14 \\ -\ 9 \\ \hline \end{array}$$

15
$$\begin{array}{r} 16 \\ -\ 8 \\ \hline \end{array}$$

Solve.

1 Write the numbers that complete the unknown number puzzle.

3	5	8	10	12	24	54

×	9		2
6		18	
	45	15	◯
	72	24	16

Explain how you found the number in the circle.

2 There are 56 books on a library cart. Each student helper puts 7 books on a shelf. How many student helpers are there?

For numbers 2a–2d, choose Yes or No to tell whether the equation could be used to solve the problem.

2a. $56 \times 7 = \boxed{}$ ○ Yes   ○ No

2b. $56 \div 7 = \boxed{}$ ○ Yes   ○ No

2c. $7 \times \boxed{} = 56$ ○ Yes   ○ No

2d. $7 \div \boxed{} = 56$ ○ Yes   ○ No

3 Raul makes a sign for the school fair. It has a length of 9 inches and a width of 8 inches. What is the area of the sign?

Draw a rectangle to help solve the problem. Label your drawing.

Write an equation to solve the problem.

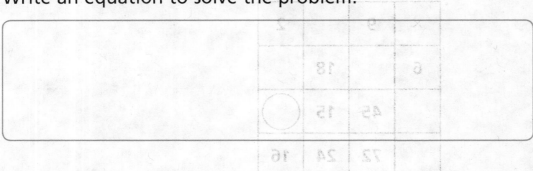

Area of the sign: _____ square inches

4 For numbers 4a–4c, select True or False for each statement.

4a. The first step to solve $3 + 2 \times 4$ is $3 + 2$.   ○ True ○ False

4b. The first step to solve $5 \times 4 \div 2$ is 5×4.   ○ True ○ False

4c. The first step to solve $(9 - 6) \div 3$ is $9 - 6$.   ○ True ○ False

5 Write a problem that can be solved using the given equation. Then solve.

$$7 \times 6 = \boxed{}$$

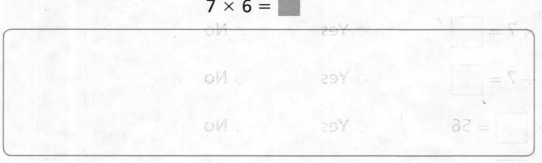

Solution: _____ tickets

6 Select the equation below where the unknown number is 8. Select all that apply.

(A) 7 × ▮ = 63

(D) ▮ × 9 = 72

(B) 4 × ▮ = 32

(E) 24 ÷ ▮ = 3

(C) 36 ÷ 4 = ▮

(F) 18 ÷ 2 = ▮

7 For numbers 7a–7d, choose Yes or No to tell whether the product is correct.

7a. 3 × 30 = 900   ○ Yes   ○ No

7b. 5 × 40 = 200   ○ Yes   ○ No

7c. 2 × 40 = 800   ○ Yes   ○ No

7d. 9 × 60 = 540   ○ Yes   ○ No

8 Carrie finds 7 seashells at the beach. Her brother finds 8 seashells. They divide the seashells equally among 3 people. How many seashells did each person get? Write an equation to solve the problem.

Equation: _____

_____ seashells

9 A toy store sells 7 different model cars. Each model car comes in 5 different colors. How many different model cars are there?

Part A

Solve the problem.

_____ different model cars

Part B

Choose the type of problem and the operation you use to solve.

The type is | array / equal groups / area | . The operation is | multiplication / division | .

Write another problem that is the same type.

[ ]

10 Write a question for the given information. Then write an equation and solve.

A museum has 297 visitors on Friday. It has 468 visitors on Saturday.

Solution: _____ visitors

11 How can you use a pattern to find 6×9 if you know 3×9? Complete the given part of the multiplication table to help you explain.

×	1	2	3	4	5	6	7	8	9
3									
6									

12 Select the equations that show square numbers. Select all that apply.

Ⓐ $2 \times 5 = 10$

Ⓑ $4 \times 4 = 16$

Ⓒ $8 \times 8 = 64$

Ⓓ $6 \times 6 = 36$

Ⓔ $8 \times 4 = 32$

Ⓕ $5 \times 5 = 25$

Draw a picture for one of the equations you chose.
Explain why it is a square number.

13 Read the problem. Write the first step question and answer. Then write an equation to solve the problem.

A school buys games for 6 classrooms. The school buys 3 board games, 4 puzzle games, and 1 video game for each classroom. How many games does the school buy?

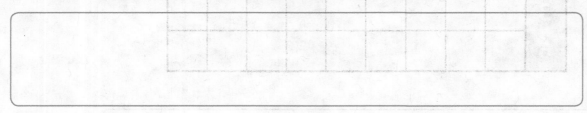

_____ games

14 Draw a line to match each expression on the left with an expression on the right that has the same value.

2 × 4 × 4 •   • 5 × 6

7 × 7   •   • 7 × 5 + 7 × 2

2 + 2 × 4 •   • 2 + 2

5 × 3 × 2 •   • 8 × 4

8 ÷ 4 + 2 •   • 2 + 8

15 Choose the equations that make the statements true.

You know that

3 × 9 = 27
3 × 5 = 15
8 × 6 = 48
4 × 7 = 28

. So, you know that

24 ÷ 3 = 8
18 ÷ 9 = 2
36 ÷ 6 = 6
48 ÷ 8 = 6

.

Play a Target Game

The object of this target game is to score 100 points, or as close to 100 points as possible without going over.

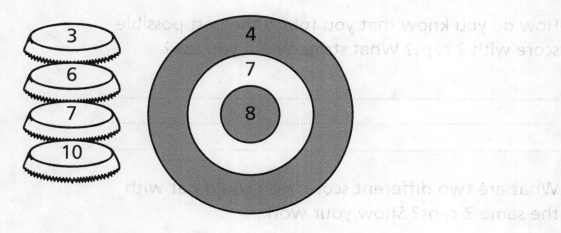

- You may drop two, three, or four bottle caps onto the target. To calculate the points for each drop, multiply the points on the cap by the points on the ring. For example, if the 3 cap lands on the 4 ring, the score would be 3 × 4 = 12.

- To find your final score, add the points for all your drops.

   Example: If the 3 bottle cap lands on the 4 ring, and the 7 bottle cap lands on the 8 ring, you could calculate your score using this equation.

   (3 × 4) + (7 × 8) =

      12   +   56   = 68

- Repeat the process by tossing other caps. Keep track of your scores and your equations for finding your scores.

1 What is the best possible score you can get with
2 bottle caps? Show your work.

_____

_____

2 How do you know that you found the best possible
score with 2 caps? What strategy did you use?

_____

_____

_____

3 What are two different scores you could get with
the same 3 caps? Show your work.

_____

_____

_____

_____

4 Can you score exactly 100 points with 3 caps?
Show your work. Show your work.

_____

_____

_____

5 Michael says that he can score exactly 100 points
with 4 bottle caps. Is that true? Show your work.

_____

_____

_____

Dear Family:

Your child is currently participating in math activities that help him or her to understand place value, rounding, and addition, subtraction, and multiplication of greater numbers.

- **Place Value Drawings:** Students learn to represent numbers with drawings that show how many hundreds, tens, and ones are in the numbers. Hundreds are represented by boxes. Tens are represented by vertical line segments, called ten sticks. Ones are represented by small circles. The drawings are also used to help students understand regrouping in addition and subtraction. Here is a place value drawing for the number 178.

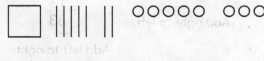

1 hundred   7 tens   8 ones

The 7 ten sticks and 8 circles are grouped in 5s so students can see the quantities easily and avoid errors.

- **Secret Code Cards:** Secret Code Cards are a set of cards for hundreds, tens, and ones. Students learn about place value by assembling the cards to show two- and three-digit numbers. Here is how the number 148 would be assembled.

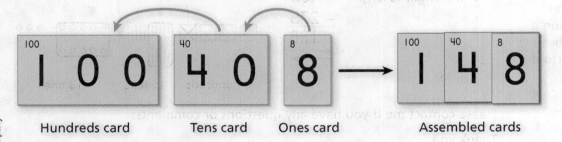

Hundreds card   Tens card   Ones card   Assembled cards

Estimate Sums and Differences Students learn to estimate sums and differences by rounding numbers. They also use estimates to check that their actual answers are reasonable.

	Rounded to the nearest hundred	Rounded to the nearest ten
493	500	490
129	100	130
+ 369	+ 400	+ 370
991	Estimate: 1,000	Estimate: 990

Addition Methods: Students may use the common U.S. method, referred to as the New Groups Above Method, as well as two alternative methods. In the New Groups Below Method, students add from right to left and write the new ten and new hundred on the line. In the Show All Totals Method, students add in either direction, write partial sums and then add the partial sums to get the total. Students also use proof drawings to demonstrate grouping 10 ones to make a new ten and grouping 10 tens to make a new hundred.

The New Groups Below Method shows the teen number 13 better than the New Groups Above Method, where the 1 and 3 are separated. Also, addition is easier in New Groups Below, where you add the two numbers you see and just add 1.

New Groups Above:

1 ← the new ten
46
+ 37
83

New Groups Below:

46
+ 37
83
← the new ten
Add right to left.

Show All Totals:

46
+ 37
70
13
83
Add left to right.

Proof Drawing:

8 tens   3 ones
the new ten

Subtraction Methods: Students may use the common U.S. method in which the subtraction is done right to left, with the ungrouping done before each column is subtracted. They also learn an alternative method in which all the ungrouping is done *before* the subtracting. If they do all the ungrouping first, students can subtract either from left to right or from right to left.

The Ungroup First Method helps students avoid the common error of subtracting a smaller top number from a larger bottom number.

1. Ungroup first.
2. Subtract (from left to right or from right to left).

15
3 5 13
4̶6̶3̶
− 275
1 88

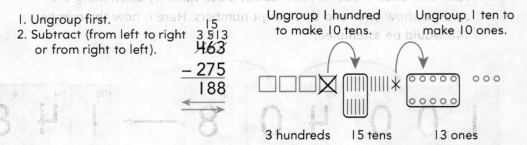

Ungroup 1 hundred to make 10 tens.   Ungroup 1 ten to make 10 ones.

3 hundreds   15 tens   13 ones

Please contact me if you have any questions or comments.
Thank you.

Sincerely,
Your child's teacher

Estimada familia:

Su niño está participando en actividades matemáticas que le servirán para comprender el valor posicional, el redondeo y la suma, resta y multiplicación de números mayores.

- **Dibujos de valor posicional:** Los estudiantes aprenden a representar números por medio de dibujos que muestran cuántas centenas, decenas y unidades contienen. Las centenas están representadas con casillas, las decenas con segmentos verticales, llamados palitos de decenas, y las unidades con círculos pequeños. Los dibujos también se usan para ayudar a los estudiantes a comprender cómo se reagrupa en la suma y en la resta. Este es un dibujo de valor posicional para el número 178.

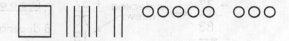

1 centena   7 decenas   8 unidades

Los palitos de decenas y los círculos se agrupan en grupos de 5 para que las cantidades se puedan ver más fácilmente y se eviten errores.

- **Tarjetas de código secreto:** Las tarjetas de código secreto son un conjunto de tarjetas con centenas, decenas y unidades. Los estudiantes aprenden acerca del valor posicional organizando las tarjetas de manera que muestren números de dos y de tres dígitos. Así se puede formar el número 148:

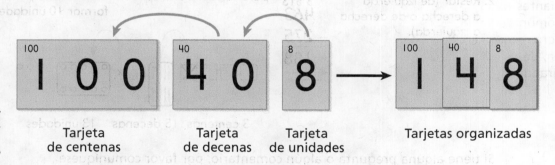

| Tarjeta de centenas | Tarjeta de decenas | Tarjeta de unidades | Tarjetas organizadas |

Estimar sumas y diferencias: Los estudiantes aprenden a estimar sumas y diferencias redondeando números. También usan las estimaciones para comprobar que sus respuestas son razonables.

	Redondear a la centena más próxima	Redondear a la decena más próxima
493	500	490
129	100	130
+ 369	+ 400	+ 370
991	Estimación: 1,000	Estimación: 990

Métodos de suma: Los estudiantes pueden usar el método común de EE. UU., conocido como Grupos nuevos arriba, y otros dos métodos alternativos. En el método de Grupos nuevos abajo, los estudiantes suman de derecha a izquierda y escriben la nueva decena y la nueva centena en el renglón. En el método de Mostrar todos los totales, los estudiantes suman en cualquier dirección, escriben sumas parciales y luego las suman para obtener el total. Los estudiantes también usan dibujos de comprobación para demostrar cómo se agrupan 10 unidades para formar una nueva decena, y 10 decenas para formar una nueva centena.

El método de Grupos nuevos abajo muestra el número 13 mejor que el método de Grupos nuevos arriba, en el que se separan los números 1 y 3. Además, es más fácil sumar con Grupos nuevos abajo, donde se suman los dos números que se ven y simplemente se añade 1.

Grupos nuevos arriba:

$$1 \leftarrow \text{la decena nueva}$$
$$\begin{array}{r} 46 \\ + 37 \\ \hline 83 \end{array}$$

Grupos nuevos abajo:

$$\begin{array}{r} 46 \\ + 37 \\ \hline 83 \end{array}$$ ← la decena nueva

Sumar de derecha a izquierda.

Mostrar todos los totales:

$$\begin{array}{r} 46 \\ + 37 \\ \hline 70 \\ 13 \\ \hline 83 \end{array}$$

Sumar de izquierda a derecha.

Dibujo de comprobación:

la decena nueva

8 decenas 3 unidades

Métodos de resta: Los estudiantes pueden usar el método común de EE. UU., en el cual la resta se hace de derecha a izquierda, desagrupando antes de restar cada columna. También aprenden un método alternativo en el que desagrupan todo *antes* de restar. Si los estudiantes desagrupan todo primero, pueden restar de izquierda a derecha o de derecha a izquierda.

El método de Desagrupar primero ayuda a los estudiantes a evitar el error común de restar un número pequeño de arriba, de un número más grande de abajo.

1. Desagrupar primero.
2. Restar (de izquierda a derecha o de derecha a izquierda).

$$\begin{array}{r} \overset{\;\;\;15}{\overset{3\;513}{4\;6\;3}} \\ - 275 \\ \hline 188 \end{array}$$

Desagrupar 1 centena para formar 10 decenas.

Desagrupar 1 decena para formar 10 unidades.

3 centenas   15 decenas   13 unidades

Si tiene alguna pregunta o algún comentario, por favor comuníquese conmigo. Gracias.

Atentamente,
El maestro de su niño

compatible numbers

expanded form

equal (=)

greatest

estimate

hundreds

A number written to show
the value of each of its digits.

Examples:
347 = 300 + 40 + 7
347 = 3 hundreds + 4 tens + 7 ones

Numbers that are easy
to compute mentally.
Compatible numbers can be
used to check if answers are
reasonable.

Example:
692 + 234

Some compatible numbers for the
addends are 700 and 200 or 700 and 234.

---

56   29   64
64 is the greatest number.

A symbol used to compare
two amounts or values. It
shows that what is on the
left of the sign is equal to
or the same value as what
is on the right of the sign.

Example:
3,756 = 3,756
3,756 *is equal* to 3,756.

□ □ □ | | | | ° ° ° ° °

3 hundreds

347 has 3 hundreds.

↑

hundreds

A reasonable guess about
how many or about how
much.

hundred thousands

ones

input-output table

place value

least

round

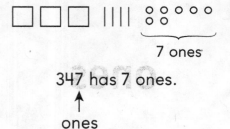

347 has 7 ones.

↑
ones

Hundred Thousands	Ten Thousands	Thousands	Hundreds	Tens	Ones
5	4	6	7	8	2

There are 5 hundred thousands in 546,782.

The value assigned to the place that a digit occupies in a number.

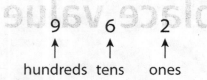

9   6   2
↑   ↑   ↑
hundreds tens ones

A table that displays ordered pairs of numbers that follow a specific rule.

Example:

Rule: Add 4	
Input	Output
3	7
5	9
9	13
11	15
15	19

To find about how many or how much by expressing a number to the nearest ten, hundred, thousand, and so on.

72   41   89
41 is the least number.

standard form

thousands

tens

unit square

ten thousands

Hundred Thousands	Ten Thousands	Thousands	Hundreds	Tens	Ones
5	4	6	7	8	2

There are 6 thousands in 546,782.

The name of a number written using digits.

Example:
1,829

A square whose area is 1 square unit.

4 tens

347 has 4 tens.

↑
tens

Hundred Thousands	Ten Thousands	Thousands	Hundreds	Tens	Ones
5	4	6	7	8	2

There are 4 ten thousands in 546,782.

1	2	10	20
1	2	1 0	2 0

3	4	30	40
3	4	3 0	4 0

5	6	50	60
5	6	5 0	6 0

7	8	70	80
7	8	7 0	8 0

9	90	100	
9	9 0	1 0 0	

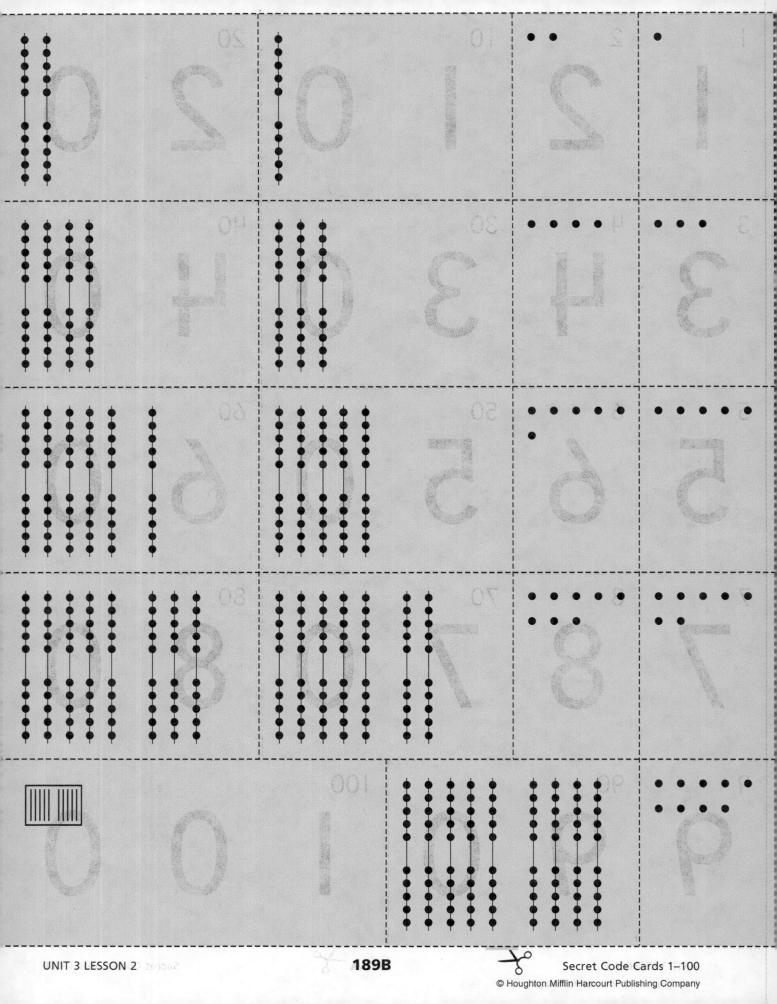

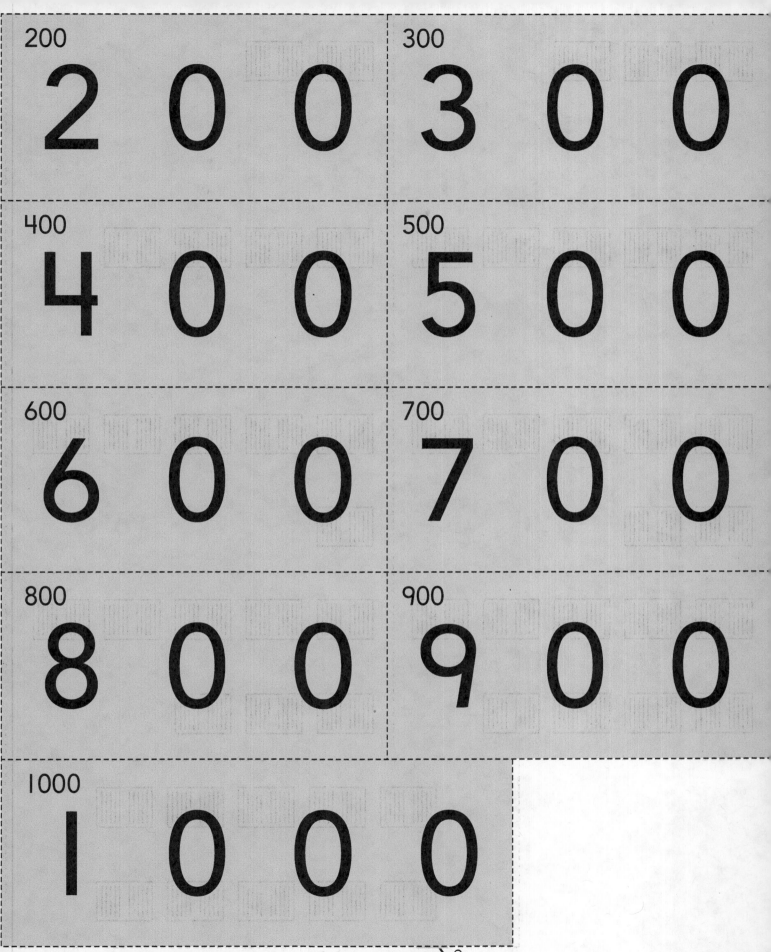

200   2 0 0

300   3 0 0

400   4 0 0

500   5 0 0

600   6 0 0

700   7 0 0

800   8 0 0

900   9 0 0

1000   1 0 0 0

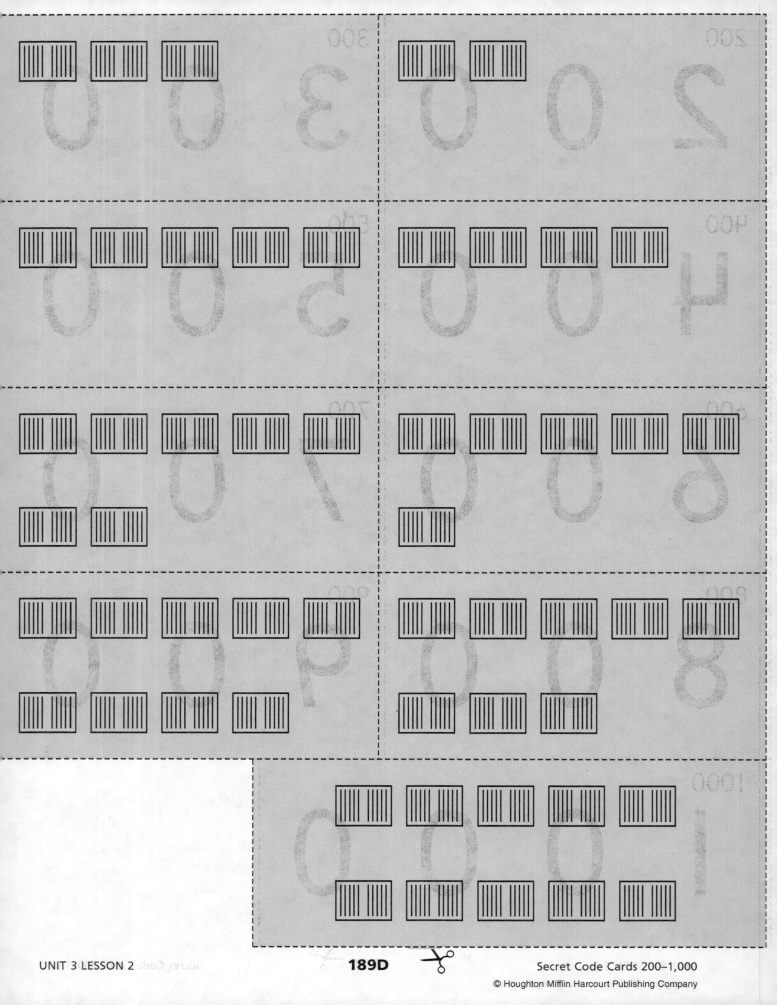

189D

Secret Code Cards 200–1,000

Name _____

What's the Error?

Dear Math Students,

I was asked to build the number 238 with Secret Code Cards. I made the number with these cards.

200 2 0 0   3   8

200 2   3   8

My teacher says that what I showed is not correct. Can you help me?

Your friend,
Puzzled Penguin

10 **Write an answer to Puzzled Penguin.**

_____

_____

_____

_____

✔ Check Understanding

Use the number 456 to complete the sentences. Build the number with Secret Code Cards to check your answer.

The value of the digit 4 is _____.

The value of the digit 5 is _____.

The value of the digit 6 is _____.

190

Name _____

What's the Error?

Dear Math Students,

Today my teacher asked me to estimate the answer to this problem:

Ms. Smith's class brought in 384 cans for the food drive.
Mr. Alvarez's class brought in 524 cans. About how many
cans did the two classes bring in?

$$
\begin{array}{r}
384 \rightarrow 300 \\
+\ 524 \rightarrow +\ 500 \\
\hline
800
\end{array}
$$

About 800 cans were brought in.

Is my answer correct? If not, please correct my work and tell me what I did
wrong.

Your friend,
Puzzled Penguin

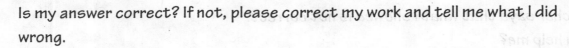

33 Write an answer to Puzzled Penguin.

_____

_____

Estimate the Number of Objects

**Jar D has 100 Beans. Estimate how
many beans are in the other jars.**

34 Jar A _____

35 Jar B _____

36 Jar C _____

Jar A   Jar B   Jar C   Jar D
100
Beans

✓ **Check Understanding**

Round each number to the nearest ten.

83 _____   98 _____   245 _____   362 _____

Name _____

Write the correct answer.

1 Round to the nearest hundred.

678

_____

2 Round to the nearest ten.

524

_____

3 Write the number shown by the place value drawing.

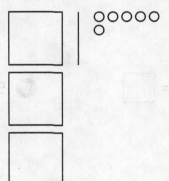

_____

4 Round to the nearest ten.

567

_____

5 Gerard has 365 baseball cards. He puts as many of them as he can into piles of 100. How many piles of 100 does he make?

_____

Name _____

Multiply.

1 1 × 3 = ☐

2 3 × 2 = ☐

3 4 × 3 = ☐

4 4 × 1 = ☐

5 2 × 5 = ☐

6 6 × 1 = ☐

7 6 × 6 = ☐

8 8 × 4 = ☐

9 5 × 7 = ☐

10 9 × 3 = ☐

11 8 × 8 = ☐

12 6 × 9 = ☐

13 7 × 10 = ☐

14 10 × 10 = ☐

15 8 × 9 = ☐

© Houghton Mifflin Harcourt Publishing Company

Name _____

What's the Error?

Dear Math Students,

Today I found the answer to 168 + 78, but I don't
know if I added correctly. Please look at my work.
Is my answer right? If not, please correct my work
and tell what I did wrong.

$$\begin{array}{r} 168 \\ +\ 78 \\ \hline 948 \end{array}$$

Your friend,
Puzzled Penguin

5 Write an answer to Puzzled Penguin.

_____

_____

PATH to FLUENCY Line Up the Places to Add

**Write each addition vertically. Line up the places
correctly. Then add and make a proof drawing.**

6 179 + 38 = _____

7 650 + 345 = _____

8 407 + 577 = _____

✓ Check Understanding

Explain why it is important to line up place
values before adding.

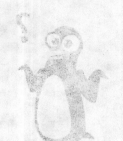

MATH TO FLUENCY

Check Understanding

Write the correct answer.

Show your work.

1. The bookstore sold 273 books in the morning and 385 books in the afternoon before it closed. How many books did it sell that day?

   _____

2. What new groups will need to be made to add 345 and 276?

   _____

   _____

3. Holly's farm has 143 goats and 287 sheep. How many animals does the farm have in all? Write an equation and solve the problem.

   _____

Add.

4. $227 + 98 =$ _____

5. $47 + 26 =$ _____

Name _____

PATH to
FLUENCY

Divide.

1. $3 \div 3 = \boxed{}$

2. $8 \div 2 = \boxed{}$

3. $9 \div 3 = \boxed{}$

4. $16 \div 2 = \boxed{}$

5. $25 \div 5 = \boxed{}$

6. $28 \div 4 = \boxed{}$

7. $32 \div 8 = \boxed{}$

8. $40 \div 4 = \boxed{}$

9. $48 \div 6 = \boxed{}$

10. $56 \div 7 = \boxed{}$

11. $63 \div 9 = \boxed{}$

12. $54 \div 6 = \boxed{}$

13. $64 \div 8 = \boxed{}$

14. $72 \div 8 = \boxed{}$

15. $90 \div 9 = \boxed{}$

What's the Error?

Dear Math Students,

Today I found the answer to 134 – 58, but I don't know if I did it correctly. Please look at my work. Is my answer right? If not, please correct my work and tell what I did wrong.

```
 134
– 58
─────
 124
```

Your friend,
Puzzled Penguin

5 Write an answer to Puzzled Penguin.

_____

_____

PATH to FLUENCY Subtraction Detective

To avoid making subtraction mistakes, look at the top number closely. Do all the ungrouping *before* you subtract. The magnifying glass around the top number helps you remember to be a "subtraction detective."

Subtract. Show your ungroupings numerically and with proof drawings.

6
(371)
– 86

7
(163)
– 47

8
(459)
–175

 Check Understanding
Complete. Always subtract the _____
number from the _____ number.

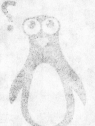

```
  134
−  58
  124
```



```
  371
−  86
```

```
  163
−  47
```

```
  459
− 175
```

Subtract.

1 765 − 56 = _____

2 72 − 35 = _____

Solve.

3 524 people watch the town parade. 178 of them are children. How many people watching the parade are adults?

_____

4 Roberto has a collection of 243 CDs. He scratched 152 of them. How many of his CDs are not scratched?

_____

5 Amaya has 476 pennies. Then she finds 359 more pennies. How many pennies does she have now?

_____

Name _____

Multiply or divide.

1 $1 \div 1 = $ ☐

2 $3 \times 5 = $ ☐

3 $6 \div 2 = $ ☐

4 $4 \times 3 = $ ☐

5 $9 \div 3 = $ ☐

6 $8 \times 2 = $ ☐

7 $12 \div 3 = $ ☐

8 $7 \times 6 = $ ☐

9 $8 \div 1 = $ ☐

10 $7 \times 3 = $ ☐

11 $20 \div 4 = $ ☐

12 $5 \times 7 = $ ☐

13 $36 \div 9 = $ ☐

14 $9 \times 2 = $ ☐

15 $54 \div 9 = $ ☐

Identify Place Value Through Hundred Thousands

Write each number in the place-value chart.

1 12,072   **2** 6,908   **3** 90,542   **4** 175,163

	Hundred Thousands	Ten Thousands	Thousands	Hundreds	Tens	Ones
1.						
2.						
3.						
4.						

Write the value of the underlined digit.

5 1̲3,456 _____   **6** 190,7̲65 _____

7 8̲8,763 _____   **8** 4,5̲67 _____

9 25,78̲3 _____   **10** 95,4̲26 _____

Write Numbers Different Ways

Write each number in standard form.

11 sixty thousand, one hundred eight _____

12 one hundred sixty-six thousand, eighty _____

Write each number in word form.

13 17,893 _____

14 175,635 _____

Write each number in expanded form.

15 23,059 _____

16 103,814 _____

Name _____

More and Less

Write the number that is 10,000 more and the number that is 10,000 less.

17 87,630   10,000 more _____   10,000 less _____

18 19,455   10,000 more _____   10,000 less _____

Write the number that is 1,000 more and the number that is 1,000 less.

19 5,176   1,000 more _____   1,000 less _____

20 26,709   1,000 more _____   1,000 less _____

Write the number that is 100 more and the number that is 100 less.

21 2,547   100 more _____   100 less _____

22 30,169   100 more _____   100 less _____

What's the Error?

Dear Math Students,

Today my teacher asked me to find the number that is 1,000 more than 15,319, but I don't know if my answer is correct. I wrote:

1,000 more than 15,319 is 25,319.

Your friend,
Puzzled Penguin

23 Write an answer to Puzzled Penguin.

_____

_____

_____

Factor the Tens to Multiply Ones and Tens

This 3 × 40 rectangle contains 12 groups of 10 square units, so its area is 120 square units.

	$1 \times 10 = 10$	$1 \times 10 = 10$	$1 \times 10 = 10$	$1 \times 10 = 10$	
1	$1 \times 10 = 10$	$1 \times 10 = 10$	$1 \times 10 = 10$	$1 \times 10 = 10$	1
1	$1 \times 10 = 10$	$1 \times 10 = 10$	$1 \times 10 = 10$	$1 \times 10 = 10$	1

40 = 10 + 10 + 10 + 10

10 + 10 + 10 + 10

3 How can we show this numerically? Complete the steps.

$3 \times 40 = (3 \times 1) \times (\underline{\hspace{1cm}} \times 10)$

$= (\underline{\hspace{1cm}} \times \underline{\hspace{1cm}}) \times (1 \times 10)$

$= \underline{\hspace{1cm}} \times 10 = 120$

4 On your MathBoard, draw a 40 × 3 rectangle and find its area.

5 How is the 40 × 3 rectangle similar to the 3 × 40 rectangle? How is it different?

_____

_____

_____

_____

6 Write out the steps for finding 4 × 30 by factoring the tens. Use your MathBoard if you need to.

_____

_____

_____

Name _____

Use Rectangles to Multiply

**Draw a rectangle for each problem on your MathBoard.
Find the tens product, the ones product, and the total.**

14 8×38

_____

_____

_____

15 3×29

_____

_____

_____

16 4×28

_____

_____

_____

17 7×34

_____

_____

_____

18 2×38

_____

_____

_____

19 3×28

_____

_____

_____

20 5×30

_____

_____

_____

21 5×28

_____

_____

_____

Solve each problem.

22 Lucille put 9 rows of tile on her mudroom floor.
Each row has 16 tiles. How many tiles are on
Lucille's mudroom floor?

Show your work.

_____

23 A pizzeria can make pizzas on thin crusts, thick
crusts, or flatbreads. The pizzeria has a total
of 57 different ways to top the pizzas.
How many different combinations of crusts and
pizza toppings can the pizzeria make?

_____

24 Complete this word problem. Then solve it.

_____ has _____ boxes of _____.

There are _____ _____ in each box.

How many _____ does _____

have altogether? _____

242 Multiply 2-Digit Numbers by 1-Digit Numbers

Name _____

What's the Error?

Dear Math Students,

Today I found the answer to 4 × 29.
Here is how I found the answer.

	2	9
4	4 × 2 = 8	4 × 9 = 36

4 × 29 = 44

Is my answer correct? If not, please correct
my work and tell me what I did wrong.

Your friend,
Puzzled Penguin

29 Write an answer to the Puzzled Penguin.

_____

_____

Practice 2–Digit by 1–Digit Multiplication

Use an area model to find the answer.

30 96 × 2 = _____

31 50 × 3 = _____

32 78 × 5 = _____

33 3 × 52 = _____

✓ Check Understanding

Explain how the rectangle you draw to solve
Problem 33 is similar to the rectangle you can
draw to solve 52 × 3.

PATH to FLUENCY **Use an Area Model to Solve**

For each acre of land that a farmer cuts, he gets 127 bales of hay. The farmer cuts his land 4 times every year. What is the total number of bales of hay the farmer will get from each acre this year?

6 Draw rectangles to represent the problem.

7 Explain how to use the area model to solve the problem above.

_____

_____

_____

8 Use your rectangle drawing and the steps you described to find the answer to the problem.

_____

Write the equation.

9 If the farmer has 9 acres of land, how many bales of hay will the farmer cut each year? Complete the area model to find the answer.

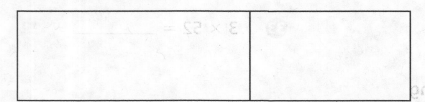

Equation: _____

Name _____

PATH to FLUENCY Use Rectangles to Multiply

Draw an area model for each problem on your MathBoard. Find the hundreds product, the tens product, the ones product, and the total.

14 8 × 387

_____

_____

_____

15 3 × 299

_____

_____

_____

16 4 × 528

_____

_____

_____

17 5 × 467

_____

_____

_____

18 2 × 838

_____

_____

_____

19 6 × 506

_____

_____

_____

Solve.

20 During the grand opening, an ice cream shop is giving away 5 free ice creams to the first 275 people through the door. What is the total number of ice creams that the shop is giving away?

_____

✓ **Check Understanding**

Complete. An area model for 2 × 413 shows the hundreds part is _____, the tens part is _____, and the ones part is _____, for a total area of _____.

Name _____

© Houghton Mifflin Harcourt Publishing Company

VOCABULARY
rule
input-output table

PATH to FLUENCY Complete Input-Output Tables

Use the rule to complete each input-output table.

1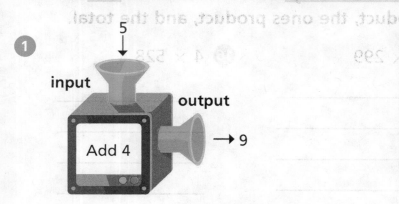

5 → input

output → 9

Add 4

Rule: Add 4	
Input	Output
5	9
6	
8	
10	
13	

2

3 → input

output → 9

Multiply by 3

Rule: Multiply by 3	
Input	Output
3	9
4	
5	
7	
9	

3

Rule: Add 8	
Input	Output
7	15
10	
24	
31	
50	

4

Rule: Subtract 10	
Input	Output
21	11
42	
59	
77	
95	

5

Rule: Multiply by 4	
Input	Output
3	12
4	
6	
8	
10	

6

Rule: Subtract 15	
Input	Output
16	1
31	
35	
49	
70	

Name _____

Find the Rule

Find the rule for each input-output table. Then complete the table.

7

Rule:	
Number of Bicycles	**Number of Wheels**
Input	Output
1	2
2	
3	
4	
5	

8

Rule:	
Input	**Output**
15	16
21	22
32	33
45	
49	

9

Rule:	
Input	**Output**
16	10
20	14
46	40
59	
84	

10

Rule:	
Input	**Output**
2	10
3	15
4	20
7	
10	

11 Blair is selling tickets to the school play. He records the number of tickets he sells to each family and the amount of money he collects. Complete the table. Then use the table to find the cost of each ticket.

Tickets Sold	2	3	5	7		10
Amount Collected		$21	$35	$49	$63	

Answer: _____

Check Understanding

Create an input-output table that uses the rule add 10.

Rule	Add 10				
Input					
Output					

250 Input-Output Tables

PATH to FLUENCY
Find the Rule

Find the rule for each input-output table. Then complete the table.

Rule: _____

Number of Bicycles Input	Number of Wheels Output
1	2
2	
3	
4	
5	

9 Rule: _____

Input	Output
15	16
21	22
32	33
45	
49	

10 Rule: _____

Input	Output
16	10
20	14
46	40
59	
84	

11 Rule: _____

Input	Output
2	10
3	15
4	20
7	
10	

12 Blair is selling tickets to the school play. He records the number of tickets he sells to each family and the amount of money he collects. Complete the table. Then use the table to find the cost of each ticket.

Tickets Sold	2	3	5	7	10
Amount Collected		$21	$35	$49	$63

Answer: _____

Check Understanding

Create an input-output table that uses the rule add 10.

Rule	Add 10			
Input				
Output				

1 Write the number that is 10,000 more than 89,086.

_____

2 Round to the nearest thousand to estimate the difference.

36,969

−   3,489

For questions 3 and 4, draw a model to solve.

3 An orchard has 8 rows of apple trees. There are 24 apple trees in each row. How many apple trees does the orchard have in all?

_____

4 Yolanda's book of puzzles has 365 pages. Each page has 3 puzzles. How many puzzles are in the book?

_____

5 Use the rule to complete the table.

Rule: Add 10	
Input	Output
3	13
13	
43	
63	
93	

PATH to FLUENCY

Multiply or divide.

1 $7 \div 1 =$ ☐

2 $8 \times 5 =$ ☐

3 $6 \div 3 =$ ☐

4 $9 \times 3 =$ ☐

5 $3 \div 3 =$ ☐

6 $8 \times 7 =$ ☐

7 $15 \div 3 =$ ☐

8 $9 \times 6 =$ ☐

9 $36 \div 6 =$ ☐

10 $4 \times 3 =$ ☐

11 $28 \div 4 =$ ☐

12 $5 \times 9 =$ ☐

13 $72 \div 9 =$ ☐

14 $6 \times 2 =$ ☐

15 $63 \div 9 =$ ☐

252

1 Select the way that shows three hundred fifty-seven. Mark all that apply.

(A) 357

(B) 3 hundreds + 57 tens

(C) 3 hundreds + 5 tens + 7 ones

(D)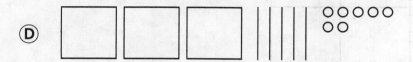

(E) 300 + 5 + 7

2 Make a place value drawing for the number.

691

3 The museum sells 15,564 posters. It sells 18,836 calendars. Round each number to the nearest thousand to estimate how many more calendars the museum sells than posters.

about _____ more calendars

4 Write the number in the box that shows how it should be rounded to the nearest hundred.

| 479 | 440 | 655 | 405 | 643 |

400	500	600	700

5 Use the rule to complete the table.

Rule: Multiply by 6	
Input	Output
2	12
3	
6	
7	
8	

6 Use the model to multiply 426 by 7.

426 =   □   □   □

7 × 426 = □

7 Subtract.

700 − 255 =

	7	0	0
−			

8 Select the number that has the digit 5 in the thousands place. Select all that apply.

(A) 64,500   (C) 25,700

(B) 59,700   (D) 16,705

For numbers 9 and 10, add or subtract. Make a proof drawing to show that your answer is correct.

9   497
      + 326

10 690
      − 493

Name _____

For numbers 11 and 12, add or subtract.   *Show your work.*

11   437
    + 273

Which method did you use to add?

I used the | New Groups Above |
            | New Groups Below | Method.
            | Show All Totals |

12   617
    − 549

Did you ungroup to subtract? Explain why or why not.

13 Andre buys 860 bricks. He buys 575 red bricks and
147 tan bricks. The rest of the bricks are gray. Write and
solve an equation to find how many gray bricks Andre
buys.

Equation: _____

_____ gray bricks

14 A company sells 6,409 cases of fruit. It sells 3,620 cases
of oranges and the rest are cases of grapefruit. How
many cases of grapefruit does the company sell?

_____ cases

15 Pia collects 245 acorns in a jar. For numbers 15a–15d, select True or False for each statement.

15a. Pia collects 193 more acorns.
She now has 338 acorns. ○ True ○ False

15b. Pia gives 160 acorns to Ana.
She now has 85 acorns. ○ True ○ False

15c. Pia collects 286 more acorns.
She uses 143 to decorate a tray.
She now has 388 acorns. ○ True ○ False

15d. Pia gives her two sisters 85 acorns
each. She now has 160 acorns. ○ True ○ False

16 Li earns 321 points in the first round of a math contest. He earns another 278 points in the second round and 315 points in the third round. Li says he has 804 points.

Is Li's answer reasonable? Explain.

Find the actual answer to check if you are correct.

17 Darian sells 293 bags of popcorn and 321 bags of peanuts.

Part A

How many bags of popcorn and peanuts does Darian sell?

_____ bags

Part B

Write a subtraction word problem related to how many bags of popcorn and peanuts Darian sells. Then find the answer without doing any calculations.

18 Sanaz makes 28 puppets for the craft fair. She needs 2 buttons on each puppet. How many buttons does Sanaz need in all?

_____ buttons

Raise Money

The students at Kevin's school are collecting pennies for a service project. They plan to use the money to buy flowers to plant at a local park. They need 1,000 pennies to buy each flat of flowers.

1 Kevin has collected 873 pennies. Round 873 to the nearest 100. Is the rounded number less than 1,000? Explain.

2 What would you have to add to 873 to get 1,000? How do you know your answer is reasonable?

3 Write an addition word problem related to Problem 2. Explain how the problems are related.

4 June, Ella, and Joshua also are collecting pennies
for the service project. June collected 324 pennies,
Ella collected 442 pennies, and Joshua collected
248 pennies.

Part A

Estimate to decide whether these three students
collected enough pennies to buy a flat of flowers.

Part B

Find the actual answer to check if you are correct.
Explain your strategy.

Part C

How many more pennies do the students need
to collect to buy a second flat of flowers? Show
your work.

Part D

Write an addition word problem related to
Part C. Explain how the problems are related.

© Houghton Mifflin Harcourt Publishing Company

Dear Family:

In this unit, your child will be introduced to fractions. Students will build fractions from unit fractions and explore fractions as parts of a whole.

Unit Fraction

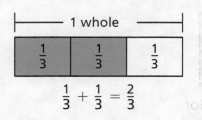

$$\frac{1}{3} + \frac{1}{3} = \frac{2}{3}$$

Fraction of a Whole

$\underset{\longleftarrow}{3}$ ← numerator
$\underset{4}{}$ ← denominator

Students will compare and order fractions with either the same denominator or the same numerator.

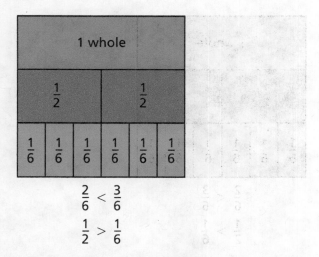

$$\frac{2}{6} < \frac{3}{6}$$

$$\frac{1}{2} > \frac{1}{6}$$

Students will also generate measurement data with halves and fourths and relate the fractions to length, time, and money. They graph their data in a line plot.

You can help your child become familiar with units of length, time, and money by working with these concepts together. For example, you might estimate and measure the length of something in inches or the amount of time something takes in seconds.

Please contact me if you have any questions or comments.

Sincerely,
Your child's teacher

Estimada familia:

En esta unidad, se le presentarán por primera vez las fracciones a su niño. Los estudiantes formarán fracciones con fracciones unitarias y explorarán las fracciones como partes de un entero.

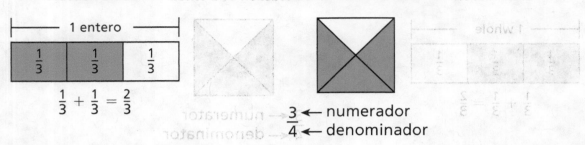

Fracción unitaria

Fracción de un entero

1 entero

$\frac{1}{3}$ $\frac{1}{3}$ $\frac{1}{3}$

$$\frac{1}{3} + \frac{1}{3} = \frac{2}{3}$$

$\frac{3}{4}$ ← numerador
← denominador

Los estudiantes compararán y ordenarán fracciones del mismo denominador o del mismo numerador.

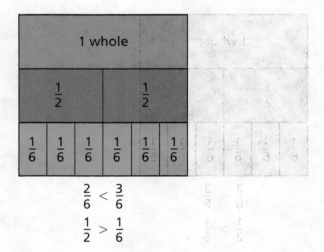

1 whole

$\frac{1}{2}$ $\frac{1}{2}$

$\frac{1}{6}$ $\frac{1}{6}$ $\frac{1}{6}$ $\frac{1}{6}$ $\frac{1}{6}$ $\frac{1}{6}$

$$\frac{2}{6} < \frac{3}{6}$$

$$\frac{1}{2} > \frac{1}{6}$$

Los estudiantes también generarán datos de medición con mitades y cuartos y relacionarán las fracciones a longitud, tiempo y dinero. Graficarán sus datos en un diagrama de puntos.

Puede ayudar a su niño a familiarizarse con las unidades de longitud, tiempo y dinero trabajando con estos conceptos en conjunto. Por ejemplo, es posible estimar y medir la longitud de algo en pulgadas o el tiempo que toma algo en segundos..

Si tiene alguna duda o algún comentario, por favor comuníquese conmigo.

       Atentamente,
       El maestro de su niño

denominator

frequency
table

elapsed time

horizontal
bar graph

fraction

inch (in.)

A table that shows how many times each event, item, or category occurs.

Frequency Table	
Age	Tally
7	1
8	3
9	5
10	4
11	2

The bottom number in a fraction that shows the total number of equal parts in the whole.

Example:

$\frac{1}{3}$ ←——— denominator

A bar graph with horizontal bars.

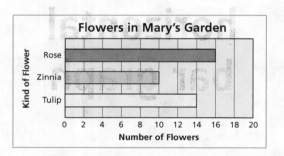

The time that passes between the beginning and the end of an activity.

A customary unit used to measure length.

12 inches = 1 foot

A number that names part of a whole or part of a set.

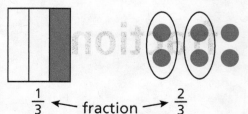

$\frac{1}{3}$ ←— fraction —→ $\frac{2}{3}$

key

mixed number

line plot

numerator

line segment

tally chart

A whole number and a fraction.

$1\frac{3}{4}$ is a mixed number.

A part of a map, graph, or chart that explains what symbols mean.

The top number in a fraction that shows the number of equal parts counted.

Example:

$\frac{1}{3}$ ◄———————— numerator

A diagram that shows frequency of data on a number line. Also called a *dot plot*.

A chart used to record and organize data with tally marks.

Tally Chart	
Age	Tally
7	I
8	III
9	IЖ
10	IIII
11	II

A part of a line. A line segment has two endpoints.

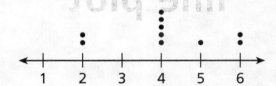

unit fraction

vertical bar graph

A fraction whose numerator
is 1. It shows one equal part
of a whole.

Example:

$\frac{1}{4}$

A bar graph with vertical bars.

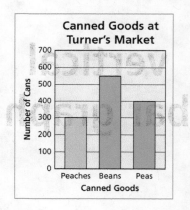

Fraction Rectangles

Cut out the bottom rectangle first.
Then cut on the dotted lines to make 4 rectangles.
Wait to cut out the top rectangle.

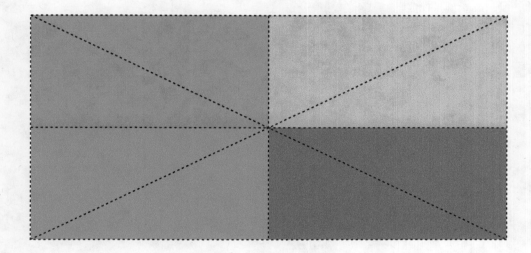

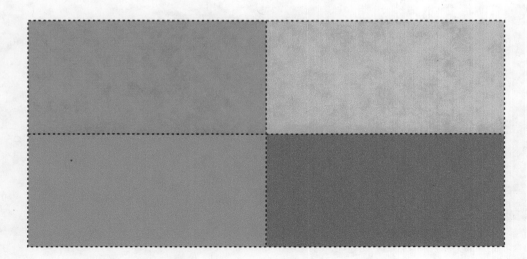

Cut Out Rectangles

Cut out the bottom rectangle first.
Then cut on the dotted lines to make 4 rectangles.
Wait to cut out the top rectangle.

263B Understand Fractions

Name _____

Explore Unit Fractions

Use your rectangles from page 263A to make the whole shape. Count the equal parts. What unit fraction of the whole shape is one of the rectangles?

1

Number of equal parts _____   Unit fraction _____

2

Number of equal parts _____   Unit fraction _____

3

Number of equal parts _____   Unit fraction _____

Name _____

Unit Fractions and Fraction Bars

You can represent a **fraction** with a fraction bar. The **denominator** tells how many equal parts the whole is divided into. The **numerator** tells how many equal parts you are talking about.

1 whole

$\dfrac{1}{3}$ ← numerator
← denominator

Shade 1 part.

A **unit fraction** has a numerator of 1. Shade the rest of the fraction bars at the right below to represent unit fractions. What patterns do you see?

| | → | | 1 one |

1 whole   Shade 1 whole.

| | → | | $\dfrac{1}{2}$ one half |

Divide the whole into 2 equal parts.   Shade 1 part.

| | → | | $\dfrac{1}{3}$ one third |

Divide the whole into 3 equal parts.   Shade 1 part.

| | → | | $\dfrac{1}{4}$ one fourth |

Divide the whole into 4 equal parts.   Shade 1 part.

| | → | | $\dfrac{1}{5}$ one fifth |

Divide the whole into 5 equal parts.   Shade 1 part.

| | → | | $\dfrac{1}{6}$ one sixth |

Divide the whole into 6 equal parts.   Shade 1 part.

| | → | | $\dfrac{1}{7}$ one seventh |

Divide the whole into 7 equal parts.   Shade 1 part.

| | → | | $\dfrac{1}{8}$ one eighth |

Divide the whole into 8 equal parts.   Shade 1 part.

Name

Build Fractions from Unit Fractions

Write the unit fractions for each whole. Next, shade the correct number of parts. Then show each shaded fraction as a sum of unit fractions.

9 ⟶ Shade 2 parts.

Divide the whole into 5 equal parts.

$$\frac{1}{5} + \frac{1}{5} + \frac{1}{5} + \frac{1}{5} + \frac{1}{5}$$

$$\frac{1}{5} + \frac{1}{5} = \frac{2}{5}$$

10 ⟶ Shade 2 parts.

Divide the whole into 3 equal parts.

11 ⟶ Shade 5 parts.

Divide the whole into 7 equal parts.

12 ⟶ Shade 7 parts.

Divide the whole into 8 equal parts.

13 ⟶ Shade 3 parts.

Divide the whole into 6 equal parts.

✔ Check Understanding

A fraction bar is divided into 8 equal parts.
What unit fraction represents each part? _____.
Write an equation that shows 5 parts shaded.

Name _____

Use Fraction Bars

Divide the fraction bar into unit fractions. Shade each fraction bar to show the fraction. Write the sum of the unit fractions under the shaded parts.

1 $\frac{1}{6}$

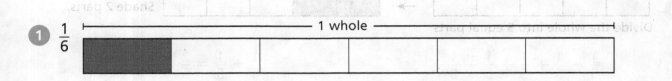

2 $\frac{2}{3}$

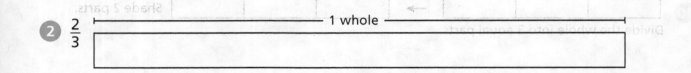

3 $\frac{7}{8}$

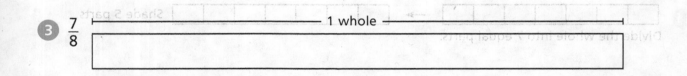

4 $\frac{2}{4}$

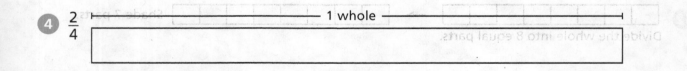

5 $\frac{5}{6}$

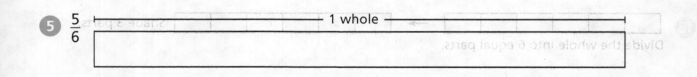

6 $\frac{3}{8}$

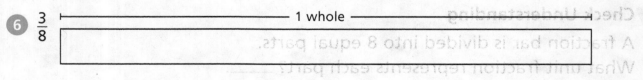

Name _____

Use Number Lines

First, divide each number line into the correct unit fractions. Then label each point. Show the target fraction by looping the unit fractions that make it.

7 $\frac{1}{6}$
0 ←———————————————→ 1

8 $\frac{2}{3}$
0 ←———————————————→ 1

9 $\frac{7}{8}$
0 ←———————————————→ 1

10 $\frac{2}{4}$
0 ←———————————————→ 1

11 $\frac{5}{6}$
0 ←———————————————→ 1

12 $\frac{3}{8}$
0 ←———————————————→ 1

✓ Check Understanding

Explain how Exercise 6 and Exercise 12 can both be used to show $\frac{3}{8}$.

Name _____

Locate Fractions Less Than 1

Divide each number line into the correct unit fractions. Then label each point. Show the target fraction by looping the unit fractions that make it.

1 $\frac{1}{4}$

2 $\frac{1}{8}$

3 $\frac{3}{4}$

4 $\frac{5}{6}$

5 $\frac{2}{3}$
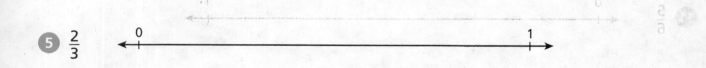

Plot the target fractions $\frac{2}{3}$ and $\frac{5}{6}$ on the number line below.

6
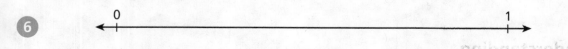

Name _____

Locate Fractions Greater Than 1

Divide each number line into the correct unit fractions. Then label each point. Show the target fraction by looping the unit fractions that make it.

7 $\frac{5}{4}$

8 $\frac{8}{3}$

9 $\frac{5}{1}$

10 $\frac{6}{2}$

Introduce Mixed Numbers

A fraction greater than 1 that cannot be named as a whole number can be named as a mixed number. **Mixed numbers** have a whole-number part and a fraction part.

Examples of mixed numbers:

$1\frac{1}{2}$

$3\frac{2}{3}$

$4\frac{2}{4}$

Complete.

11 $\frac{5}{4} = \frac{4}{4} + \frac{1}{4}$

$\frac{8}{3} = \frac{3}{3} + \frac{3}{3} + \frac{\square}{3}$

$\frac{8}{6} = \frac{\square}{6} + \frac{\square}{6}$

$= 1 + \frac{1}{4}$

$= 1 + 1 + \square$

$= 1 + \square$

$= \square$

$= \square$

$= \square$

Name _____

Find 1

**Divide each number line into the correct unit fractions.
Label each point. Then locate 1 on the number line.**

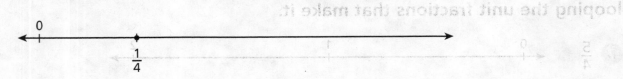

12

0

$\frac{1}{4}$

13

0

$\frac{1}{3}$

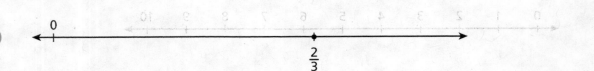

14

0

$\frac{2}{3}$

15

0

$\frac{9}{6}$

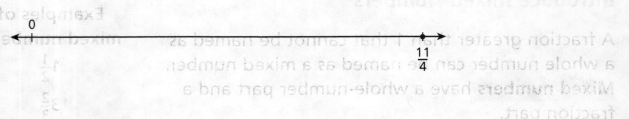

16

0

$\frac{11}{4}$

17 Explain how you located 1 for Exercise 15.

_____

_____

_____

Name ______________________________

Find Fractions

Divide each number line into the correct unit fractions. Then label each point. Use loops to show the target fraction.

18 $\frac{3}{4}$

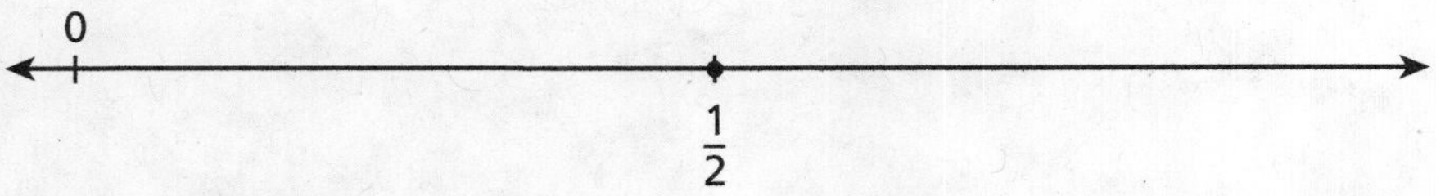

19 $\frac{5}{6}$

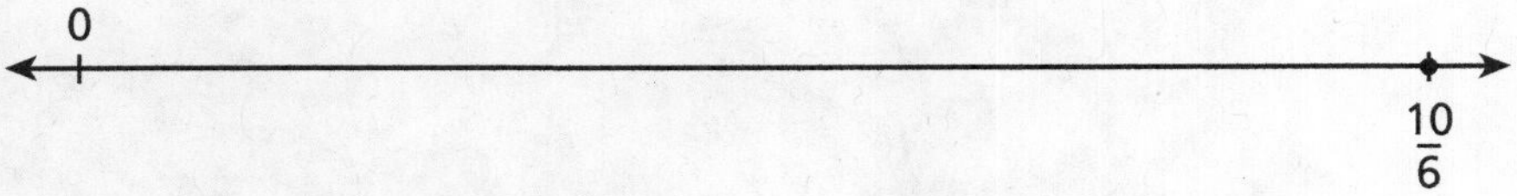

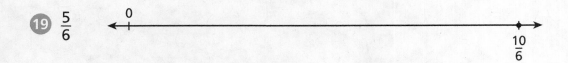

20 $\frac{3}{8}$

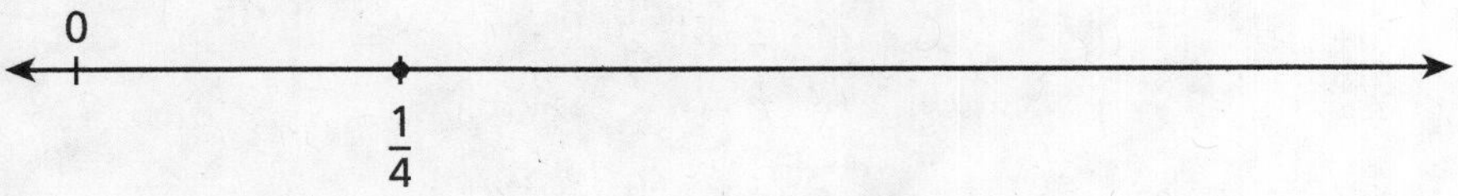

21 $\frac{5}{3}$

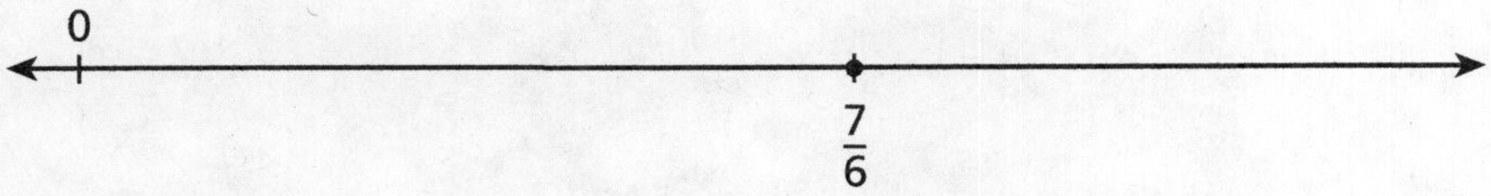

22 $\frac{1}{6}$

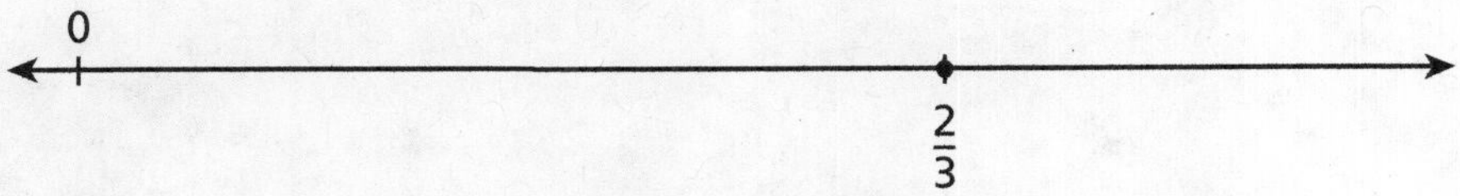

23 $\frac{10}{8}$

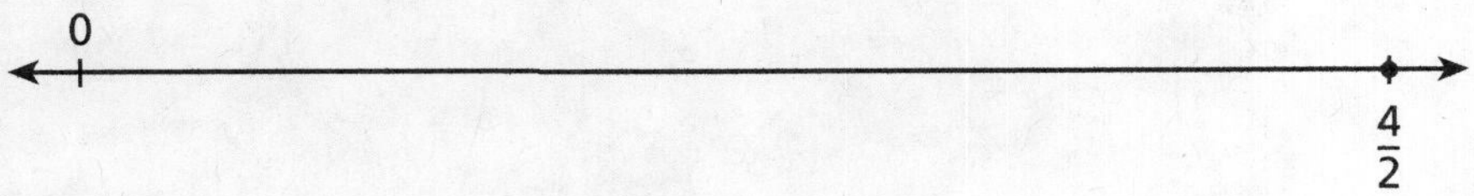

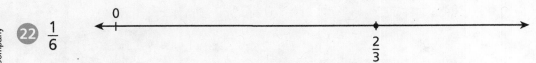

Check Understanding

Complete the sentence. The two fractions used to find 1 on the number line in Problem 23 are __________ and __________.

Find Fractions

Divide each number line into the correct unit fractions.
Then label each point. Use loops to show the target fraction.

Check Understanding

Complete the sentence. The two fractions used to find 1

on the number line in Problem 23 are _____ and _____

Fraction Circles

Each circle is the same size and represents the same whole. So, you can use these circles to compare fractions. Label each unit fraction. Then cut out the fraction circles on the dashed lines.

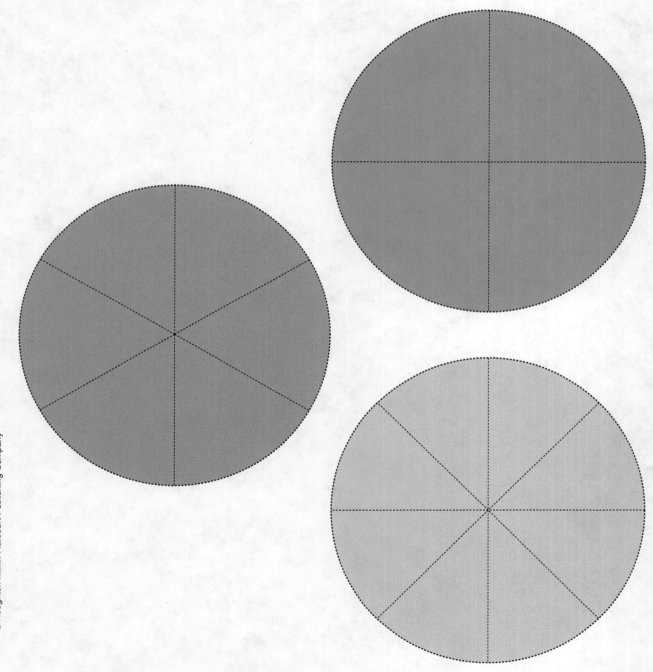

275A   Compare Fractions

Fraction Circles

Each circle is the same size and represents the same whole. So, you can use these circles to compare fractions. Label each unit fraction. Then cut out the fraction circles on the dashed lines.

Name _____

Compare and Order Fractions

Compare. Use <, >, or =.

7 $\frac{2}{2}$ ◯ $\frac{2}{3}$ **8** $\frac{1}{3}$ ◯ $\frac{5}{3}$ **9** $\frac{3}{2}$ ◯ $\frac{3}{6}$ **10** $\frac{5}{6}$ ◯ $\frac{4}{6}$

Order the fractions from least to greatest.

11 $\frac{5}{8}$ $\frac{3}{8}$ $\frac{7}{8}$ **12** $\frac{7}{3}$ $\frac{7}{6}$ $\frac{7}{5}$ **13** $\frac{2}{5}$ $\frac{1}{5}$ $\frac{3}{5}$

____, ____, ____   ____, ____, ____   ____, ____, ____

What's the Error?

Dear Math Students,

Today my teacher asked me to compare $\frac{3}{7}$ and $\frac{3}{9}$ and to explain my thinking.

I wrote $\frac{3}{7} = \frac{3}{9}$. My thinking is that both fractions have 3 unit fractions so they must be equal.

Is my work correct? If not, please correct my work and tell me what I did wrong. How do you know my answer is wrong?

Your friend,
Puzzled Penguin

14 Write an answer to Puzzled Penguin.

_____

_____

_____

✓ Check Understanding

Explain how comparing two fractions with the same denominator is different from comparing two fractions with the same numerator.

276 Compare Fractions

Name _____

VOCABULARY
line segment

Units of Length

Loop length units and fractions of units to show the length of the line segment. Write the length.

_____

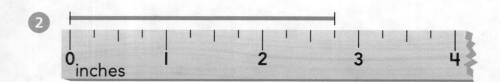

_____

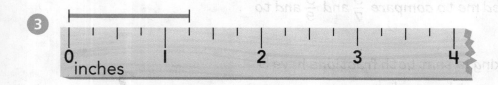

_____

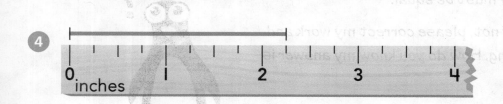

_____

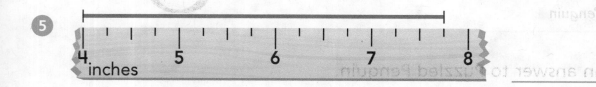

_____

6 Why is this ruler wrong?

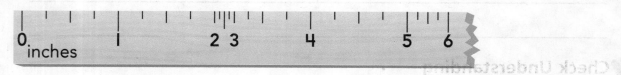

_____

_____

Name _____

Make a Line Plot

Use the box below to record the actual measure for the line segments that each classmate drew on page 278.

17 Use the measurement data from the box above to complete the line plot below.

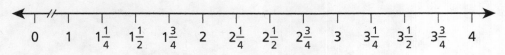

Length of Line Segments (in inches)

18 How many of the line segments have a measure of $2\frac{1}{2}$ inches? _____

19 Which length appears the most often on the line plot? _____

✓ Check Understanding

Describe how to measure a line segment to the nearest $\frac{1}{4}$ inch.

Name _____

Show the shaded fraction as a sum of unit fractions.

1

Divide the fraction bar into the correct number of equal parts.

2 8 equal parts

Shade the fraction bar to show the fraction. First divide the fraction bar into the correct unit fractions.

3 $\frac{1}{3}$

|←——————— 1 whole ———————→|

Mark the number line to show the fraction. First divide the number line into correct unit fractions.

4 $\frac{5}{3}$

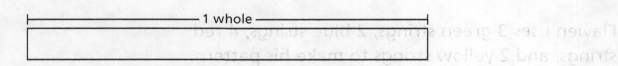

0   1   2   3

Compare. Use <, >, or =.

5 $\frac{1}{6} \bigcirc \frac{1}{2}$

UNIT 4 Big Idea 1

Name _____

1. Flavien uses string in the colors and lengths shown below to create a pattern. Measure the length of each of the strings shown to the nearest $\frac{1}{4}$ inch.

_____

[ ] inches

_____

[ ] inches

_____

[ ] inches

_____

[ ] inches

2. Flavien uses 3 green strings, 2 blue strings, 4 red strings, and 2 yellow strings to make his pattern. Use the length measurements from the previous question to complete the line plot below.

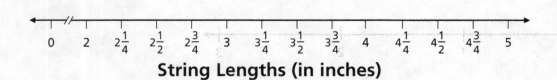

String Lengths (in inches)

Dear Family:

In math class, your child is beginning lessons about time. This topic is directly connected to home and community and involves skills your child will use often in everyday situations.

Students are reading time to the hour, half-hour, quarter-hour, five minutes, and minute, as well as describing the time before the hour and after the hour.

For example, you can read 3:49 both as minutes after the hour and minutes before the hour.

Forty-nine minutes after three   **Eleven minutes before four**

Students will be using clocks to solve problems about elapsed time.

Help your child read time and find elapsed time. Ask your child to estimate how long it takes to do activities such as eating a meal, traveling to the store, or doing homework. Have your child look at the clock when starting an activity and then again at the end of the activity. Ask how long the activity took.

Your child will also learn to add and subtract time on a number line.

If you have any questions or comments, please contact me.

Sincerely,
Your child's teacher

Estimada familia:

En la clase de matemáticas su niño está comenzando lecciones que le enseñan sobre la hora. Este tema se relaciona directamente con la casa y la comunidad, y trata de destrezas que su niño usará a menudo en situaciones de la vida diaria.

Los estudiantes leerán la hora, la media hora, el cuarto de hora, los cinco minutos y el minuto; también describirán la hora antes y después de la hora en punto.

Por ejemplo, 3:49 se puede leer de dos maneras:

Las tres y cuarenta y nueve   **Once para las cuatro**

Los estudiantes usarán relojes para resolver problemas acerca del tiempo transcurrido en diferentes situaciones.

Ayude a su niño a leer la hora y hallar el tiempo transcurrido. Pídale que estime cuánto tiempo tomarán ciertas actividades, tales como comer una comida completa, ir a la tienda o hacer la tarea. Pida a su niño que vea el reloj cuando comience la actividad y cuando la termine. Pregúntele cuánto tiempo tomó la actividad.

Su niño también aprenderá a sumar y restar tiempo en una recta numérica.

Si tiene alguna pregunta o algún comentario, por favor comuníquese conmigo.

Atentamente,
El maestro de su niño

Name _____

Make an Analog Clock

Attach the clock hands to the clock face using a prong fastener.

Make an Analog Clock

Attach the clock hands to the clock face using a prong fastener.

● hour

● minute

Name

Show Time to 15 Minutes

Draw the hands on the analog clock. Write the time on the digital clock.

13 nine fifteen

☐ : ☐

14 half past seven

☐ : ☐

15 three o'clock

☐ : ☐

16 seven thirty

☐ : ☐

17 one forty-five

☐ : ☐

18 fifteen minutes after two

☐ : ☐

Times of Daily Activities

19 Complete the table.

Time	Light or Dark	Part of the Day	Activity
3:15 A.M.			
8:00 A.M.			
2:30 P.M			
6:15 P.M			
8:45 P.M			

Name _____

Times Before and After the Hour to 1 Minute

Write the time as minutes *after* an hour and minutes *before* an hour.

10

_____

_____

_____

11

_____

_____

_____

12

_____

_____

_____

13

_____

_____

_____

14

_____

_____

_____

15

_____

_____

_____

✓ Check Understanding

Use the analog clock to show 7:31. Write the time
as minutes *after* the hour and minutes *before* the hour.

_____

_____

290

Name _____

Elapsed Time in Minutes and Hours

VOCABULARY
elapsed time

1 Find the end time.

Start Time	Elapsed Time	End Time
1:00 P.M.	2 hours	
4:15 A.M.	4 hours	
4:55 P.M.	18 minutes	
2:15 A.M.	1 hour and 55 minutes	
11:55 A.M.	2 hours and 17 minutes	

2 Find the **elapsed time**.

Start Time	Elapsed Time	End Time
2:30 P.M.		4:42 P.M.
7:45 A.M.		8:15 A.M.
2:17 P.M.		7:17 P.M.
11:00 A.M.		2:00 P.M.
11:55 A.M.		4:25 P.M.

3 Find the start time.

Start Time	Elapsed Time	End Time
	3 hours	4:15 P.M.
	15 minutes	2:45 P.M.
	2 hours and 35 minutes	11:55 A.M.
	1 hour and 20 minutes	3:42 A.M.

Name _____

Add Time

Solve using a number line.   *Show your work.*

1 Keisha went into a park at 1:30 P.M. She hiked for
1 hour 35 minutes. Then she went to the picnic area for
45 minutes and left the park. What time did Keisha leave
the park?

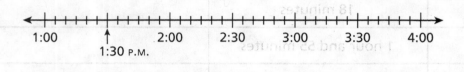

2 Loren arrived at the children's museum at 1:15 P.M. First,
he spent 30 minutes looking at the dinosaur exhibit.
Next, he watched a movie for 20 minutes. Then he spent
15 minutes in the museum gift shop. What time did Loren
leave the museum? How long was he in the museum?

3 Caleb started working in the yard at 8:45 A.M. He raked for
1 hour 45 minutes and mowed for 45 minutes. Then he
went inside. What time did he go inside? How long did
he work in the yard?

293

Subtract Time

Solve using a number line.

Show your work.

4 Hank finished bowling at 7:15 P.M. He bowled for
2 hours 35 minutes. At what time did he start bowling?

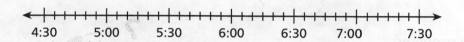

5 The school music program ended at 8:35 P.M. It lasted for
1 hour 50 minutes. What time did the program start?

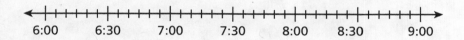

6 Lia served the salad at 3:15 P.M. It cooled in the refrigerator
for 35 minutes. She spent 15 minutes gathering the
ingredients from the garden and 15 minutes chopping
the vegetables. What time did Lia start working on
the salad?

✓ **Check Understanding**

Explain how you know to jump forward or
backward when adding and subtracting on the
number line.

Name _____

What's the Error?

Dear Math Students,

Today I was asked to find the time Jim got to
the doctor's office if he woke up at 7:55 A.M., spent
45 minutes getting ready, and then drove 20 minutes to the
doctor's office.

Here is how I solved the problem.

From 7:55 on a clock, I counted up 45 minutes to 8:45,
then I counted up 20 minutes to 9:05. Jim got to the
doctor's office at 9:05 A.M.

Is my answer correct? If not, please correct my work
and tell me what I did wrong. How do you know my
answer is wrong?

Your friend,
Puzzled Penguin

6 **Write an answer to the Puzzled Penguin.**

_____

_____

_____

Solve.

7 Wayne left home at 3:50 P.M. to go to the park. It took
30 minutes to get to the park. He spent 45 minutes
at the park. What time did he leave the park?

_____

8 Leslie finished her project at 11:05 A.M. She spent 1 hour
10 minutes making a poster and 35 minutes writing a
report. What time did Leslie start her project?

_____

© Houghton Mifflin Harcourt Publishing Company

Name _____

Write the correct answer.

1 Write the time as minutes *after* an hour.

_____

2 Write the time as minutes *before* an hour.

_____

3 Carol leaves her house at 4:30 P.M. and drives for one hour to the grocery store. She shops for 20 minutes and then drives for one hour to get home. At what time does she get home?

Show your work.

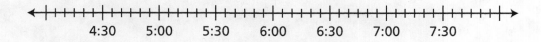

4:30   5:00   5:30   6:00   6:30   7:00   7:30

_____

4 Stephen leaves the house at 2:00 P.M. to walk the dog to the park. He walks for an hour. He lets the dog run around in the park for 50 minutes and then walks the dog home. He arrives home at 5:30 P.M. How long did it take Stephen to walk home?

2:00   3:00   4:00   5:00   6:00   7:00   8:00

_____

5 Band practice starts at 3:15 P.M. and ends at 3:50 P.M. How long does practice last?

_____

Name _____

Add or subtract.

1 14 + 23 = ☐

2 48 − 20 = ☐

3 27 + 11 = ☐

4 56 − 32 = ☐

5 30 + 16 = ☐

6 49 − 43 = ☐

7   46
   + 25

8   42
   − 19

9   59
   + 18

10   60
   − 35

11   44
   + 38

12   74
   − 69

13   76
   + 19

14   91
   − 58

15   53
   + 47

Dear Family:

In the rest of the lessons in this unit, your child will be learning to show information in various ways. Students will learn to read and create pictographs and bar graphs. They will organize and display data in frequency tables and line plots. Students will also learn how to use graphs to solve real world problems.

Examples of pictographs, bar graphs, and line plots are shown below.

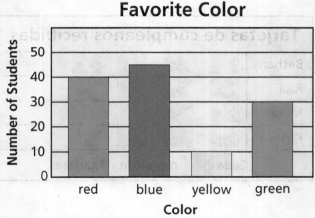

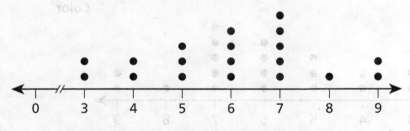

Number of Letters in a Name

Your child is learning how graphs are used in the world around us. You can help your child learn by sharing graphs that appear in newspapers, magazines, or online.

Thank you for helping your child learn how to read, interpret, and create graphs.

Sincerely,
Your child's teacher

301 Read and Create Pictographs and Bar Graphs

Estimada familia:

Durante el resto de las lecciones de esta unidad, su niño aprenderá a mostrar información de varias maneras. Los estudiantes aprenderán a leer y a crear pictografías y gráficas de barras. Organizarán y mostrarán datos en tablas de frecuencia y en diagramas de puntos. También aprenderán cómo usar las gráficas para resolver problemas cotidianos.

Debajo se muestran ejemplos de pictografías, gráficas de barras y diagramas de puntos.

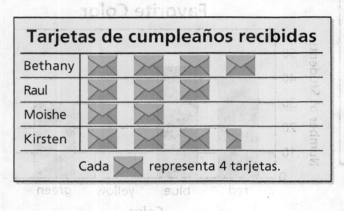

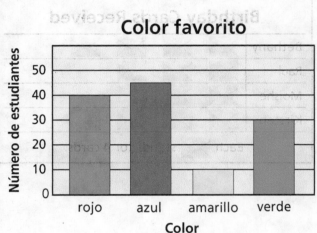

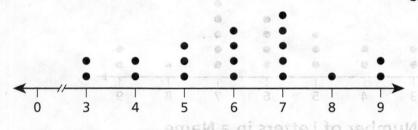

Número de letras en un nombre

Su niño está aprendiendo cómo se usan las gráficas en la vida cotidiana. Puede ayudarlo mostrándole gráficas que aparezcan en periódicos, revistas o Internet.

Gracias por ayudar a su niño a aprender cómo leer, interpretar y crear gráficas.

Atentamente,
El maestro de su niño

Name _____

Make a Pictograph

7 **Use the data about Kanye's Playlists to make your own pictograph.**

Kanye's Playlists	
Type	Number of Playlists
Jazz	12
Rap	16
Classical	4

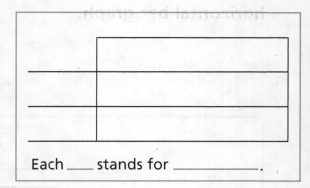

Each ____ stands for _____.

8 How many playlists in all does Kanye have?

_____

9 How many more rap playlists does Kanye have than classical?

_____

10 How many fewer jazz playlists does Kanye have than rap?

_____

11 How many pictures would you draw to show that Kanye has 9 country playlists?

_____

Name _____

Create Bar Graphs

16 Use the information in this table to complete the horizontal bar graph.

Favorite Way to Exercise	
Activity	Number of Students
Biking	12
Swimming	14
Walking	10

17 Use the information in this table to complete the vertical bar graph.

Favorite Team Sport	
Sport	Number of Students
Baseball	35
Soccer	60
Basketball	40

Create Bar Graphs with Multidigit Numbers

13 Use the information in the table on the right to make a horizontal bar graph.

Joe's Cap Collection	
Type	**Caps**
Baseball	60
Basketball	35
Golf	20

14 Use the information in the table on the right to make a vertical bar graph.

Summer Bike Sales	
Type of Bike	**Number Sold**
Road Bike	200
Mountain Bike	600
Hybrid Bike	450

Name _____

Create Line Plots with Fractions

5 Have 10 classmates spread their fingers apart as far as possible, and measure from the tip of the thumb to the tip of the little finger to the nearest $\frac{1}{2}$ inch. Record the data in the tally chart below and then make a frequency table.

Tally Chart	
Length	**Tally**

Frequency Table	
Length	**Number of Classmates**

6 Use the data to make a line plot.

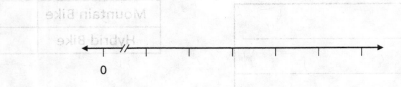

Hand Span Lengths (in inches)

7 Which length occurred the most often? _____

8 What is the difference between the greatest length and the least length?

_____

9 Write a question that can be answered by using the data in the line plot.

_____

_____

Name

Take a Survey and Make a Pictograph

10 Ask 10 classmates to tell whether winter, spring, summer, or fall is their favorite season. Record their answers in the tally chart below and then make a frequency table.

Favorite Season

Tally Chart	
Season	**Tally**
Winter	
Spring	
Summer	
Fall	

Favorite Season

Frequency Table	
Season	**Number of Classmates**
Winter	
Spring	
Summer	
Fall	

11 Use the data from above to make a pictograph.

_____	
_____	
_____	
_____	

Key: Each ☺ stands for _____.

12 Suppose you ask two more students to tell their favorite season and both of them answered, "Winter." How would the pictograph need to change?

_____

_____

315 Represent and Organize Data

Use Measurement Data to Make a Bar Graph

13 Estimate the distance around 4 classmates' wrists in centimeters. Then measure the distance around their wrists to the nearest centimeter. Complete the table.

Distance Around the Wrist to the Nearest Centimeter		
Student	Estimate in centimeters	Measurement in centimeters

14 Use the measurement data to make a bar graph.

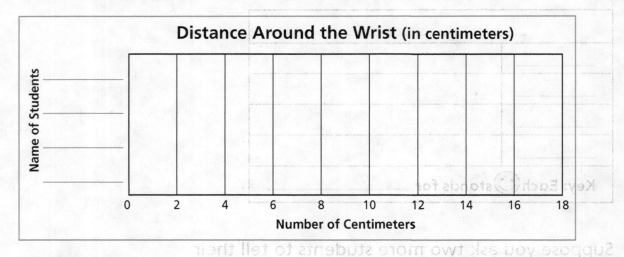

Check Understanding

Complete.

The bar graph above shows that _____ students have a distance around their wrists of less than 14 centimeters.

316

Represent and Organize Data

Math and Sports

Many students take part in a track and field day at school each year. One event is the standing broad jump. In the standing broad jump, the jumper stands directly behind a starting line and then jumps. The length of the jump is measured from the starting line to the mark of the first part of the jumper to touch the ground.

Complete.

1 Your teacher will tell you when to do a standing broad jump. Another student should measure the length of your jump to the nearest $\frac{1}{2}$ foot and record it on a slip of paper.

2 Record the lengths of the students' jumps in the box below.

Name _____

How Far Can a Third Grader Jump?

To analyze how far a third grader can jump, the data needs to be organized and displayed.

3 Use the lengths of the students' jumps to complete the tally chart and the frequency table.

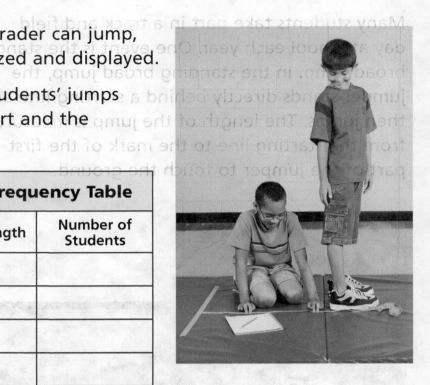

Tally Chart	
Length	Tally
	|
	||||
	|||| |||
	|||
	||
	|

Frequency Table	
Length	Number of Students

4 Make a line plot.

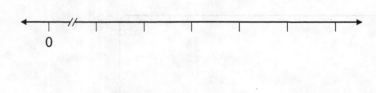

1 Use the data in the table to complete the bar graph.

Students	
Grade	**Number of Students**
2nd	25
3rd	40
4th	80
5th	50

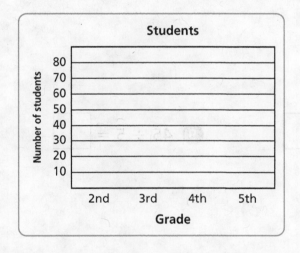

Students

2 Use the data in the table to complete the line plot.

Time Spent at After School Activities	
Hours	**Number of students**
$\frac{1}{2}$	4
1	3
$1\frac{1}{2}$	2
2	1
$2\frac{1}{2}$	3
3	5

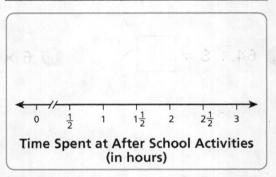

Time Spent at After School Activities (in hours)

The animals that Gary saw while hiking are shown in the pictograph on the right. Use the pictograph to answer questions 3 and 4.

3 How many toads did Gary see?

_____

4 How many more frogs than turtles did Gary see?

_____

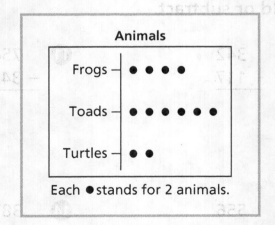

Animals

Each ● stands for 2 animals.

Unit 4 Big Idea 3

Name _____

Multiply or divide.

1 $8 \div 2 = \boxed{}$

2 $3 \times 5 = \boxed{}$

3 $7 \times 6 = \boxed{}$

4 $4 \times 10 = \boxed{}$

5 $60 \div 10 = \boxed{}$

6 $7 \div 1 = \boxed{}$

7 $64 \div 8 = \boxed{}$

8 $6 \times 9 = \boxed{}$

9 $45 \div 5 = \boxed{}$

Add or subtract.

10
$$\begin{array}{r} 342 \\ + 117 \\ \hline \end{array}$$

11
$$\begin{array}{r} 754 \\ - 342 \\ \hline \end{array}$$

12
$$\begin{array}{r} 263 \\ + 474 \\ \hline \end{array}$$

13
$$\begin{array}{r} 556 \\ - 438 \\ \hline \end{array}$$

14
$$\begin{array}{r} 387 \\ + 476 \\ \hline \end{array}$$

15
$$\begin{array}{r} 803 \\ - 598 \\ \hline \end{array}$$

1 Select the letter that shows the shaded fraction.
Mark all that apply.

(A) $\frac{1}{4}$

(B) $\frac{4}{3}$

(C) $\frac{3}{4}$

(D) $\frac{1}{4} + \frac{1}{4} + \frac{1}{4}$

(E) $\frac{4}{1} + \frac{4}{1} + \frac{4}{1}$

2 For numbers 2a–2d, choose Yes or No
to tell whether the words say the time
on the clock.

2a. twenty-six minutes before eleven   ○ Yes   ○ No

2b. thirty-four minutes after twelve   ○ Yes   ○ No

2c. thirty-four minutes after eleven   ○ Yes   ○ No

2d. twenty-six minutes before twelve   ○ Yes   ○ No

3 Use a straightedge to divide the fraction bar
into 6 equal parts. Then shade four parts.

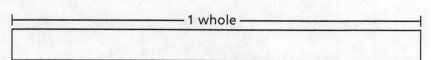

What fraction does the shaded fraction bar represent?

_____

Show the fraction as the sum of unit fractions.

_____

4 Kyle starts his homework at 6:30 P.M. He spends 35 minutes doing math homework and 40 minutes doing science homework. At what time does Kyle finish his homework? How much time does he spend on homework? Use the number line to help you.

6:30   7:00   7:30   8:00   8:30   9:00   9:30

Kyle finishes his homework at _____ P.M.

He spends | 1 hour 5 minutes
1 hour 15 minutes | on homework.
1 hour 25 minutes

5 Locate the fraction on the number line.

$\frac{3}{4}$ 0   1

© Houghton Mifflin Harcourt Publishing Company

6 The bar graph shows the number of plants sold at a nursery.

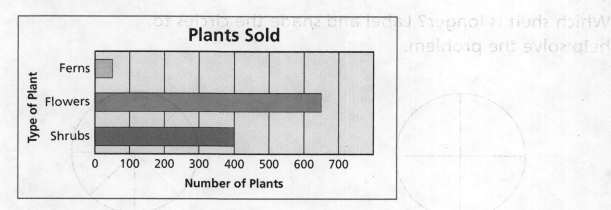

How many more flowers does the nursery sell than ferns and shrubs combined?

_____ more flowers

Write and answer another question using data from the graph.

7 Estimate the length of the marker in inches. Then measure it to the nearest $\frac{1}{4}$ inch.

Estimate: _____ in.   Actual: _____ in.

© Houghton Mifflin Harcourt Publishing Company

8 Jeff has two shelves. The length of the wood shelf is
   $\frac{2}{4}$ meter and the length of the metal shelf is $\frac{2}{8}$ meter.

   Which shelf is longer? Label and shade the circles to
   help solve the problem.

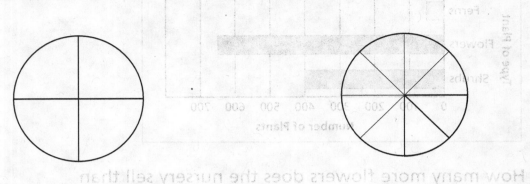

   The _____ shelf is longer.

9 Tom measures the distances some
   softballs were thrown from home
   plate. The results are shown in the
   line plot. For numbers 9a–9d, select
   True or False for each statement.

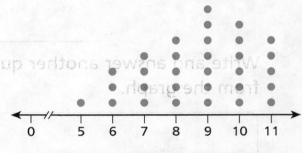

   **Distance from Home Plate
   (in feet)**

   9a. 8 softballs are thrown 5 feet.   ○ True   ○ False

   9b. 13 softballs are thrown less   ○ True   ○ False
        than 9 feet.

   9c. 11 softballs are thrown farther   ○ True   ○ False
        than 9 feet.

   9d. 4 feet is the difference between the   ○ True   ○ False
        least and greatest distances thrown.

10 Use the data in the table to complete the pictograph and bar graph.

T-Shirt Sales			
Size	Small	Medium	Large
Number of Shirts	40	70	50

T-Shirt Sales

Small	
Medium	
Large	

Key: _____

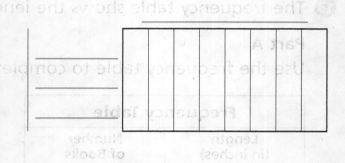

Which graph would you choose to show the data? Why?

11 Write the start time or end time to complete the chart.

8:48 A.M.	3:25 A.M.	12:50 P.M.
8:53 A.M.	3:35 P.M.	1:10 P.M.

Start Time	Elapsed Time	End Time
8:15 A.M.	38 minutes	
	55 minutes	4:20 A.M.
10:45 A.M.	2 hours 25 minutes	

12 Diane has $\frac{5}{4}$ meter of blue ribbon and $\frac{3}{4}$ meter of red ribbon.
Write a comparison. Which ribbon is longer?

Comparison: _____

The _____ ribbon is longer.

13 The frequency table shows the lengths of some books in a classroom.

Part A

Use the frequency table to complete the line plot.

Frequency Table	
Length (in inches)	Number of Books
5	2
$5\frac{1}{2}$	3
6	6
$6\frac{1}{2}$	5
7	8
$7\frac{1}{2}$	5
8	7

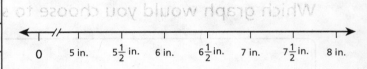

Part B

Most book lengths are between which two measures?

_____ inches and _____ inches

What if you measure three more book lengths at $7\frac{1}{2}$ inches and
add the data to the line plot? How would your answer change?

Plan a Class Craft Fair

Imagine that your class is having a Craft Fair. You will help plan the schedule for all the activities. Use the information in the table and in Steps A–C to find the start time for each event.

1 Complete the table showing the start time for each event and its duration.

Step A Add 10 minutes between activities to prepare for the next craft.

Step B Include a reasonable amount of time for setting up the first activity and for cleaning up at the end of the fair.

Step C Decide on a good time for the Craft Fair to begin.

Craft Fair Schedule		
Event	Start Time	Amount of time
Set-up		
Make Craft-Stick Towers		35 minutes
Make Puppets		25 minutes
Paint Pictures		20 minutes
Clean-up		

2 Explain how you decided the time the Craft Fair will begin.

_____

_____

3 The table shows the names of students and the heights of their craft-stick towers. Use the data in the table to complete the bar graph.

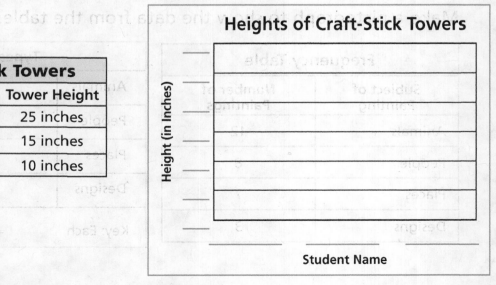

Craft-Stick Towers	
Student Name	Tower Height
Lee	25 inches
Juan	15 inches
Mei	10 inches

Heights of Craft-Stick Towers

Height (in inches)

Student Name

© Houghton Mifflin Harcourt Publishing Company

4 Making puppets took most of the students longer than the 25 minutes that was planned. This table shows the time students spent making puppets.

Make a line plot to show the times.

Frequency Table	
Length of Time (in minutes)	Number of Students
25	2
26	5
27	3
28	7
29	3
30	9
31	1

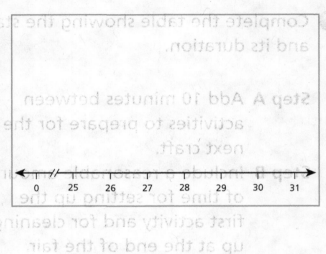

Do you think the class should plan more time for puppet making next year? Explain.

_____

_____

5 The teacher made a table to show the number of each type of painting students painted.

Make a pictograph to show the data from the table.

Frequency Table	
Subject of Painting	Number of Paintings
Animals	12
People	8
Places	7
Designs	3

Types of Paintings	
Animals	
People	
Places	
Designs	
Key: Each _____ = _____.	

Dear Family:

Your child is currently learning about perimeter and area. Students find the area of a rectangle by counting the number of square units inside the figure and find the perimeter of a rectangle by counting linear units around the outside of the figure. They develop methods to find the perimeter and area of a rectangle.

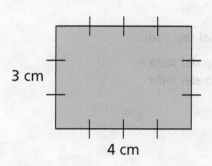

Perimeter = distance around the rectangle

Perimeter = side length + side length + side length + side length

$P = 4 \text{ cm} + 3 \text{ cm} + 4 \text{ cm} + 3 \text{ cm}$

$P = 14 \text{ cm}$

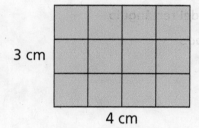

Area = square units inside the rectangle

Area = side length × side length

$A = 4 \text{ cm} \times 3 \text{ cm}$

$A = 12 \text{ sq cm}$

Students draw rectangles and discover relationships between perimeter and area, such as for a given area, the longest, skinniest rectangle has the greatest perimeter and the rectangle with sides closest to the same length or the same length has the least perimeter.

Students create shapes with tangrams and use the shapes as improvised units to measure area.

In this unit, students use fraction bars and number lines to find equivalent fractions and solve real world problems using their understanding of fraction concepts.

$$\frac{1}{2} = \frac{3}{6}$$

If you have any questions or comments, please contact me.

Thank you.

Sincerely,
Your child's teacher

Estimada familia:

Su niño está aprendiendo acerca de perímetro y área. Los estudiantes encontrarán el área de un rectángulo contando las unidades cuadradas que caben en la figura y hallarán el perímetro de un rectángulo contando las unidades lineales alrededor de la figura. Ellos desarrollarán métodos para hallar el perímetro y el área de un rectángulo.

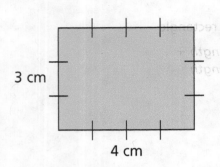

Perímetro = distancia alrededor del rectángulo

Perímetro = largo del lado + largo del lado + largo del lado + largo del lado

$P = 4\ cm + 3\ cm + 4\ cm + 3\ cm$

$P = 14\ cm$

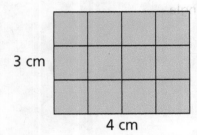

Área = unidades cuadradas dentro del rectángulo

Área = largo del lado × largo del lado

$A = 4\ cm \times 3\ cm$

$A = 12\ cm\ cuad$

Los estudiantes dibujarán rectángulos y descubrirán cómo se relacionan el perímetro y el área, por ejemplo, para un área determinada, el rectángulo más largo y angosto tiene el perímetro mayor y el rectángulo con lados de igual o casi igual longitud, tiene el perímetro menor.

Los estudiantes crearán figuras con tangramas y las usarán como medidas improvisadas para medir área.

En esta unidad, los estudiantes usarán barras de fracciones y rectas numéricas para hallar fracciones equivalentes y resolver problemas cotidianos usando los conceptos que aprendan sobre fracciones.

$$\frac{1}{2} = \frac{3}{6}$$

Si tiene alguna duda o algún comentario, por favor comuníquese conmigo.

Atentamente,
El maestro de su niño

Celsius (°C)

Fahrenheit (°F)

decompose

perimeter

equivalent fractions

temperature

A scale used to measure temperature.

Examples:
Water freezes at 32°F.
Water boils at 212°F.

A scale used to measure temperature.

Example:
Water freezes at 0°C.
Water boils at 100°C.

The distance around a figure.

Example:
Perimeter = 3 cm + 5 cm + 3 cm + 5 cm
= 16 cm

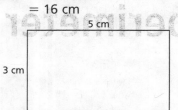

5 cm

3 cm

To separate or break apart (a geometric figure or a number) into smaller parts.

The measure of how hot or cold something is.

Fractions that name the same amount.

Example:
$\frac{1}{2}$ and $\frac{2}{4}$

equivalent fractions

thermometer

© Houghton Mifflin Harcourt Publishing Company

A tool that is used to measure temperature.

Recognize Perimeter and Area

On this page, the dots on the dot paper are
1 cm apart. Use the rectangle for Exercises 1–4.

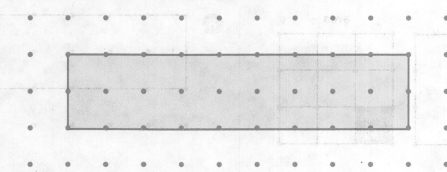

1 What part of the rectangle is
its **perimeter**?

_____

2 What part of the rectangle is
its area?

_____

3 Find the perimeter. Draw tick
marks to help.

_____

4 Find the area. Draw unit squares
to help.

_____

5 Draw a rectangle 4 cm long and
3 cm wide on the dot paper.
Find the perimeter and area.

Perimeter _____

Area _____

6 Explain how you found the area
of the rectangle in Exercise 5.

_____

_____

_____

_____

_____

Name _____

Find Perimeter and Area

Find the perimeter and area of each figure.
Remember to include the correct units in your answers.

7 perimeter   area

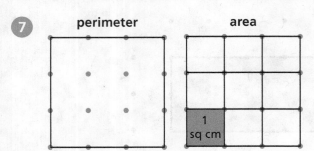

Perimeter = _____

Area = _____

8

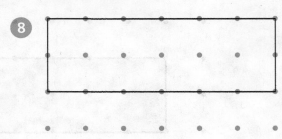

Perimeter = _____

Area = _____

9

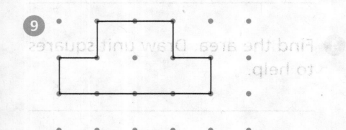

Perimeter = _____

Area = _____

10

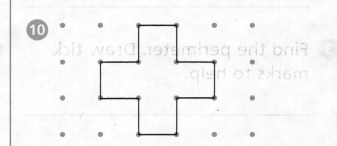

Perimeter = _____

Area = _____

11

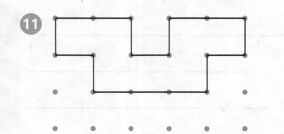

Perimeter = _____

Area = _____

12

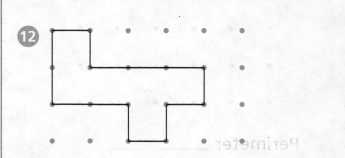

Perimeter = _____

Area = _____

Name

Tile a Rectangle

Cut out the 1-inch unit squares along the dashed lines.
Try to cut as carefully and as straight as you can.

Name _____

Tile a Rectangle

13 Use the 1-inch unit squares from page 335A
to cover the rectangle below.

Be sure there are no gaps between the unit squares.

Be sure no unit squares overlap.

14 Draw lines with a straight edge to show the unit
squares. The number of unit squares is the area
in square inches. What is the area?

_____

15 Use an inch ruler to measure the side lengths
of the rectangle. Label the length and the width.

_____

16 Write a multiplication equation to show the area.

_____

335

Name _____

Tile a Rectangle (continued)

**Cover each rectangle with 1-inch unit squares.
Count the squares to find the area. Then write
an equation to show the area.**

17

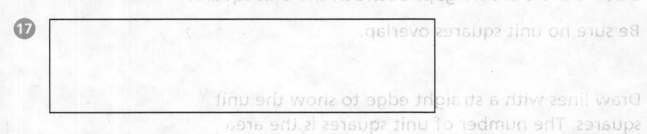

The area is _____.   The equation is _____

18

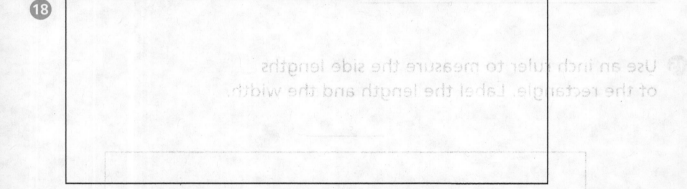

The area is _____.   The equation is _____.

19 How many 1-inch unit squares
are needed to cover a rectangle
that is 7 inches long and
4 inches wide?

_____

20 What is the area of a rectangle
that is 7 inches long and
4 inches wide?

_____

✔**Check Understanding**

Complete the sentences.

Perimeter measures _____.

Area measures _____.

Write Different Equations for Area

1 Use the drawings. Show two ways to find the area of a rectangle that is 10 units long and 6 units wide.

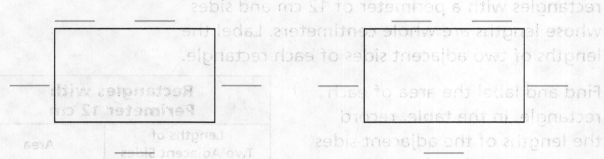

2 Write equations for your two rectangle drawings.

_____   _____

3 Suppose the rectangle is 10 feet long and 6 feet wide. What is its area?

_____

4 Suppose the rectangle is 10 meters long and 6 meters wide. What is its area?

_____

5 Use drawings and write equations to show two ways to find the area of a rectangle that is 9 yards long and 5 yards wide.

Compare Rectangles with the Same Perimeter

Complete.

1 On a centimeter dot grid, draw all possible rectangles with a perimeter of 12 cm and sides whose lengths are whole centimeters. Label the lengths of two adjacent sides of each rectangle.

2 Find and label the area of each rectangle. In the table, record the lengths of the adjacent sides and the area of each rectangle.

3 Compare the shapes of the rectangles with the least area and greatest area.

| Rectangles with Perimeter 12 cm ||
Lengths of Two Adjacent Sides	Area

_____

_____

4 On a centimeter dot grid, draw all possible rectangles with a perimeter of 22 cm and sides whose lengths are whole centimeters. Label the lengths of two adjacent sides of each rectangle.

5 Find and label the area of each rectangle. In the table, record the lengths of the adjacent sides and the area of each rectangle.

6 Compare the shapes of the rectangles with the least area and greatest area.

| Rectangles with Perimeter 22 cm ||
Lengths of Two Adjacent Sides	Area

_____

_____

Name _____

Compare Rectangles with the Same Area

7 On a centimeter dot grid, draw all possible rectangles with an area of 12 sq cm and sides whose lengths are whole centimeters. Label the lengths of two adjacent sides of each rectangle.

Rectangles with Area 12 sq cm	
Lengths of Two Adjacent Sides	Perimeter

8 Find and label the perimeter of each rectangle. In the table, record the lengths of the adjacent sides and the perimeter of each rectangle.

9 On a centimeter dot grid, draw all possible rectangles with an area of 18 sq cm and sides whose lengths are whole centimeters. Label the lengths of two adjacent sides of each rectangle.

Rectangles with Area 18 sq cm	
Lengths of Two Adjacent Sides	Perimeter

10 Find and label the perimeter of each rectangle. In the table, record the lengths of the adjacent sides and the perimeter of each rectangle.

11 Compare the shapes of the rectangles with the least and greatest perimeter.

_____

_____

_____

✓ Check Understanding

Draw and label a rectangle with the greatest area possible for a perimeter of 18 inches. The sides must be whole inches.

Name _____

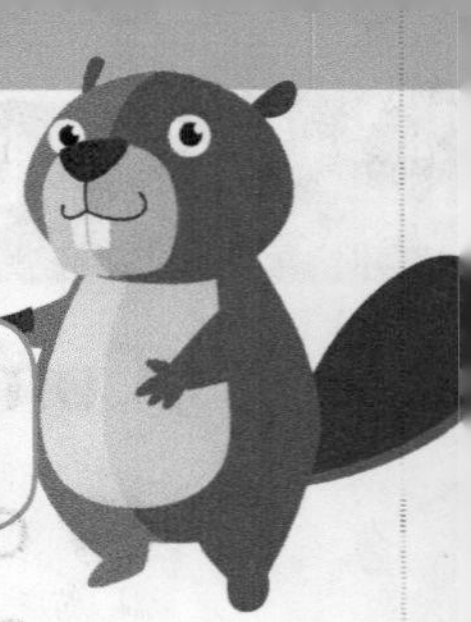

Find Area by Decomposing into Rectangles

**Decompose each figure into rectangles.
Then find the area of the figure.**

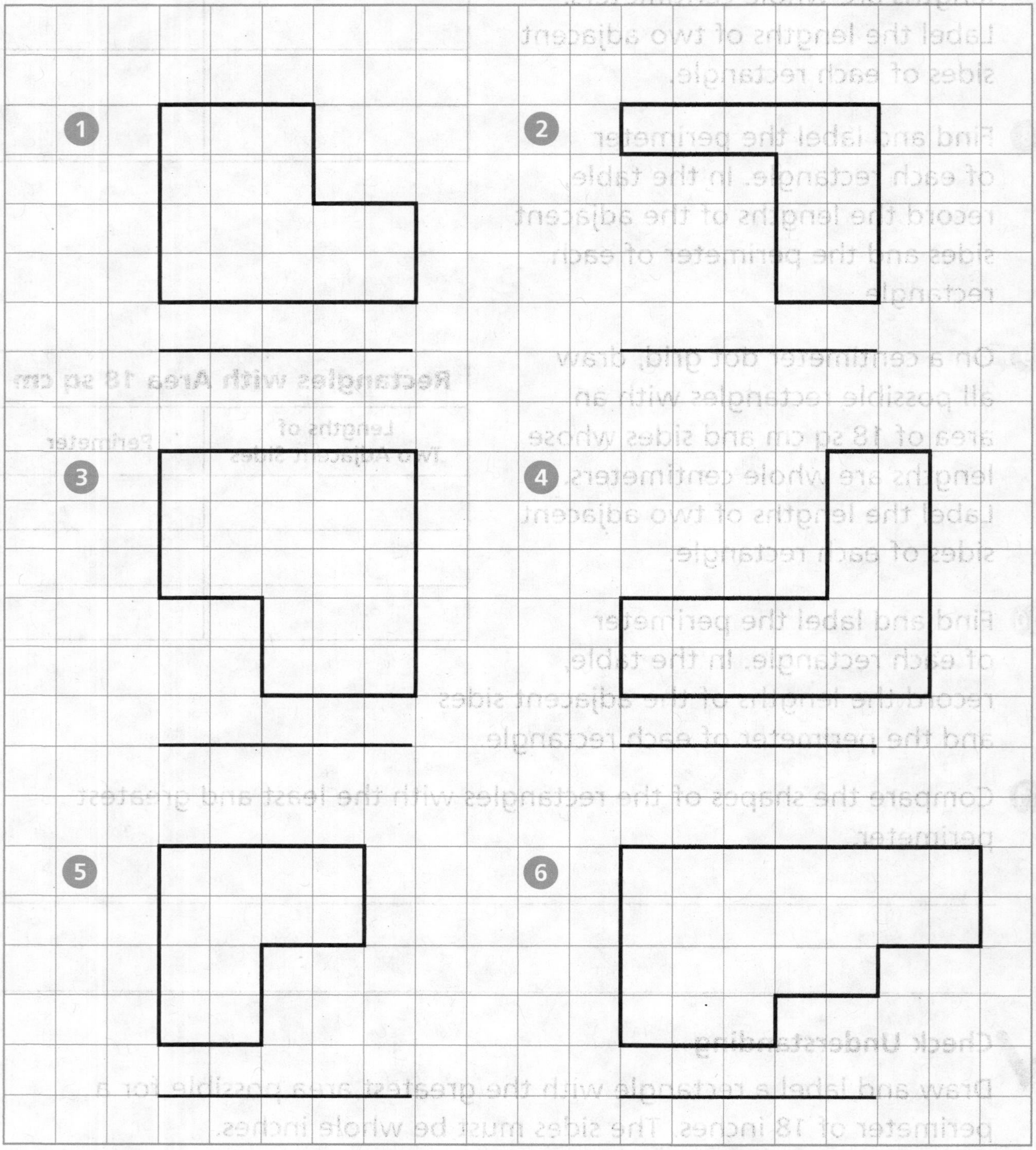

①

②

③

④

⑤

⑥

Name _____

Find Area by Decomposing into Rectangles (continued)

Decompose each figure into rectangles. Then find the area of the figure.

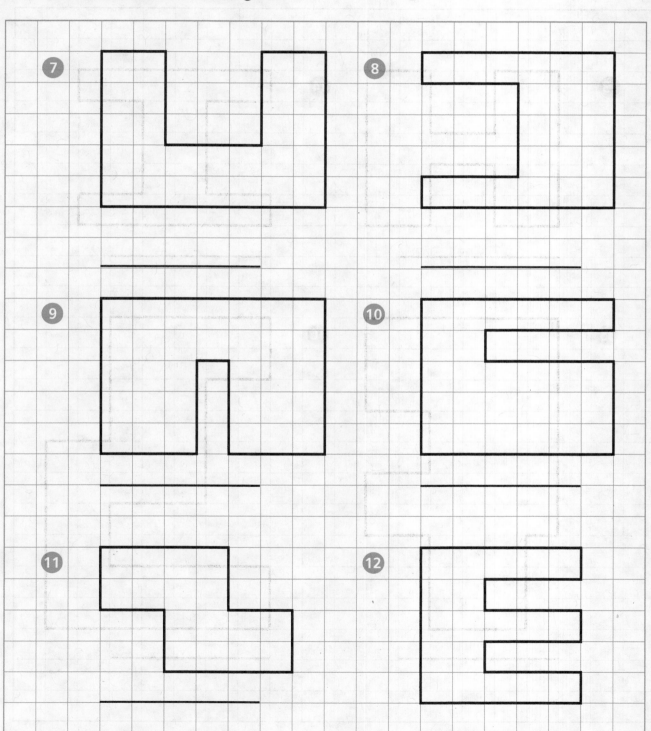

Name _____

Find Area by Decomposing into Rectangles (continued)

Decompose each figure into rectangles.
Then find the area of the figure.

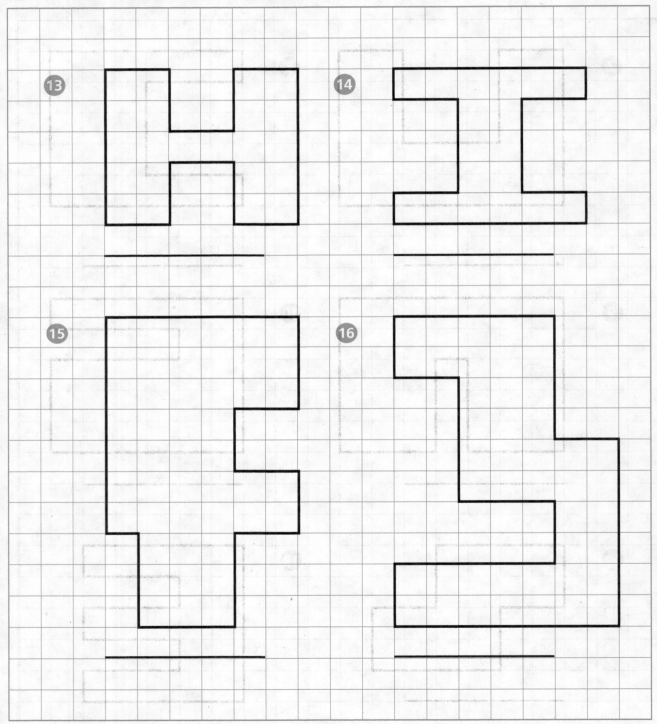

What's the Error?

Dear Math Students,

Today my teacher asked me to find the area of a figure. I knew that I could decompose the figure into rectangles. This is what I did.

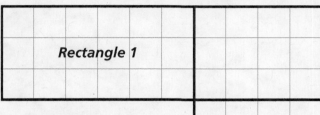

Area of Rectangle 1:
$3 \times 6 = 18$ square units

Area of Rectangle 2:
$5 \times 4 = 20$ square units

Area of Figure:
$18 + 20 = 38$ square units

Is my work correct? If not, please correct my work and tell me what I did wrong. How do you know my answer is wrong?

Your friend,
Puzzled Penguin

17 Write an answer to Puzzled Penguin.

_____

_____

_____

_____

✓ Check Understanding

Decompose the figure Puzzled Penguin decomposed into rectangles a different way and find the area of the figure.

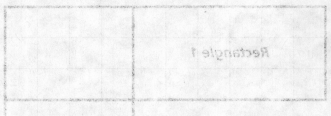

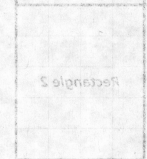

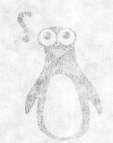

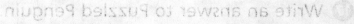

Name

Rectangle 1

Rectangle 2

Check Understanding

Name _____

Explore Tangrams

Cut one tangram figure into pieces along the dotted lines. Try to cut as carefully and as straight as you can. Save the other figures to use later.

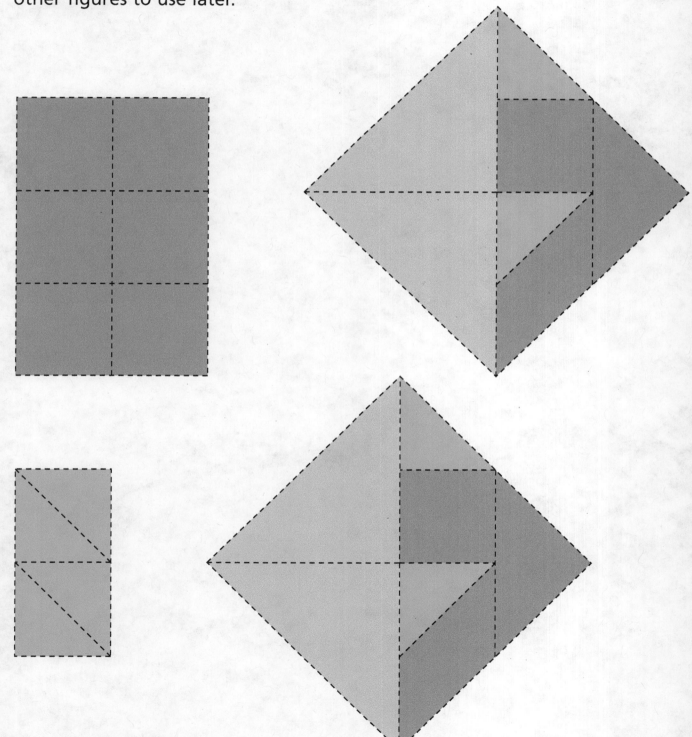

351A Tangram Shapes and Area

Cut one tangram figure into pieces along the dotted lines.
Try to cut as carefully and as straight as you can. Save the
other figures to use later.

351B

Tangram Shapes and Area

Name

Solve Tangram Puzzles

Use the tangram pieces from page 351A.

1 Make this bird. When you finish, draw lines to show how you placed the pieces.

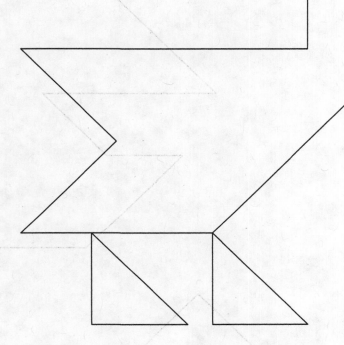

2 Make this rectangle. Draw lines to show how you placed the pieces. Hint: You do not need all the pieces.

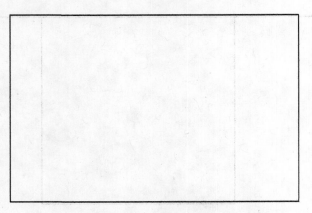

Name _____

Solve Tangram Puzzles (continued)

**Use the tangram pieces. Draw lines to show
how you placed the pieces.**

3 Make this boat.

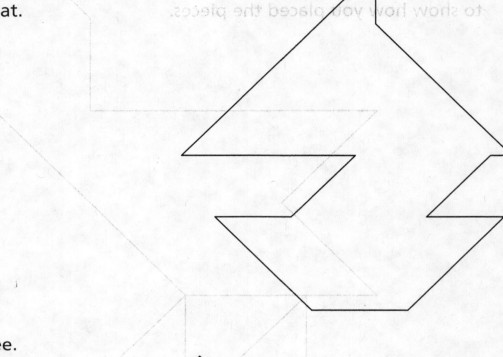

4 Make this tree.

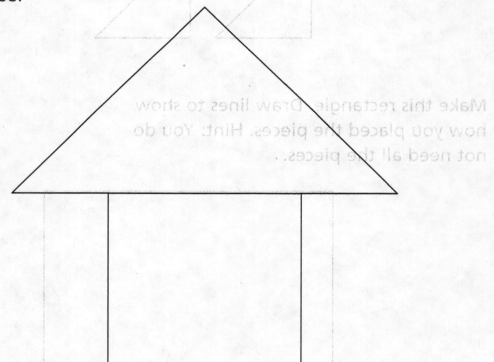

Tangram Shapes and Area

Name _____

Use Tangram Pieces to Find Area

5 Use all seven tangram pieces. Cover this rectangle.

6 What is the area of the rectangle?

_____

7 Use any tangram pieces. Cover this rectangle.

8 What is the area of the rectangle?

_____

© Houghton Mifflin Harcourt Publishing Company

353 Tangram Shapes and Area

Name

Use Tangram Pieces to Find Area (continued)

Use any tangram pieces. Cover each rectangle.

9

What is the area of the rectangle?

_____

10

What is the area of the square?

_____

Tangram Shapes and Area

Name _____

Use Tangram Pieces to Find Area (continued)

Use any tangram pieces. Cover each figure.

What is the area of the rectangle?

_____

What is the area of the square?

_____

What is the area of the figure?

_____

355

Name _____

Use Tangram Pieces to Find Area (continued)

Use any tangram pieces. Cover each figure.

14 **What is the area of the triangle?**

_____

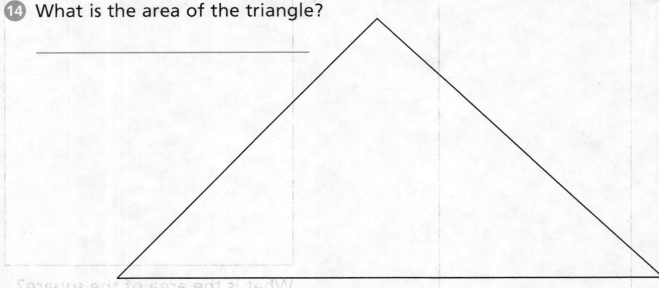

15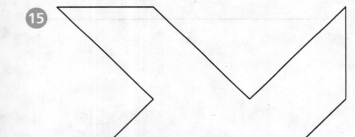

What is the area of the figure?

_____

✓ **Check Understanding**

What is the area of a figure made with all seven

tangram pieces? _____

356   Tangram Shapes and Area

Write the correct answer.

Show your work.

1 What is the area of the figure?

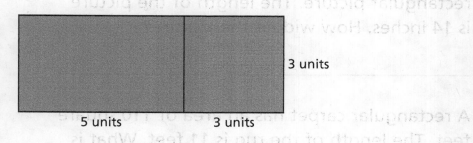

5 units   3 units   3 units

_____

2 The area of a rectangle is 80 square units. The length of one of the shorter sides is 8 units. What is the length of one of the longer sides?

_____

3 Rectangles A and B have the same areas. Rectangle A is 3 inches wide and 8 inches long. If Rectangle B is 4 inches wide, how long is it?

_____

Use the centimeter dot grid for Exercises 4–5.

4 Which figure has an area of 18 square centimeters?

_____

5 What is the perimeter of each figure?

_____

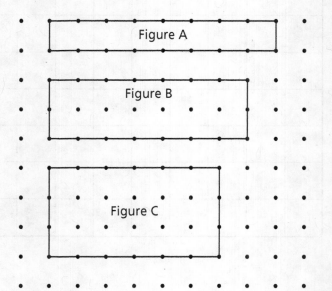

Figure A

Figure B

Figure C

Name _____

Solve.

1 Marcy uses 48 inches of ribbon to frame a rectangular picture. The length of the picture is 14 inches. How wide is the picture?

_____

2 A rectangular carpet has an area of 110 square feet. The length of the rug is 11 feet. What is the width of the rug?

_____

3 On the centimeter grid below, draw two different rectangles with a perimeter of 12 centimeters. Label the area of each figure.

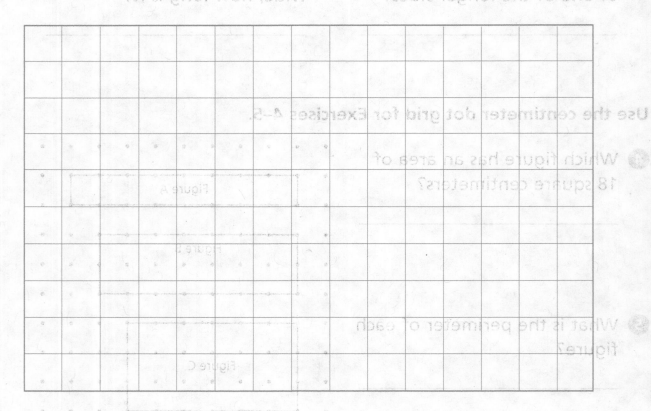

Make Fraction Strips

359B Fraction Strips

Name _____

Thirds and Sixths

Use your thirds and sixths strips to answer Exercises 5–6.

5 How many sixths are in one third? _____

Complete these two equations:

_____ sixths = 1 third $\dfrac{\square}{6} = \dfrac{1}{3}$

6 How many sixths are in two thirds? _____

Complete these two equations:

_____ sixths = 2 thirds $\dfrac{\square}{6} = \dfrac{2}{3}$

What's the Error?

Dear Math Students,

Today my teacher asked me to name a fraction that is equivalent to $\dfrac{1}{2}$.

I wrote $\dfrac{2}{6} = \dfrac{1}{2}$.

Is my answer correct? If not, please correct my work and tell me what I did wrong.

Your Friend,
Puzzled Penguin

7 Write an answer to Puzzled Penguin.

_____

_____

_____

 Check Understanding

Name another fraction equivalent to $\dfrac{1}{2}$ that Puzzled Penguin could have written. _____

Name _____

Equivalent Fractions on Number Lines

1 Complete each number line. Show all fractions including each fraction for 1.

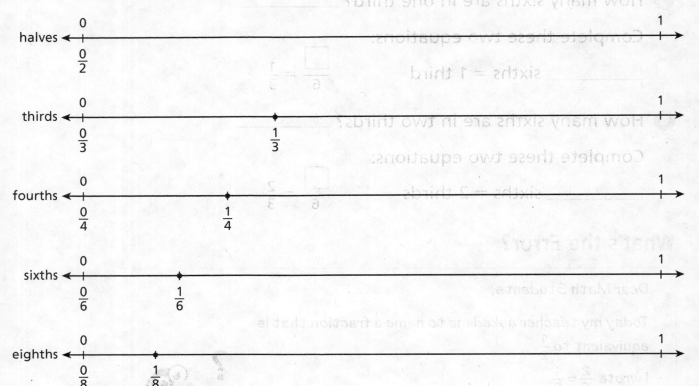

2 Write an equivalence chain with fractions that equal $\frac{2}{2}$.

_____

3 Why are the fractions in the equivalence chain for $\frac{2}{2}$ equal?

_____

4 Why does the length of unit fractions grow smaller as their denominators get larger?

_____

_____

361

Equivalent Fractions

Name _____

Fraction of a Set

Write a fraction to answer each question.

10 What fraction of the buttons are large buttons?

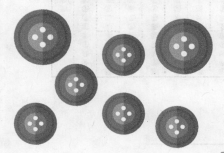

_____

11 What fraction of the balls are soccer balls?

_____

Write two fractions to answer each question.

12 What fraction of the coins are pennies?

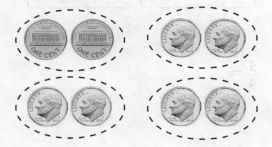

_____ _____

13 What fraction of the pieces of fruit are pears?

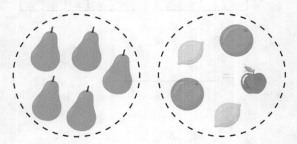

_____

Shade the given fraction of each set.

14 $\frac{7}{11}$

15 $\frac{2}{9}$

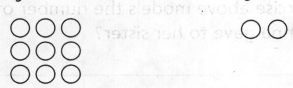

16 $\frac{1}{5}$

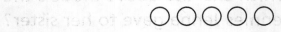

365 Problem Solving with Fractions

Name _____

Represent Fractions of a Dollar

Shade each whole to show the given fraction and write the money amount.

28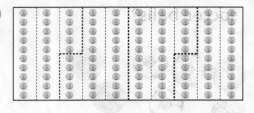

$\frac{2}{4}$ = _____

29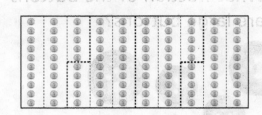

$\frac{1}{4}$ = _____

30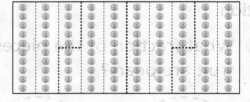

$\frac{4}{4}$ = _____

31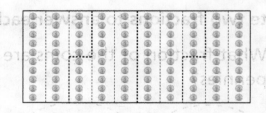

$\frac{3}{4}$ = _____

✔ **Check Understanding**

Jenna has 100 pennies. She gives $\frac{3}{4}$ of her pennies to her sister. How many pennies does Jenna give to her sister?

_____

Which exercise above models the number of pennies Jenna gave to her sister?

_____

368 Problem Solving with Fractions

Name _____

Complete.

1 How many sixths are in one third? _____

Complete these two equations:

_____ sixths = 1 third

$$\frac{\square}{6} = \frac{1}{3}$$

2 How many eighths are in one half? _____

Complete these two equations:

_____ eighths = 1 half

$$\frac{\square}{8} = \frac{1}{2}$$

3 Write an equivalence chain with three fractions that equal $\frac{1}{4}$.

_____

_____

Complete the number line. Show the fraction for 1.

4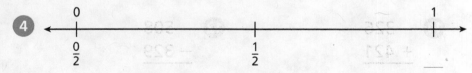

Solve.   *Show your work.*

5 Monica buys $\frac{2}{3}$ pound of apples. Nicole buys $\frac{5}{6}$ pound of peaches. Do the apples or the peaches weigh more? Explain your answer.

_____

_____

Name _____

Multiply or divide.

1 $7 \times 0 =$ ☐

2 $12 \div 2 =$ ☐

3 $8 \times 3 =$ ☐

4 $16 \div 4 =$ ☐

5 $3 \times 7 =$ ☐

6 $42 \div 6 =$ ☐

7 $6 \times 8 =$ ☐

8 $81 \div 9 =$ ☐

9 $8 \times 7 =$ ☐

Add or subtract.

10
$$\begin{array}{r} 885 \\ -\ 345 \\ \hline \end{array}$$

11
$$\begin{array}{r} 326 \\ +\ 421 \\ \hline \end{array}$$

12
$$\begin{array}{r} 508 \\ -\ 329 \\ \hline \end{array}$$

13
$$\begin{array}{r} 264 \\ +\ 338 \\ \hline \end{array}$$

14
$$\begin{array}{r} 623 \\ -\ 365 \\ \hline \end{array}$$

15
$$\begin{array}{r} 478 \\ +\ 385 \\ \hline \end{array}$$

Name _____

373B

Use the thermometer for Exercises 1–2.

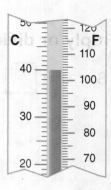

1 Write the temperature using °C.

_____

2 It is predicted that the temperature will be lower by 8° C next week. What is the predicted temperature in degrees Celsius?

_____

3 Nancy's thermometer shows that the temperature outside is 80° F. Name a possible activity that Nancy could do outdoors?

_____

4 Gianni paid for a $1.65 pen with two $1 bills. How much change should he get?

_____

5 Abdul buys a sandwich for $4.15. He uses a $5 bill to pay. How much change should he receive?

_____

Name _____

Multiply or divide.

1 $8 \times 0 = \boxed{}$

2 $18 \div 3 = \boxed{}$

3 $9 \times 3 = \boxed{}$

4 $16 \div 8 = \boxed{}$

5 $7 \times 7 = \boxed{}$

6 $48 \div 6 = \boxed{}$

7 $5 \times 9 = \boxed{}$

8 $72 \div 9 = \boxed{}$

9 $3 \times 7 = \boxed{}$

Add or subtract.

10
$$\begin{array}{r} 489 \\ -\ 345 \\ \hline \end{array}$$

11
$$\begin{array}{r} 363 \\ +\ 128 \\ \hline \end{array}$$

12
$$\begin{array}{r} 208 \\ -\ 192 \\ \hline \end{array}$$

13
$$\begin{array}{r} 568 \\ +\ 338 \\ \hline \end{array}$$

14
$$\begin{array}{r} 453 \\ -\ 365 \\ \hline \end{array}$$

15
$$\begin{array}{r} 406 \\ +\ 314 \\ \hline \end{array}$$

1 A park ranger has 32 feet of fencing to fence four sides of a rectangular recycling site. What is the greatest area of the recycling site that the ranger can fence? Explain how you know.

2 Use the fractions to label each point on the number line.

3 Select the fraction that would be included in an equivalence chain for $\frac{6}{6}$. Mark all that apply.

(A) $\frac{3}{3}$ (D) $\frac{5}{5}$

(B) $\frac{3}{6}$ (E) $\frac{6}{1}$

(C) $\frac{4}{4}$

4 Steve makes a banner with an area of 8 square feet. On the grid, draw all possible rectangles with an area of 8 square feet and whose side lengths are whole feet. Label the lengths of two adjacent sides of each rectangle. Label each rectangle with its perimeter.

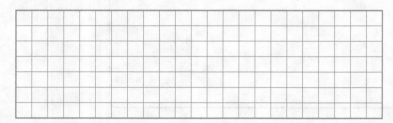

Compare the perimeters of the banners. What do you notice about their shapes?

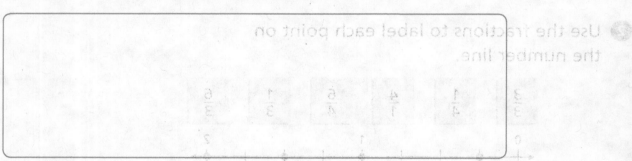

5 Draw a line from the fraction on the left to match the equivalent fraction or number on the right.

$\frac{4}{6}$ •   • 8

$\frac{8}{1}$ •   • $\frac{2}{3}$

$\frac{3}{4}$ •   • 1

$\frac{2}{8}$ •   • $\frac{6}{8}$

$\frac{2}{2}$ •   • $\frac{1}{4}$

6 Mark the number line to show the fractions. First divide the number line into correct unit fractions.

0 _____ 1

7 What fraction of the coins are pennies?

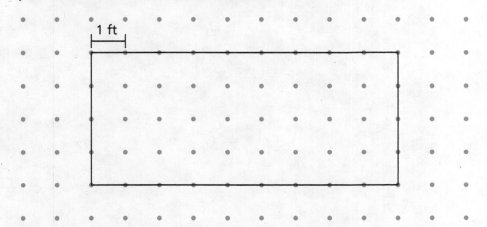

_____

8 Mr. Gomez hangs a mural on the classroom wall. Find the perimeter and area of the mural.

1 ft

Perimeter: _____ feet

Area: _____ square feet

9 Liana plants a vegetable garden in two sections. She plants corn in a section that is 5 meters long and 6 meters wide. She plants squash in a section that is 3 meters long and 6 meters wide.

Part A

Describe one way to find the area of the garden. Then find the area.

Area: _____ square meters

Part B

Draw a picture of the garden to show your answer is correct.

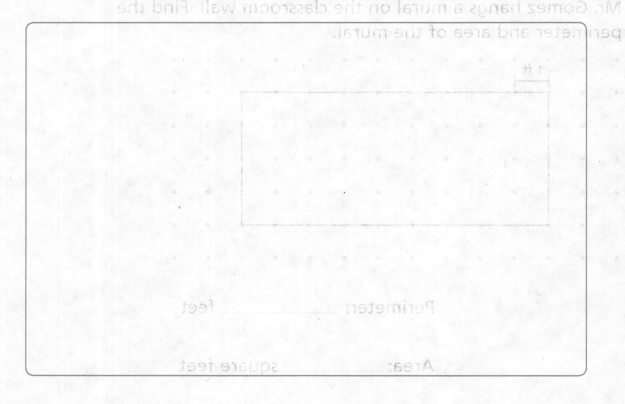

10 Dan walks $\frac{5}{8}$ mile to school. Beth walks $\frac{3}{4}$ mile to school.

Part A

Who walks farther? Label and shade the circles to help solve the problem.

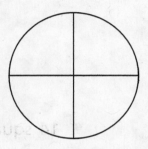 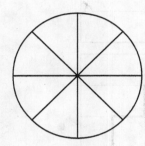

_____ walks farther.

Part B

Suppose Dan walks $\frac{6}{8}$ mile instead of $\frac{5}{8}$ mile. Who walks farther? How do the circles help you decide?

11 The thermometer shows the temperature at 3:00 P.M.

11a What temperature does the thermometer show in degrees Fahrenheit? _____

11b At 2:00 A.M. it is predicted that the temperature will be 16° lower. What is the predicted temperature in degrees Fahrenheit for 2:00 A.M.? _____

Name _____

12 Draw a line from the figure to the area of the figure.

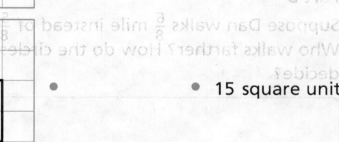

•   • 13 square units

•   • 14 square units

•   • 15 square units

13 Riki buys some tomatoes for $2.19. She pays with three $1 bills. How much change should she receive?

_____

14 Rino needs $\frac{1}{2}$ cup of pineapple juice for a shake. What are two other fractions equivalent to $\frac{1}{2}$?

Dog Park

The town of Springfield is planning to create a rectangular dog park. The park will be 8 yards long and 10 yards wide.

1 How much fencing is needed to go around the park?

_____

2 What is the area of the planned park?

_____

3 Half of the park will have a lawn and one fourth of the park will be covered with gravel. Shade the model below to show the lawn and the part with gravel.

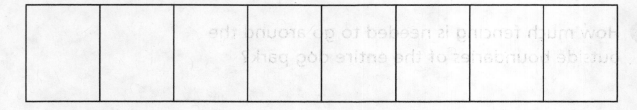

4 The remaining area of the park will have benches. What fraction of the total area will have benches?

_____

5 Write two equivalent fractions to represent the area of the park with the lawn.

_____

The town of Springfield plans to make the dog park larger.

6 The town will add 20 square yards of land next to the original park. Draw and label the possible dimensions of the addition.

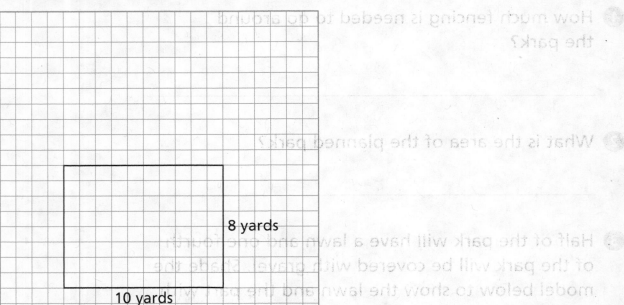

8 yards

10 yards

7 How much fencing is needed to go around the outside boundaries of the entire dog park?

8 Use the grid below to design your own dog park. Each square represents 1 square unit. The area of your park must be 24 square units. Label the drawing with the perimeter of the park.

© Houghton Mifflin Harcourt Publishing Company

Dear Family:

In this unit, your child will solve addition, subtraction, multiplication, and division problems involving unknown addends and factors.

- If one of the addends is unknown, it can be found by subtracting the known addend from the total or by counting on from the known addend to the total.

- If the total is unknown, it can be found by adding the addends.

- If one of the factors is unknown, it can be found by dividing the product by the other factor.

- If the product is unknown, it can be found by multiplying the factors.

Math Mountains are used to show a total and two addends. Students can use the Math Mountain to write an equation and then solve the equation to find the unknown.

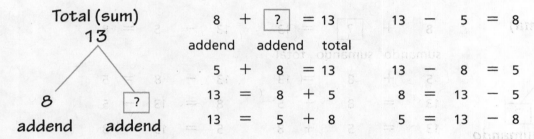

$$8 + \boxed{?} = 13 \qquad 13 - 5 = 8$$
$$\text{addend} \quad \text{addend} \quad \text{total}$$
$$5 + 8 = 13 \qquad 13 - 8 = 5$$
$$13 = 8 + 5 \qquad 8 = 13 - 5$$
$$13 = 5 + 8 \qquad 5 = 13 - 8$$

Equations with numbers alone on the left are also emphasized to help with the understanding of algebra.

Comparison Bars are used to solve problems that involve one amount that is more than or less than another amount. Drawing Comparison Bars can help a student organize the information in the problem in order to find the unknown smaller amount, the unknown larger amount, or the difference.

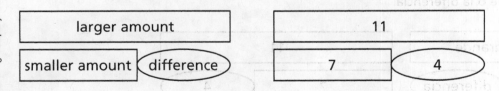

Please contact me if you have any questions or comments.

Sincerely,
Your child's teacher

Estimada familia:

En esta unidad, su niño resolverá sumas, restas, multiplicaciones y divisiones con sumandos o factores desconocidos.

- Si uno de los sumandos se desconoce, puede hallarse restando el sumando conocido del total, o contando hacia adelante desde el sumando conocido hasta llegar al total.

- Si el total se desconoce, puede hallarse sumando los sumandos.

- Si uno de los factores se desconoce, puede hallarse dividiendo el producto entre el otro factor.

- Si el producto se desconoce, puede hallarse multiplicando los factores.

Para mostrar un total y dos sumandos se usan las **Montañas matemáticas**. Los estudiantes puede usarlas para escribir una ecuación, y al resolverla, hallar el elemento desconocido.

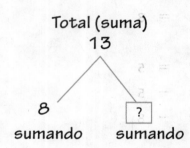

Total (suma)
13

8 — sumando
? — sumando

$$8 + \boxed{?} = 13 \qquad 13 - 5 = 8$$
sumando sumando total

$$5 + 8 = 13 \qquad 13 - 8 = 5$$
$$13 = 8 + 5 \qquad 8 = 13 - 5$$
$$13 = 5 + 8 \qquad 5 = 13 - 8$$

Se hace énfasis en las ecuaciones que tienen números solos en el lado izquierdo, para facilitar la comprensión del álgebra.

Para resolver problemas con una cantidad que es más o menos que otra, se usan **Barras de comparación**. Estas barras sirven para organizar la información del problema, y hallar así, la cantidad desconocida más pequeña, la más grande o la diferencia.

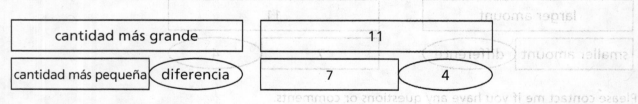

Si tiene alguna pregunta o algún comentario, por favor comuníquese conmigo.

Atentamente,
El maestro de su niño

addend

sum

total

One of two or more numbers to be added together to find a sum.

Example: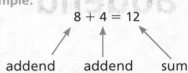

$$8 + 4 = 12$$

addend   addend   sum

The answer when adding two or more addends.

Example:

$$37 + 52 = 89$$

addend   addend   sum

The answer when adding two or more addends. The sum of two or more numbers.

Example:

$$672 + 228 = 900$$

addend   addend   total or sum

Represent Word Problems with Math Tools

The equations and Math Mountains below
show the word problems on page 390.

Add To	**Take From**

Add To

$$80 \quad + \quad 60 \quad = \quad \boxed{}$$
Chris's   Mom's   total
group   group

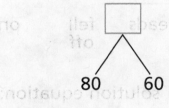

80   60

Take From

$$140 \quad - \quad 80 \quad = \quad \boxed{}$$
total   ate   now

140

80    $\boxed{}$

Put Together/Take Apart

$$70 \quad + \quad 50 \quad = \quad \boxed{}$$
Alison's   Taylor's   total
class   class

70   50

Put Together/Take Apart

$$120 \quad - \quad 70 \quad = \quad \boxed{}$$
total   tables   cooler

$$70 \quad + \quad \boxed{} \quad = \quad 120$$
tables   cooler   total

120

70    $\boxed{}$

7 Write the unknown numbers in the boxes.

8 How are these math tools the same? How are they different?

_____

9 **Math Journal** Write a word problem for this

equation: $110 - 40 = \boxed{}$. Then solve it.

Represent Unknown Start Problems with Math Tools

The equations and Math Mountains below show the word problems on page 397.

Add To: Unknown Start

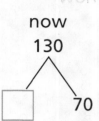

now
130

start   more

Situation Equation:

☐ + 70 = 130

start   more   now

solution equations:

70 + ☐ = 130

130 − 70 = ☐

Take From: Unknown Start

beads

70   60

fell   on
off

Situation Equation:

☐ − 70 = 60

beads   fell   on
off

solution equation:

60 + 70 = ☐

Add To: Unknown Start

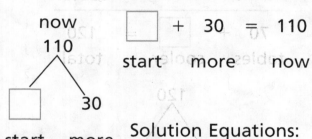

now
110

start   more

Situation Equation:

☐ + 30 = 110

start   more   now

Solution Equations:

30 + ☐ = 110

110 − 30 = ☐

Take From: Unknown Start

start

30   80

friend   now

Situation Equation:

☐ − 30 = 80

start   friend   now

Solution Equation:

80 + 30 = ☐

5 Write the unknown numbers in the boxes.

_____

6 How are these math tools alike? How are they different?

_____

_____

Name _____

What's the Error?

Dear Math Students,

As part of my math homework, I solved this problem:

Carlos has 19 fish. He has 14 fewer fish than Daniel. How many fish does Daniel have?

Here is what I did: 19 − 14 = 5   Daniel has 5 fish.

Is my answer right? If not, please correct my work, and tell me what I did wrong.

Your friend,
Puzzled Penguin

Carlos	19
Daniel	? 14

1 Write an answer to Puzzled Penguin.

_____

_____

Solve Comparison Problems with Misleading Language

Solve each problem on a separate piece of paper.

2 Unknown Smaller Amount
Daniel has 23 fish. He has 15 more fish than Carlos. How many fish does Carlos have?

3 Unknown Larger Amount
Gina ran 12 laps. She ran 8 fewer laps than Bettina. How many laps did Bettina run?

4 Unknown Smaller Amount
Bettina ran 20 laps. She ran 8 more laps than Gina. How many laps did Gina run?

5 Unknown Larger Amount
Sara read 18 books this year. She read 13 fewer books than Lupe. How many books did Lupe read this year?

Name _____

Solve Problems with Extra Information

Read each problem. Cross out any extra information. Then solve.

1 Emma solved 9 math problems and answered 7 reading questions. Her sister solved 8 math problems. How many math problems did they solve in all?

_____

2 Mark had 6 shirts and 5 pairs of pants. Today his aunt gave him 4 more shirts and another pair of pants. How many shirts does he have now?

_____

3 A parking lot had 179 cars and 95 trucks. Then 85 cars left the lot. How many cars are in the parking lot now?

_____

4 Laura had some roses in a vase. From her garden, she picked 7 more roses and 6 daisies. Now she has 12 roses in all. How many roses did she have at first?

_____

5 Nikko had 245 pennies and 123 nickels. His brother gave him 89 more pennies and 25 more nickels. How many pennies does Nikko have now?

_____

407 Word Problems with Extra, Hidden, or Not Enough Information

Name _____

Solve Problems with Hidden Information

Read each problem. Circle the hidden information. Then solve.

6 Samuel had 16 new horseshoes in the shed yesterday. Today, he put a new set of horseshoes on his horse Betsy. How many horseshoes are left in the shed?

_____

7 Maya is going on a vacation with her family for a week and 3 days. How many days will she be on vacation?

_____

8 Julie bought a dozen eggs at the market. She gave 3 of them to Serge. How many eggs does Julie have left?

_____

9 Lisa had 3 quarters and 2 dimes. Then she found 3 nickels and 12 pennies. What is the value of the coins in cents she has now?

_____

10 Marissa is moving away. She is going to move back in 1 year and 21 days. How many days will she be gone?

_____

Name _____

Solve the problem. Label your answer.

Show your work.

1. Marie drove 43 miles. Sherry drove 15 miles. How many more miles did Marie drive than Sherry?

_____

2. George had some money in his wallet. He spent $35 but still has $27 left. How much money did he have in his wallet before he spent any of it?

_____

3. There are 63 potatoes in a sack. There are 29 rotten potatoes in the sack. How many are not rotten?

_____

4. Jessica scored 38 points fewer than Elizabeth. Jessica scored 54 points. How many points did Elizabeth score?

_____

Read the problem. Circle the hidden information. Then solve.

5. Omar buys a dozen oranges at the market. He uses 5 of them to make juice. How many oranges does Omar have left?

_____

411

Name _____

Multiply or divide.

1 $4 \times 1 = \boxed{}$

2 $2 \div 1 = \boxed{}$

3 $3 \times 2 = \boxed{}$

4 $9 \div 3 = \boxed{}$

5 $5 \times 6 = \boxed{}$

6 $24 \div 4 = \boxed{}$

7 $8 \times 5 = \boxed{}$

8 $63 \div 7 = \boxed{}$

9 $9 \times 9 = \boxed{}$

Add or subtract.

10
$$\begin{array}{r} 478 \\ -\ 265 \\ \hline \end{array}$$

11
$$\begin{array}{r} 243 \\ +\ 536 \\ \hline \end{array}$$

12
$$\begin{array}{r} 562 \\ -\ 348 \\ \hline \end{array}$$

13
$$\begin{array}{r} 635 \\ +\ 258 \\ \hline \end{array}$$

14
$$\begin{array}{r} 824 \\ -\ 659 \\ \hline \end{array}$$

15
$$\begin{array}{r} 579 \\ +\ 323 \\ \hline \end{array}$$

Name _____

What's the Error?

Dear Math Students,

My teacher gave me this problem:

Luther had 11 sheets of color paper. There were 6 orange sheets, and the rest were blue. Today he used 2 sheets of blue paper. How many sheets of blue paper does Luther have now?

Here is what I did: 11 – 6 = 5
Luther now has 5 blue sheets.

Is my answer correct? If not, please correct my work and tell me what I did wrong.

Your friend,
Puzzled Penguin

1 Write an answer to Puzzled Penguin.

_____

Solve Two-Step Word Problems

Solve each problem. Label your answers.

2 The bus had 14 passengers. When it stopped, 5 people got off and 8 people got on. How many people are riding the bus now?

3 There are 15 fish in a tank. 12 have stripes, and the others are do not. How many more striped fish are there than fish without stripes?

Sports News

Danielle plays on a third grade basketball team in a league. Her team made the news when they scored 47 points, 41 points, and 53 points in a three-game tournament.

Write a two-step equation and solve the problem.

4 How many points did Danielle's team score altogether?

_____

5 Describe how you can use mental math to decide if your answer to Problem 4 is reasonable.

_____

_____

_____

6 Danielle's scorecard shows her statistics for the three games. Use the information in the table to write equations to find the unknown numbers. Then complete the table.

	Number of 1-pt Free Throws	Number of 2-pt Field Goals	Total Points
Game 1	5	7	
Game 2		6	18
Game 3	3		21

Name _____

Complete.

1 Lila makes bags of stickers that are exactly the same for 5 friends. She uses a total of 45 stickers. Each bag has 2 butterfly stickers and the rest are flower stickers. How many flower stickers are in each bag? Write a first-step question and answer. Then solve the problem.

_____

_____

2 Troy saves money for a bike that costs $126. He saves $58 one month and $43 the next month. How much more money does Troy need to buy the bike?
Answer: $15
Is the answer reasonable? Explain.

_____

3 The Downtown bus has 16 passengers. When it stops, 4 people get off and 7 people get on. How many passengers are on the Downtown bus now?

_____

Write an equation and solve the problem.

4 Lauren has 109 rare coins. She sells 37 coins. She wants to put the rest of the coins in an album. Each page in the album holds 8 coins. How many pages will she use?

_____

_____

5 Peyton cuts a pipe into two pieces. One piece has a length of 13 feet. The other piece is 9 feet shorter. How long was the pipe Peyton cut?

_____

_____

Name _____

PATH to
FLUENCY

Multiply or divide.

1 $4 \div 2 = \boxed{}$

2 $2 \times 4 = \boxed{}$

3 $72 \div 8 = \boxed{}$

4 $3 \times 8 = \boxed{}$

5 $25 \div 5 = \boxed{}$

6 $8 \times 4 = \boxed{}$

7 $40 \div 8 = \boxed{}$

8 $9 \times 6 = \boxed{}$

9 $80 \div 8 = \boxed{}$

Add or subtract.

10   211
     + 167

11   472
     − 231

12   527
     + 268

13   682
     − 537

14   636
     + 289

15   911
     − 685

1 Mr. Taylor arranges some chairs in rows. He puts the same number of chairs in each of 7 rows and puts 7 chairs in the last row. He sets up 70 chairs. How many chairs does he put in each of the 7 equal rows?

Choose the equation that can be used to solve the problem.

I can use the equation

$$(7 \times c) + 7 = 70$$

$$(70 \div 7) + 7 = c$$

$$(7 \times c) - 7 = 70$$

.

Solve the problem.

_____ chairs

2 Marisol picks 150 flowers. She picks 80 red flowers and the rest are yellow. She sells 45 yellow flowers. How many yellow flowers does she have now?

For numbers 2a–2e, choose Yes or No to tell whether the equation can be used to find the number of yellow flowers Marisol has now.

2a.　$150 - 80 - 45 = y$　　○ Yes　　　○ No

2b.　$150 + 80 - 45 = y$　　○ Yes　　　○ No

2c.　$150 + 80 + 45 = y$　　○ Yes　　　○ No

2d.　$150 = 80 + 45 + y$　　○ Yes　　　○ No

2e.　$150 = 80 - 45 + y$　　○ Yes　　　○ No

3 Mark makes 18 picture frames this month. He makes 7 fewer picture frames than Sara. How many picture frames does Sara make?

Draw comparison bars to represent the problem. Then solve.

_____ picture frames.

4 David and Marne pick cucumbers at a farm. David picks 93 cucumbers. How many cucumbers does Marne pick?

What information is not helpful for solving the problem?

(A) how many more cucumbers David picks

(B) how many fewer cucumbers Marne picks

(C) how many cucumbers are grown at the farm each year

(D) how many cucumbers David and Marne pick

Rewrite the problem to include the necessary information. Then solve it.

5 There are 240 boys and girls in a soccer league. There are 130 girls. How many boys are there?

Write an equation with a variable to represent the problem. Then draw a Math Mountain to solve the problem.

_____ boys

6 On Wednesday, Jonah sees 30 birds and 4 rabbits. Of the birds, 13 are robins and the rest are pigeons. On Thursday, he sees some more pigeons. He has now seen 21 pigeons. How many pigeons did he see on Thursday?

Part A Write the information in the correct box.

| 30 birds | 4 rabbits | 13 robins | 21 pigeons |

Needed Information	Extra Information

Part B Solve the problem. What strategy did you use? How did it help?

7 Susan buys 24 postcards. She sends 6 postcards to friends.
She puts the rest in 3 folders, with an equal number in
each folder. How many postcards are in each folder?

Write the first step question and answer. Then solve.

_____ postcards

8 Kato uses 56 photos to make online albums. He puts
7 photos in each album. How many albums does
Kato make?

For Exercises 8a–8d, select True or False if the equation
can be used to solve the problem.

8a. $7 \times a = 56$ ○ True   ○ False

8b. $56 \div 7 = a$ ○ True   ○ False

8c. $7 \times 56 = a$ ○ True   ○ False

8d. $56 \div a = 7$ ○ True   ○ False

9 Tara posts 35 flyers for the school carnival. Keisha posts
8 more flyers than Tara. How many flyers did Tara and
Keisha post? Choose the number that completes the
sentence.

Tara and Keisha post
| 43 |
| 62 | flyers.
| 78 |

10 Jason packs 54 grapefruit in 9 boxes for shipping. He packs the same number of grapefruit in each box. How many grapefruit does Jason pack into each box?

Use the numbers and symbols to write a situation equation and a solution equation. Then solve.

| g | 9 | 54 | × | ÷ | = |

Situation Equation: _____

Solution Equation: _____

_____ grapefruit

11 A ship can hold 3,250 cargo containers. There are 1,852 containers on the lower deck and 650 containers on the upper deck of the ship. How many more containers can be loaded on the ship? Write an equation and solve the problem.

_____

12 Parker has 452 toy dinosaurs in his collection. His sister gives him 38 more toy dinosaurs. Then he sells some of them online. Parker now has 418 toy dinosaurs. How many did he sell?

Answer: 72 toy dinosaurs

Is the answer reasonable? Tell why or why not. Then write an equation and solve the problem.

_____

13 Eva buys some items at the store and pays with pennies and nickels. Use the information in the table to write equations to find the unknown numbers. Then complete the table.

Pencil: _____

Eraser: _____

Clip: _____

	Number of Pennies	Number of Nickels	Total Cost
Pencil	6	8	¢
Eraser		4	24¢
Clip	2		37¢

14 Holly is going to the beach in 2 weeks and 4 days.

Which equation can be used to find the number of days until Holly goes to the beach?

(A) $2 \times 7 + 4 = b$; $b = 18$ days

(B) $2 \times 5 + 4 = b$; $b = 14$ days

(C) $2 + 7 + 4 = b$; $b = 13$ days

(D) $2 \times 7 - 4 = b$; $b = 10$ days

15 Omar has 5 ties and Ryan has 12 ties. How many more ties does Ryan have than Omar?

Make a comparison drawing to represent the problem. Then solve.

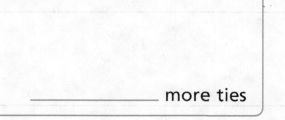

_____ more ties

Planning a Garden

Last year community gardeners planted 8 rows of
tomato plants with the same number in each row.
Then they planted 10 more plants. There was a total of
58 plants. How many plants were in each row before
they planted the additional 10?

1 Write an equation to represent the problem. Solve.

2 Could you write an equation for the problem using
other operations than the ones you used?
Explain why or why not.

3 Gardeners decided to buy stakes to help support
the tomato plants. The stakes are sold in bundles
of 12. If the gardeners bought 5 bundles of stakes,
did they buy enough stakes? How many more do
they need or how many extras do they have? Write
an equation to solve. Explain the solution.

4 Community gardeners plan to plant pumpkins this year. Write a two-step word problem about planting pumpkins that can be solved using an equation. Solve and explain the solution.

5 The gardeners plan to plant 40 pumpkin plants. They have space for 7 rows. They would like to keep an equal number of pumpkin plants in each row, if possible. Draw a picture to show the number of pumpkin plants they should plant in each row. Write an equation to match your picture.

6 How would the garden change if gardeners planted the pumpkin plants in 8 rows?

Dear Family:

In this unit, students explore ways to measure things using the customary and metric systems of measurement.

The units of measure we will be working with include:

U.S. Customary System

Capacity
1 cup (c) = 8 fluid ounces (oz)
1 pint (pt) = 2 cups (c)
1 quart (qt) = 2 pints (pt)
1 gallon (gal) = 4 quarts (qt)

Weight
1 pound (lb) = 16 ounces (oz)

Metric System

Capacity
1 liter (L) = 1,000 milliliters (mL)

Mass
1 kilogram (kg) = 1,000 grams (g)

Students will solve problems that involve liquid volumes or masses given in the same unit by adding, subtracting, multiplying, or dividing and by using a drawing to represent the problem.

You can help your child become familiar with these units of measure by working with measurements together. For example, you might use a measuring cup to explore how the cup can be used to fill pints, quarts, or gallons of liquid.

Thank you for helping your child learn important math skills. Please contact me, if you have any questions or comments.

Sincerely,
Your child's teacher

Estimada familia:

En esta unidad los niños estudian cómo medir cosas usando el sistema usual de medidas y el sistema métrico decimal.

Las unidades de medida con las que trabajaremos incluirán:

Sistema usual

Capacidad
1 taza (tz) = 8 onzas líquidas (oz)
1 pinta (pt) = 2 tazas (tz)
1 cuarto (ct) = 2 pintas (pt)
1 galón (gal) = 4 cuartos (ct)

Peso
1 libra (lb) = 16 onzas (oz)

Sistema métrico decimal

Capacidad
1 litro (L) = 1,000 mililitros (mL)

Masa
1 kilogramo (kg) = 1,000 gramos (g)

Los estudiantes resolverán problemas relacionados con volúmenes de líquido o masas, que se dan en la misma unidad, sumando, restando o dividiendo, y usando un dibujo para representar el problema.

Puede ayudar a que su niño se familiarice con estas unidades de medida midiendo con él diversas cosas. Por ejemplo, podrían usar una taza de medidas para aprender cómo se pueden llenar pintas, cuartos o galones con líquido.

Gracias por ayudar a su niño a aprender destrezas matemáticas importantes. Si tiene alguna duda o algún comentario, por favor comuníquese conmigo.

Atentamente,
El maestro de su niño

adjacent sides

convex

angle

cup (c)

concave

decagon

A polygon is convex if all of its diagonals are inside it.

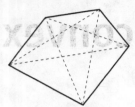

Two sides of a figure that meet at a point.

Example:
Sides *a* and *b* are adjacent.

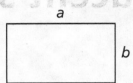

A U.S. customary unit of measure used to measure capacity.

1 cup = 8 fluid ounces
2 cups = 1 pint
4 cups = 1 quart
16 cups = 1 gallon

A figure formed by two rays or two line segments that meet at an endpoint.

A polygon with 10 sides.

A polygon for which you can connect two points inside the polygon with a segment that passes outside the polygon.

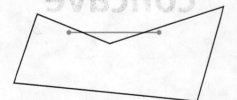

fluid ounce (fl oz)

hexagon

gallon (gal)

kilogram (kg)

gram (g)

liquid volume

A polygon with six sides.

A unit of liquid volume in the U.S. customary system that equals $\frac{1}{8}$ cup or 2 tablespoons.

A metric unit of mass.

1 kilogram = 1,000 grams

A U.S. customary unit used to measure capacity.

1 gallon = 4 quarts = 8 pints = 16 cups

A measure of how much a container can hold. Also called *capacity*.

A metric unit of mass. One paper clip has a mass of about 1 gram.

1,000 grams = 1 kilogram

liter (L)

octagon

mass

opposite sides

milliliter (mL)

ounce (oz)

A polygon with eight sides.

A metric unit used to measure capacity.

1 liter = 1,000 milliliters

Sides of a polygon that are across from each other; they do not meet at a point.

Example:
Sides *a* and *c* are opposite.

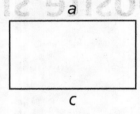

The amount of matter in an object.

A U.S. customary unit used to measure weight.

16 ounces = 1 pound

A metric unit used to measure capacity.

1,000 milliliters = 1 liter

Two lines are parallel
if they never cross or
meet. They are the same

parallel

Two lines are
perpendicular if they cross
or meet to form square
corners.

perpendicular

A quadrilateral with both
pairs of opposite sides
parallel.

parallelogram

pint (pt)

A polygon with five sides.

pentagon

A closed plane figure with
sides made up of straight
line segments.

polygon

Two lines are perpendicular if they cross or meet to form square corners.

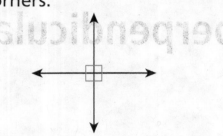

Two lines are parallel if they never cross or meet. They are the same distance apart.

A U.S. customary unit used to measure weight.

1 pint = 2 cups

A quadrilateral with both pairs of opposite sides parallel.

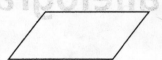

A closed plane figure with sides made up of straight line segments.

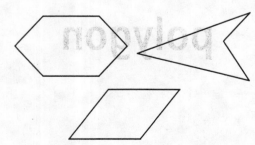

A polygon with five sides.

pound

ray

quadrilateral

rectangle

quart (qt)

rhombus

A part of a line that has one endpoint and goes on forever in one direction.

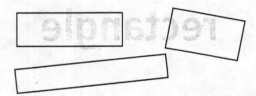

A U.S. customary unit used to measure weight.

1 pound = 16 ounces

A parallelogram that has 4 right angles.

A polygon with four sides.

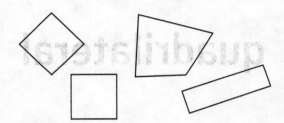

A parallelogram with equal sides.

A U.S. customary unit used to measure capacity.

1 quart = 4 cups

right angle

triangle

square

vertex

trapezoid

weight

A polygon with three sides.

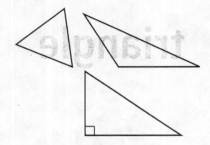

An angle that measures 90°.

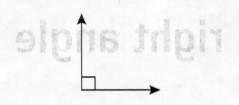

A point where sides, rays, or edges meet.

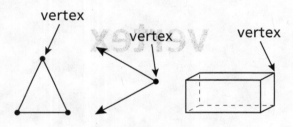

A rectangle with four sides of the same length.

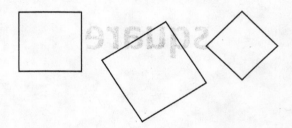

The measure of how heavy something is.

A quadrilateral with exactly one pair of parallel sides.

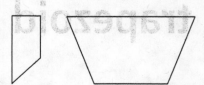

Name _____

Choose the Unit

**Choose the best unit to use to measure the liquid volume.
Write *fluid ounce*, *cup*, *pint*, *quart*, or *gallon*.**

1 a carton of heavy cream

_____

2 a flower vase

_____

3 a swimming pool

_____

4 a wash tub

_____

What's the Error?

Dear Math Students,

Today I had to choose the best unit to use to measure how much water is needed to fill a kitchen sink. I said the best unit to use is cups. Is my answer correct? If not, please correct my work and tell me what I did wrong.

Your friend,
Puzzled Penguin

5 Write an answer to Puzzled Penguin.

_____

_____

_____

6 **Math Journal** Think of a container. Choose the unit you would use to measure its capacity. Draw the container and write the name of the unit you chose. Explain why you chose that unit.

Name _____

Use Drawings to Solve Problems

Use the drawing to represent and solve the problem.

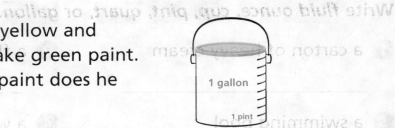

14 A painter mixes 5 pints of yellow and 3 pints of blue paint to make green paint. How many pints of green paint does he make?

_____

15 Ryan has a bottle of orange juice with 16 fluid ounces. He pours 6 fluid ounces in a cup. How many fluid ounces are left in the bottle?

_____

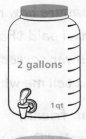

16 A restaurant makes 8 quarts of tea. They use all the tea to fill pitchers that hold 2 quarts each. How many pitchers are filled with tea?

_____

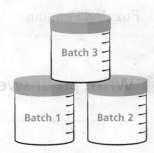

17 An ice cream machine makes 5 pints of ice cream in a batch. If 3 batches are made, how many pints of ice cream are made?

_____

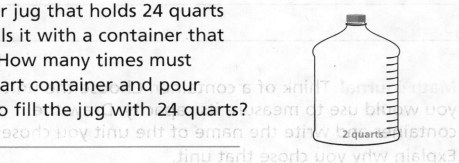

18 Fran has a water jug that holds 24 quarts of water. She fills it with a container that holds 4 quarts. How many times must she fill the 4-quart container and pour it into the jug to fill the jug with 24 quarts?

_____

Name _____

Solve Problems

**Use the drawing to represent and
solve the problem.**

Show your work.

19 Shanna bought 8 juice boxes filled with
her favorite juice. Each box holds
10 fluid ounces. How many fluid ounces
of her favorite juice did Shanna buy?

_____

20 Juana filled her punch bowl with 12 cups
of punch. She gave some of her friends
each a cup of punch. There are 7 cups of
punch left in the bowl. How many cups
did she give to friends?

_____

21 Mrs. Chavez made 20 quarts of pickles.
She made 4 quarts each day. How many
days did it take her to make the pickles?

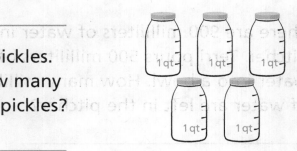

_____

22 A mid-sized aquarium holds 25 gallons of
water and a large aquarium holds
35 gallons of water. How many gallons of
water is needed to fill both aquariums?

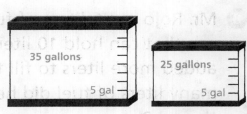

_____

✔ **Check Understanding**

Name the 5 units of liquid volume in this lesson
from largest to smallest.

_____, _____, _____,

_____, _____

Name _____

Choose the Appropriate Unit

VOCABULARY
milliliter (mL)
liter (L)

Choose the unit you would use to measure the liquid volume of each. Write *mL* or *L*.

1 a kitchen sink _____   **2** a soup spoon _____

3 a teacup _____   **4** a washing machine _____

Circle the better estimate.

5 a juice container   1 L   1 mL

6 a bowl of soup   500 L   500 mL

Use Drawings to Represent Problems

Use the drawing to represent and solve the problem.

7 There are 900 milliliters of water in a pitcher. Terri pours 500 milliliters of water into a bowl. How many milliliters of water are left in the pitcher?

_____

8 Mr. Rojo put 6 liters of fuel into a gas can that can hold 10 liters. Then he added more liters to fill the can. How many liters of fuel did he add to the can?

_____

9 Shelby needs to water each of her 3 plants with 200 milliliters of water. How many milliliters of water does she need?

_____

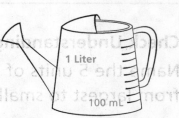

441   Metric Units of Liquid Volume

Name _____

Make Sense of Problems Involving Liquid Volume

Use the drawing to represent and solve the problem.

10 The deli sold 24 liters of juice in 3 days. The same amount was sold each day. How many liters of juice did the deli sell each day?

_____

11 Tim has a bucket filled with 12 liters of water and a bucket filled with 20 liters of water. What is the total liquid volume of the buckets?

_____

12 Sara made a smoothie and gave her friend 250 milliliters. There are 550 milliliters left. How many milliliters of smoothie did Sara make?

_____

Solve. Use a drawing if you need to.

13 Diane has 12 liters of iced tea to divide equally among 4 tables. How many liters should she put at each table?

14 Mr. Valle filled 7 jars with his famous barbeque sauce. Each jar holds 500 milliliters. How many milliliters of sauce did he have?

✓ **Check Understanding**

Describe the relationship between a liter and a milliliter.

Name _____

Choose the Appropriate Unit

Choose the unit you would use to measure the weight of each. Write *pound or ounce*.

1 a backpack full of books

_____

2 a couch

_____

3 a peanut

_____

4 a pencil

_____

Circle the better estimate.

5 a student desk   3 lb   30 lb

6 a television   20 oz   20 lb

7 a hamster   5 oz   5 lb

8 a slice of cheese   1 lb   1 oz

Use Drawings to Represent Problems

Use the drawing to represent and solve the problem.

9 Selma filled each of 3 bags with 5 ounces of her favorite nuts. How many ounces of nuts did she use altogether to fill the bags?

_____

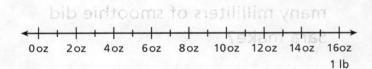

0oz 2oz 4oz 6oz 8oz 10oz 12oz 14oz 16oz
                                            1 lb

10 Two apples together weigh 16 ounces. If one apple weighs 9 ounces, how much does the other apple weigh?

_____

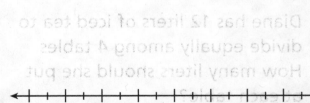
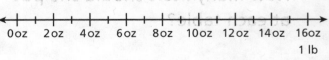

0oz 2oz 4oz 6oz 8oz 10oz 12oz 14oz 16oz
                                            1 lb

Name _____

Use Drawings to Represent Problems (continued)

Use the drawing to represent and solve the problem.

11) Noah bought 16 ounces of turkey
meat. If he uses 4 ounces to make
a turkey patty, how many patties
can he make?

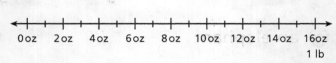

_____

12) A package of silver beads weighs
6 ounces and a package of
wooden beads weighs 7 ounces
more. How much does the
package of wooden beads weigh?

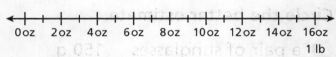

_____

Solve Word Problems

Solve. Use a drawing if you need to.

13) Ted has two dogs. Together they
weigh 88 pounds. If one dog
weighs 70 pounds, how much
does the other dog weigh?

_____

14) Emma has 20 ounces of popcorn
kernels in a bag. If she pops
4 ounces of kernels at a time,
how many times can Emma
pop corn?

_____

15) Susan mailed 3 packages. Each
package weighed 20 ounces.
What was the total weight of
the 3 packages?

_____

16) Bailey caught two fish. The
smaller fish weighs 14 ounces
and the larger fish weighs
6 ounces more. How much does
the larger fish weigh?

_____

Name _____

Choose the Appropriate Unit

VOCABULARY
mass
gram (g)
kilogram (kg)

Choose the unit you would use to measure the mass of each. Write *gram* or *kilogram*.

17 an elephant

_____

18 a crayon

_____

19 a stamp

_____

20 a dog

_____

Circle the better estimate.

21 a pair of sunglasses   150 g   150 kg

22 a horse   6 kg   600 kg

23 a watermelon   40 g   4 kg

24 a quarter   500 g   5 g

Use Drawings to Represent Problems

Use the drawing to represent and solve the problem.

25 Zach wants to buy 900 grams of pumpkin seed. The scale shows 400 grams. How many more grams does he need?

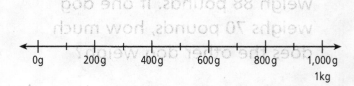

_____

26 Laura had 800 grams of fruit snacks. She put an equal amount into each of 4 containers. How many grams did she put in each container?

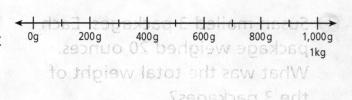

_____

Name _____

Solve Word Problems

Use the drawing to represent and solve the problem.

27 Nancy used 30 grams of strawberries and 45 grams of apples in her salad. How many grams of fruit altogether did she put in her salad?

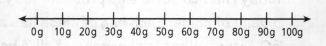

_____

28 Three people each donated a 20-kilogram bag of dog food to the animal shelter. How many kilograms of dog food was donated altogether?

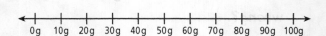

_____

Solve. Use a drawing if you need to.

29 A male leopard has a mass of 40 kilograms and a female leopard has a mass of 25 kilograms. How much greater is the mass of the male?

_____

30 Jolie made 3 necklaces that have a total mass of 180 grams. If each necklace has the same mass, what is the mass of each necklace?

_____

31 Dan bought 6 small bags of treats for his dog. Each bag has a mass of 40 grams. What is the total mass of all the bags?

_____

32 Carrie has a dog and a cat. Together they have a mass of 21 kilograms. If the cat has a mass of 9 kilograms, what is the mass of Carrie's dog?

_____

What's the Error?

Dear Math Students,

Today I had to solve this problem: Toby bought 3 bags of chips. Each bag of chips has a mass of 50 grams. What is the mass of all 3 bags of chips? Here is how I solved the problem.

50 + 3 = 53; 53 grams

Is my answer correct? If not, please correct my work and tell me what I did wrong. How do you know my answer is wrong?

Your friend,
Puzzled Penguin

33 Write an answer to the Puzzled Penguin.

_____

_____

Solve. Show your work on a separate sheet of paper.

34 A tennis ball has a mass of 60 grams. A golf ball has a mass of 45 grams. What is the total mass of the two ball?

35 How many more grams is the mass of the tennis ball than the mass of the golf ball?

36 Gary bought 10 slices of ham at the deli. Each slice weighed 2 ounces. How many ounces of ham did Gary buy?

37 Sadie had 40 grams of sunflower seeds. She divided the seeds evenly among her 5 friends. How many grams did each friend get?

447 Customary Units of Weight and Metric Units of Mass

Write the correct answer.

1 What would be the better unit to use to specify the mass of a large truck, grams or kilograms?

_____

2 What would be the better unit to use to specify the volume of water you can hold in your hand, liters or milliliters?

_____

Solve.   *Show your work.*

3 A pack of 6 markers weighs 48 grams. How much does 1 marker weigh?

_____

4 It takes 15 liters of paint to paint the shed. I have used 8 liters so far. How many more liters of paint will I need to finish painting the shed?

_____

5 A boy with a mass of 50 kilograms is riding on a surfboard with a mass of 7 kilograms. What is the mass of the boy and surfboard altogether?

_____

Name _____

Multiply or divide.

1 $3 \div 1 = \boxed{}$

2 $2 \times 6 = \boxed{}$

3 $18 \div 3 = \boxed{}$

4 $6 \times 8 = \boxed{}$

5 $32 \div 4 = \boxed{}$

6 $7 \times 10 = \boxed{}$

7 $42 \div 7 = \boxed{}$

8 $7 \times 9 = \boxed{}$

9 $72 \div 8 = \boxed{}$

Add or subtract.

10
```
  112
+ 834
```

11
```
  650
- 300
```

12
```
  534
+ 307
```

13
```
  843
- 478
```

14
```
  354
+ 618
```

15
```
  903
- 648
```

Dear Family:

Your student has been learning about geometry and measurement during this school year. The second part of Unit 7 is about angles, triangles, and other polygons, including the geometric figures called quadrilaterals. These polygons get their name because they have four (*quad-*) sides (*-lateral*).

Here are some examples of quadrilaterals students will be learning about in this unit.

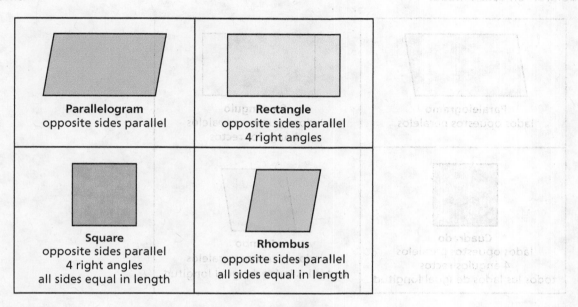

Parallelogram
opposite sides parallel

Rectangle
opposite sides parallel
4 right angles

Square
opposite sides parallel
4 right angles
all sides equal in length

Rhombus
opposite sides parallel
all sides equal in length

Students will be able to recognize and describe different quadrilaterals by their sides, angles, and vertices. Some sides may be of equal length. Some sides may be parallel; they do not meet no matter how far they are extended. Some sides may be perpendicular; where they meet is like the corner of a square.

If you have any questions, please contact me.

Thank you.

Sincerely,
Your child's teacher

Estimada familia:

Su niño ha estado aprendiendo acerca de geometría y medición. La segunda parte de la Unidad 7 trata sobre ángulos, triángulos y otros polígonos incluyendo las figuras geométricas llamadas cuadriláteros. Se llaman así porque tienen cuatro (*quadri-*) lados (*-lateris*).

Aquí se muestran algunos ejemplos de cuadriláteros que los estudiantes estudiarán en esta unidad.

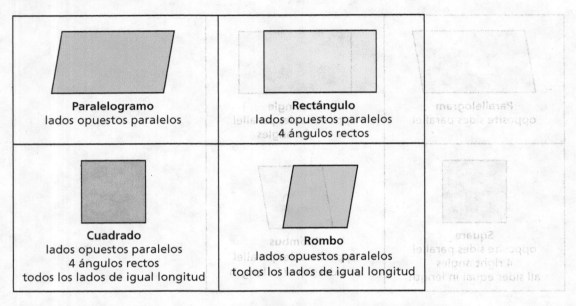

Paralelogramo
lados opuestos paralelos

Rectángulo
lados opuestos paralelos
4 ángulos rectos

Cuadrado
lados opuestos paralelos
4 ángulos rectos
todos los lados de igual longitud

Rombo
lados opuestos paralelos
todos los lados de igual longitud

Los estudiantes podrán reconocer y describir diferentes cuadriláteros según sus lados, ángulos y vértices. Algunos lados pueden tener la misma longitud. Algunos lados pueden ser paralelos; nunca se juntan, no importa cuánto se extiendan. Algunos lados pueden ser perpendiculares; donde se juntan es como el vértice de un cuadrado.

Si tiene alguna pregunta o algún comentario, por favor comuníquese conmigo.

Gracias.

Atentamente,
El maestro de su niño

Name _____

Build Quadrilaterals from Triangles

A quadrilateral is a figure with 4 sides.

Cut out each pair of triangles. Use each pair to make as many different quadrilaterals as you can. You may flip a triangle and use the back. On a separate piece of paper, trace each quadrilateral that you make.

Triangles with One Angle Larger Than a Right Angle

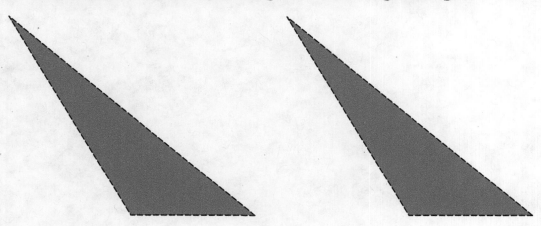

Triangles with Three Angles Smaller Than a Right Angle

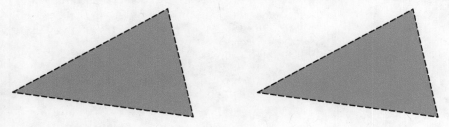

Triangles with One Right Angle

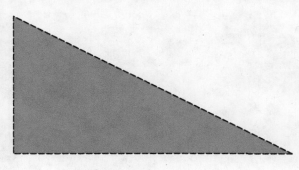
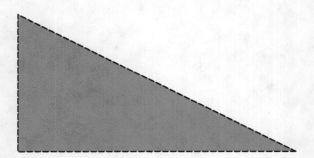

Angles, Triangles, and Other Polygons

Name _____

Build Polygons from Triangles

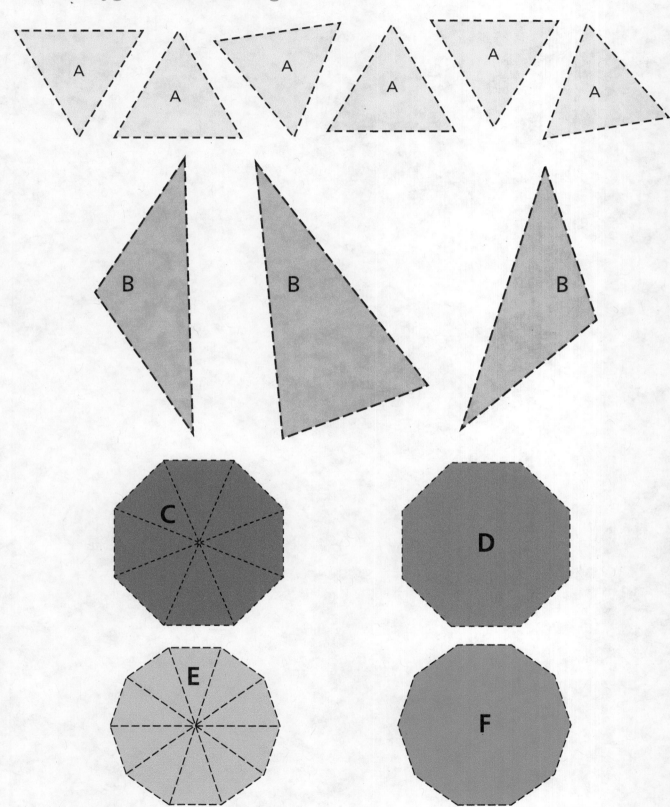

463D

Angles, Triangles, and Other Polygons

VOCABULARY
parallelogram

Describe Parallelograms

All of these figures are **parallelograms**. Both pairs of opposite sides are parallel.

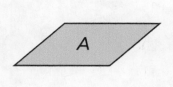 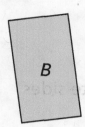  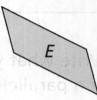

These figures are not parallelograms.

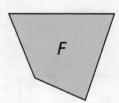 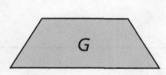 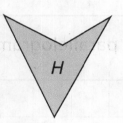  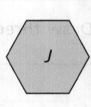

Complete the sentence.

1 A parallelogram is a quadrilateral with _____

_____

Measure Sides of Parallelograms

For each parallelogram, measure the sides to the nearest centimeter and label them with their lengths.

2

3

4

5 Look at the lengths of the sides. What patterns do

you notice? _____

Name _____

Draw Parallelograms

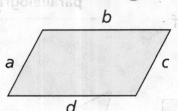

1 Write what you know about the opposite sides
of a parallelogram.

_____

_____

2 Draw three different parallelograms.

Name _____

Draw Rectangles

3 Write everything you know about the opposite sides of a rectangle.

_____

4 What do you know about the **adjacent sides** of a rectangle?

_____

5 Draw three different rectangles.

Name

Draw Squares and Rhombuses

6 Write everything you know about squares.

_____

7 Write all you know about rhombuses.

_____

_____

8 Draw two different squares and two different rhombuses.

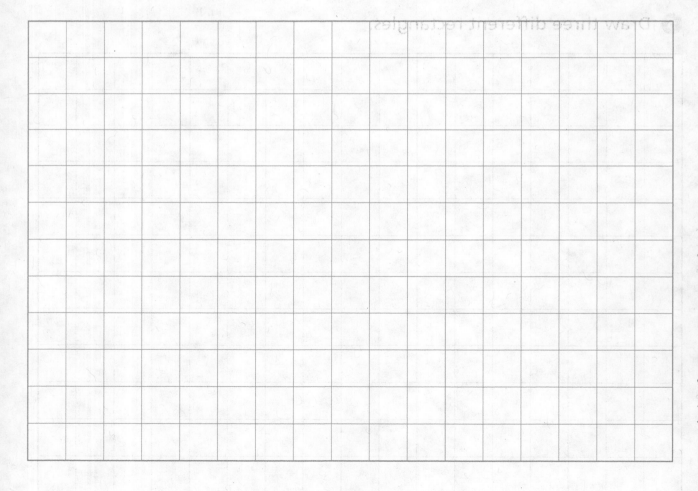

Draw Quadrilaterals

Name _____

Draw Quadrilaterals That Are Not Squares, Rectangles, or Rhombuses

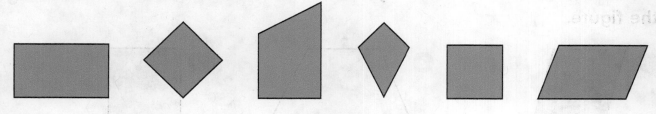

9 What is a quadrilateral?

_____

10 Name all the quadrilaterals that have at least one pair of parallel sides.

_____

11 Draw three different quadrilaterals that are not squares, rectangles, or rhombuses.

✓ **Check Understanding**

Draw a quadrilateral that is not a parallelogram.

Name _____

Name Quadrilaterals

Place a check mark beside every name that describes the figure.

1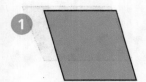

- [ ] quadrilateral
- [ ] parallelogram
- [ ] rhombus
- [ ] rectangle
- [ ] square

2

- [ ] quadrilateral
- [ ] parallelogram
- [ ] rhombus
- [ ] rectangle
- [ ] trapezoid

3

- [ ] quadrilateral
- [ ] parallelogram
- [ ] rhombus
- [ ] rectangle
- [ ] square

4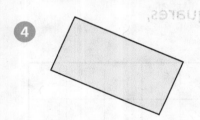

- [ ] quadrilateral
- [ ] parallelogram
- [ ] rhombus
- [ ] rectangle
- [ ] square

5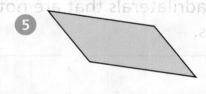

- [ ] quadrilateral
- [ ] parallelogram
- [ ] rhombus
- [ ] rectangle
- [ ] square

6

- [ ] quadrilateral
- [ ] parallelogram
- [ ] rhombus
- [ ] rectangle
- [ ] square

7

- [ ] quadrilateral
- [ ] parallelogram
- [ ] rhombus
- [ ] rectangle
- [ ] square

8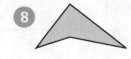

- [ ] quadrilateral
- [ ] parallelogram
- [ ] rhombus
- [ ] rectangle
- [ ] square

9

- [ ] quadrilateral
- [ ] parallelogram
- [ ] rhombus
- [ ] rectangle
- [ ] square

Name _____

Analyze Quadrilaterals

10 For each figure, put Xs under the descriptions that are always true.

	Four sides	Both pairs of opposite sides parallel	Both pairs of opposite sides the same length	Four right angles	All sides the same length
Quadrilateral					
Trapezoid					
Parallelogram					
Rhombus					
Rectangle					
Square					

Use the finished chart above to complete each statement.

11 Parallelograms have all the features of quadrilaterals *plus*

_____

_____

12 Rectangles have all the features of parallelograms *plus*

_____

13 Squares have all the features of quadrilaterals *plus*

_____

_____

14 Rhombuses have all the features of quadrilaterals *plus*

_____

_____

Name _____

Draw Quadrilaterals from a Description

Draw each figure.

15 Draw a quadrilateral that is *not* a parallelogram.

16 Draw a parallelogram that is *not* a rectangle.

17 Draw a rectangle that is *not* a square.

What's the Error?

Dear Math Students,

Today I had to draw a quadrilateral with parallel sides that
is not a rectangle, square, or rhombus.
This is my drawing.

Is my drawing correct?
If not, please help me
understand why it is wrong.

Your friend,
Puzzled Penguin

18 Write an answer to Puzzled Penguin.

_____

_____

473

Classify Quadrilaterals

Name _____

Sort and Classify Quadrilaterals

Use the category diagram to sort the figures you cut out from Student Activity Book page 475A. Write the letter of the figure in the diagram to record your work.

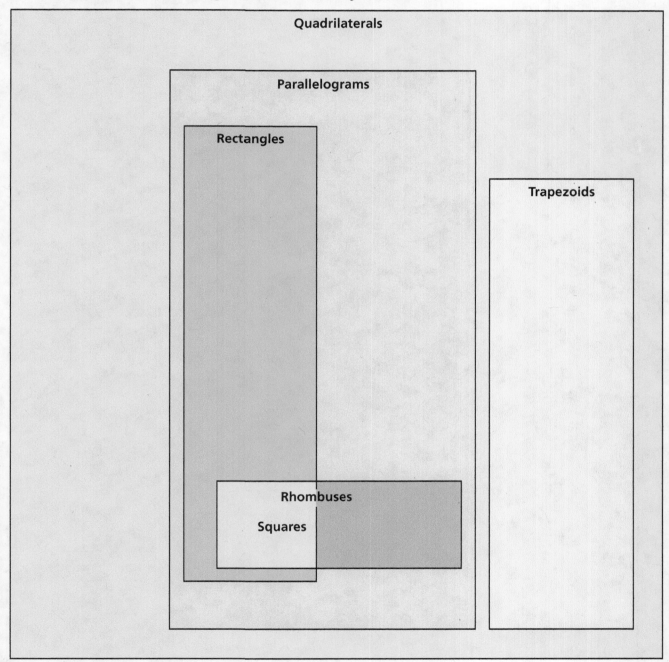

✔ Check Understanding

Complete the sentence. A rhombus is always a _____

and a _____ .

Sort and Classify Quadrilaterals

Use the category diagram to sort the figures you cut
out from Student Activity Book page 475A. Write the letter
of the figure in the diagram to record your work.

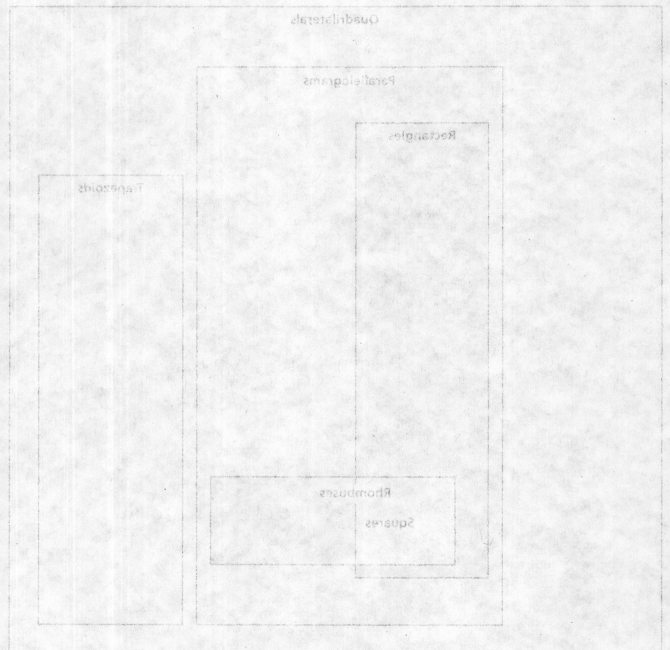

Quadrilaterals

Parallelograms

Rectangles

Trapezoids

Rhombuses

Squares

Check Understanding

Complete the sentence. A rhombus is always a _____

and a _____

Name _____

Quadrilaterals for Sorting

Cut along the dashed lines.

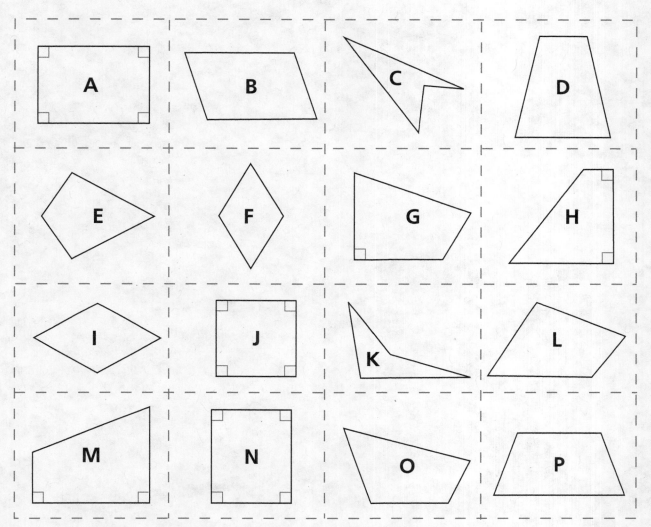

475A

<u>**Name**</u>

Design a Garden

Use the dot paper below to draw a different garden that has the same perimeter as Yoakim's combined garden. Beside it, draw a different garden that has the same area as Yoakim's garden.

⊢1 ft⊣

7 What is the area of your garden that has the same perimeter as Yoakim's garden?

_____

8 What is the perimeter of your garden that has the same area as Yoakim's garden?

_____

9 Use the centimeter dot paper at the right to draw separate areas within a garden where you would plant corn, beans, and tomatoes.

The area for corn is 12 square feet.
The area for beans is 25 square feet.
The area for tomatoes is 20 square feet.

Name _____

Write the correct answer.

1 What do a rhombus and a square have in common?

_____

2 Put a check mark beside every name that describes the figure.

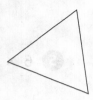

☐ quadrilateral   ☐ rhombus

☐ not a quadrilateral   ☐ trapezoid

☐ rectangle   ☐ square

3 Which triangle has a right angle?

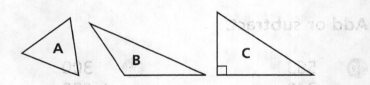

_____

4 List the figures that are quadrilaterals.

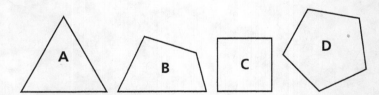

_____

5 What do the figures have in common?

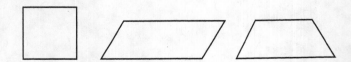

_____

Name _____

Multiply or divide.

1 2 × 4 = ☐

2 9 ÷ 3 = ☐

3 6 × 6 = ☐

4 30 ÷ 6 = ☐

5 6 × 9 = ☐

6 48 ÷ 8 = ☐

7 4 × 9 = ☐

8 72 ÷ 9 = ☐

9 8 × 7 = ☐

Add or subtract.

10   563
       − 240

11   300
       + 620

12   562
       − 428

13   529
       + 386

14   338
       − 189

15   482
       + 379

1 Write the letter for each shape in the box that describes the shape.

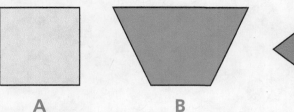
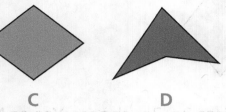
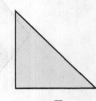

A   B   C   D   E

Quadrilateral	Parallelogram	Perpendicular sides	All sides the same length

2 Draw two different parallelograms that are not squares or rhombuses.

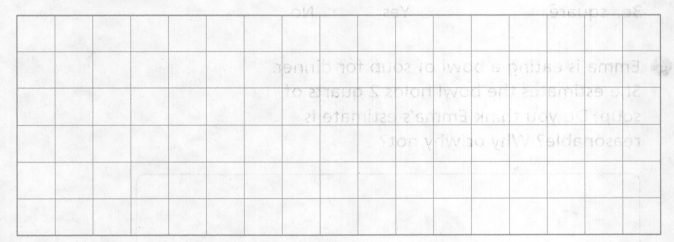

How did you decide which figures to draw?

3 Emily draws this figure.

For Exercises 3a–3e, choose Yes or No to tell whether the name describes the figure.

3a. quadrilateral   ○ Yes   ○ No

3b. rectangle   ○ Yes   ○ No

3c. parallelogram   ○ Yes   ○ No

3d. rhombus   ○ Yes   ○ No

3e. square   ○ Yes   ○ No

4 Emma is eating a bowl of soup for dinner. She estimates the bowl holds 2 quarts of soup. Do you think Emma's estimate is reasonable? Why or why not?

5 Draw a figure with 8 sides and 8 vertices.
Name the figure.

6 Write the name of the object in the box that
shows the unit you would use to measure
the mass of the object.

| loaf of bread | watermelon | person |
| house key | lion | comb |

gram	kilogram

7 Estimate the liquid volume of each object.
Draw a line from the estimate to the object.

100 liters   3 liters   300 milliliters

8 Billy needs 200 milliliters of lemonade to fill a small jar. How many milliliters of lemonade does he need to fill 6 jars of the same size?

Choose the measure to complete the sentence.

Billy needs
600
800
1,200
milliliters of lemonade.

9 Draw a quadrilateral that is both a square and a rhombus.

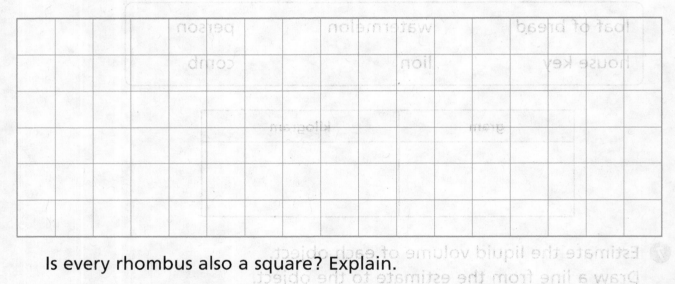

Is every rhombus also a square? Explain.

_____

10 Mia uses 40 liters of water for her garden. That is 12 more liters than Rob. How many liters of water does Rob use?

_____ liters

11 Rani uses a container that can hold 2 liters of water to fill a fish tank. The fish tank can hold 8 liters of water. How many times must she fill the smaller container to fill the fish tank?

_____ times

12 Sam uses 28 grams of chopped onions in his sauce. There are 6 grams of onions left. How many grams of onions did Sam start with?

_____ grams

13 Mei has 80 kilograms of firewood to divide equally into 10 bundles. How many kilograms of firewood should be in each bundle?

_____ kilograms

14 Chaseedah thinks this shape is a square. Anaya thinks the shape is a rectangle.

Who is correct? Explain your answer.

_____

15 Roy uses 6 grams of corn in each veggie burger. How many grams of corn does he need to make 20 veggie burgers?

_____ grams

16 Janie has three dogs. The dogs have masses of 4 kilograms, 8 kilograms, and 7 kilograms. What is the total mass of the three dogs?

_____ kilograms

17 If each bag contains 185 grams of apple chips, how many grams of apple chips are in 3 bags?

_____ grams

18 Select all the figures that have at least one set of parallel sides.

○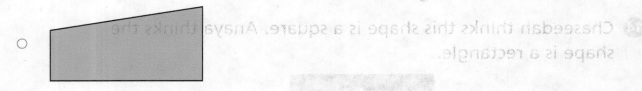

○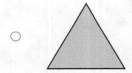

○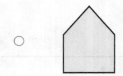

○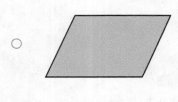

○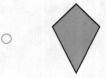

Can You Cut It?

Lucia's class is making sandwiches for a math fair. Lucia will cut the sandwiches into these three different shapes.

Shape A: a quadrilateral that is not a square

Shape B: a triangle with one right angle

Shape C: a parallelogram that is not a rectangle

1 Use your ruler to help you draw Lucia's shapes.

2 Label the shapes **Shape A**, **Shape B**, and **Shape C**.

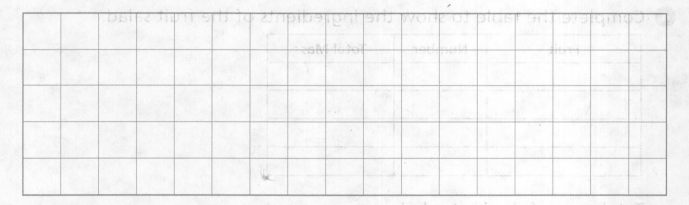

3 Combine 2 or more of the above shapes to create a different quadrilateral that Lucia can use for the sandwiches.

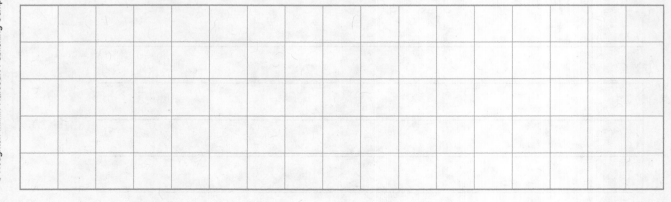

Lucia's class is also making fruit salad for the fair.
Use the chart to help plan the fruit salad.

1 apple............150 grams	1 pear......150 grams
1 tangerine........75 grams	1 plum.......65 grams
1 banana.........160 grams	1 peach....100 grams

Directions for Making Fruit Salad

• The fruit salad should have a total of 8 servings.

• Each serving should be between 90 and 100 grams.

• The fruit salad should include at least 3 different types of fruit.

4 Complete the table to show the ingredients of the fruit salad.

Fruit	Number	Total Mass

Total mass of the fruit salad: _____

5 Explain the method you used to decide how many of each
fruit to include.

_____

_____

_____

_____

_____

Be an Illustrator

Illustrator: Josh Brill

Did you ever try to use shapes to draw animals like the moose on the cover?

Over the last 10 years Josh has been using geometric shapes to design his animals. His aim is to keep the animal drawings simple and use color to make them appealing.

Add some color to the moose Josh drew. Then try drawing a cat or dog or some other animal using the shapes below.

Shape Toolbox

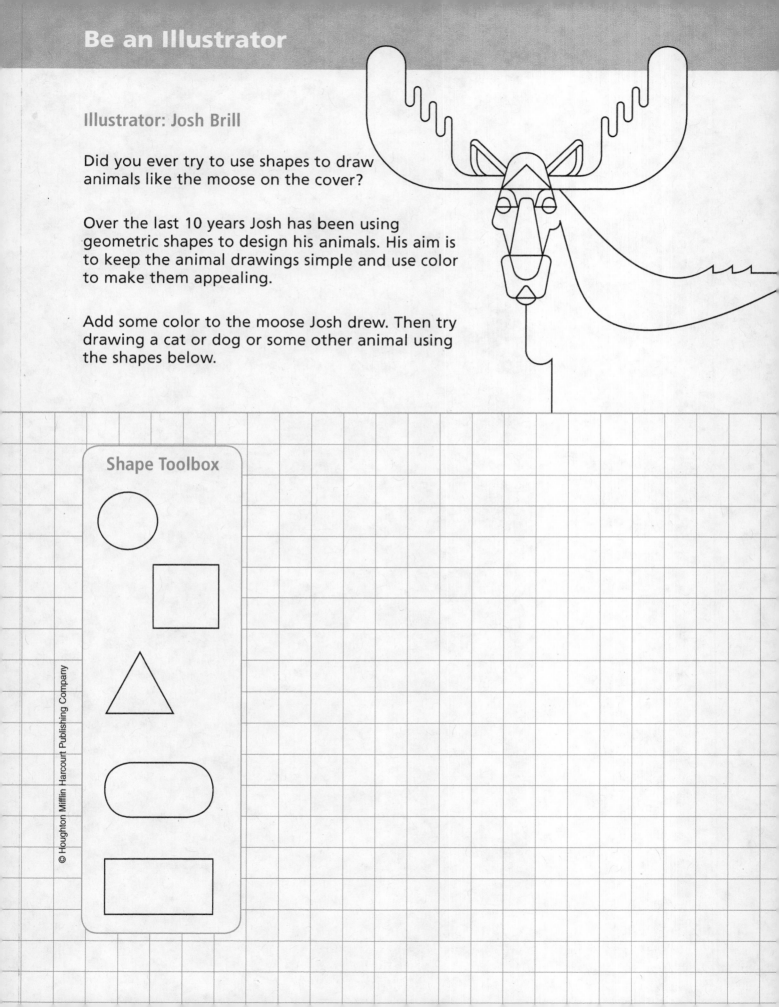